"I knew that we were in trouble then. I didn't really have any misconceptions about our ability to do anything other than play music, and I was scared. [When Brian died] I thought, 'We've fuckin' had it.' "

—John Lennon, 1970

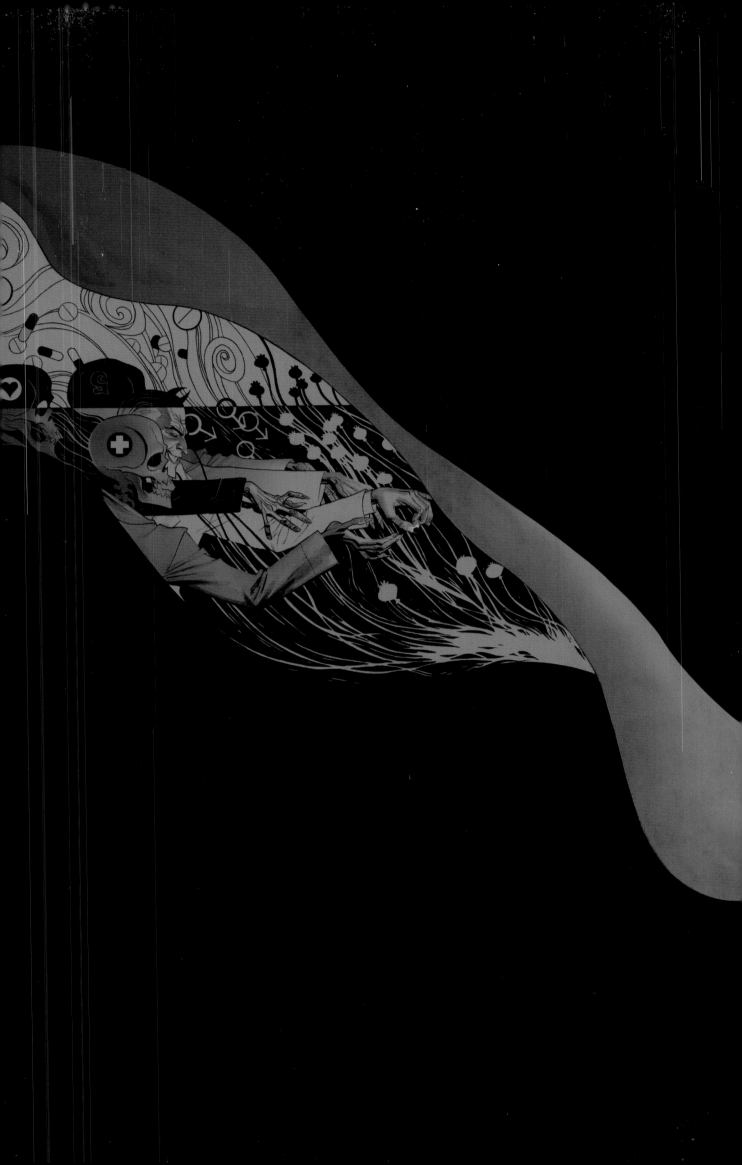

THE FIFTH BEATLE

THE BRIAN EPSTEIN STORY

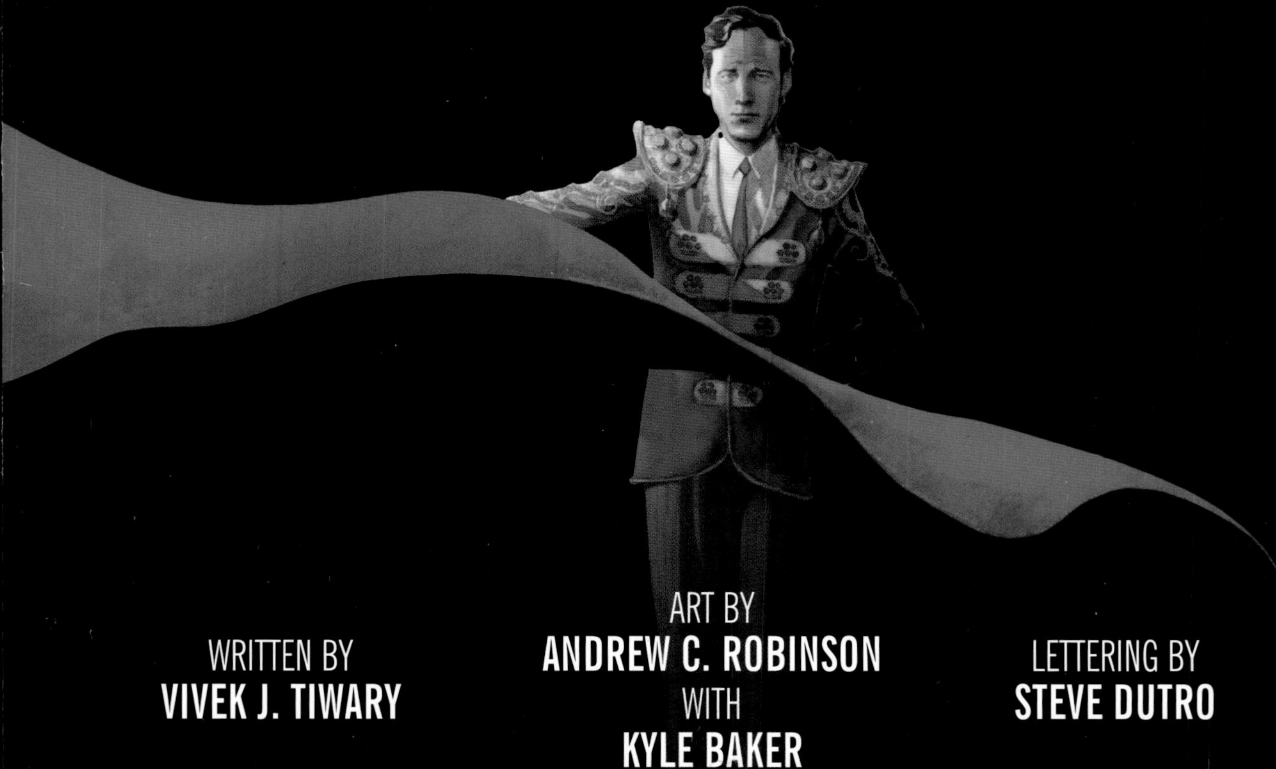

WRITTEN BY
VIVEK J. TIWARY

ART BY
ANDREW C. ROBINSON
WITH
KYLE BAKER

LETTERING BY
STEVE DUTRO

President and Publisher
MIKE RICHARDSON

Editor
PHILIP R. SIMON

Designer
JUSTIN A. COUCH

Digital Production and Retouch
CHRISTIANNE GOUDREAU

Special thanks to Shawna Gore, Mark Irwin,
Samantha Robertson, and Martha Thomases
for their editorial assistance and
dedication to this project.

Published by
M PRESS
A division of
Dark Horse Comics, Inc.
10956 SE Main Street
Milwaukie, OR 97222

DarkHorse.com | FifthBeatle.com | TiwaryEnt.com

1 3 5 7 9 10 8 6 4 2

First edition: November 2013. ISBN: 978-1-61655-256-5
Collector's Edition ISBN: 978-1-61655-265-7 | Limited Edition ISBN: 978-1-61655-257-2
To find a comics shop in your area, call the Comic Shop Locator Service toll-free at 1-888-266-4226.

Neil Hankerson, Executive Vice President · Tom Weddle, Chief Financial Officer · Randy Stradley, Vice President of Publishing · Michael Martens, Vice President of Book Trade Sales · Anita Nelson, Vice President of Business Affairs · Scott Allie, Editor in Chief · Matt Parkinson, Vice President of Marketing · David Scroggy, Vice President of Product Development · Dale LaFountain, Vice President of Information Technology · Darlene Vogel, Senior Director of Print, Design, and Production · Ken Lizzi, General Counsel · Davey Estrada, Editorial Director · Chris Warner, Senior Books Editor · Diana Schutz, Executive Editor · Cary Grazzini, Director of Print and Development · Lia Ribacchi, Art Director · Cara Niece, Director of Scheduling · Tim Wiesch, Director of International Licensing · Mark Bernardi, Director of Digital Publishing

WHEN I GOT A CALL FROM BRIAN, THAT'S WHEN I GREW WINGS

Introduction by Billy J. Kramer

I am baffled by the fact that Brian Epstein has not been posthumously inducted into the Rock and Roll Hall of Fame in the Non-Performer category. His name should be up in lights.

I witnessed Brian Epstein take an obscure group playing rock and roll in a cellar club called the Cavern and guide them to become the biggest music phenomenon the world has ever known. Simply put, as talented as they were, the Beatles may have never gotten out of Liverpool had it not been for Brian.

I used to see Brian in the evenings at Beatles shows in Liverpool, looking down and depressed after he had spent an entire day in London pounding the pavement, trying to secure them a record deal. But no record company wanted them. Still, he had such belief in their talents, and his enthusiasm never waned. He worked tirelessly on their behalf until he finally achieved his goal and secured the Beatles a recording deal with EMI.

Brian Epstein made the world pay attention to those four lads from Liverpool, and it saddens me that he has become a forgotten man in Beatles history.

The Fifth Beatle changes all that.

The Fifth Beatle captures Brian's love and dedication, his savvy business sense, and so many other traits that led to the Beatles' success. It finally gives Brian the credit that he so deserves. I only wish he were here to see that fifty years later, the legacy he left behind is as strong as ever, if not stronger.

Turn the page to meet Brian Epstein—my manager, mentor, and friend.

—BILLY J. KRAMER
New York, 2013

the beatles changed our lives, brian epstein changed theirs

he made it all possible, possible for us to be having this chat today,

brian told them who they could be and helped them become it.

we were not there on that new year's day of 1962 when the beatles auditioned for decca at their west hampstead studios.

we were not there when an a & r man, after turning down the band, chased brian out onto the street and told him that for a hundred quid he could knock the beatles into shape for another audition.

the humiliation, the pain . . . brian already had at least two social marks against him— he was jewish and gay.

christ, you know it ain't easy. dusty springfield was catholic and gay but she was able to sing her way through it.

brian had to stand in the wings and watch his lads twist and shout

but those wings became the wings of the world

from scunthorpe to shea stadium in three super fast, incredible singalong years the world was given a songbook it has never stopped singing and an idea as to what a life could be about.

brian persevered against all odds and got his lads a recording contract and that act changed all our lives for the better.

if brian had loved himself as much as he loved the beatles he may have still been with us today,

but we do have all that they did together . . .

andrew loog oldham
bogotá, mm13

WHEN I GOT A CALL FROM BRIAN, THAT'S WHEN I GREW WINGS

Introduction by Billy J. Kramer

I am baffled by the fact that Brian Epstein has not been posthumously inducted into the Rock and Roll Hall of Fame in the Non-Performer category. His name should be up in lights.

I witnessed Brian Epstein take an obscure group playing rock and roll in a cellar club called the Cavern and guide them to become the biggest music phenomenon the world has ever known. Simply put, as talented as they were, the Beatles may have never gotten out of Liverpool had it not been for Brian.

I used to see Brian in the evenings at Beatles shows in Liverpool, looking down and depressed after he had spent an entire day in London pounding the pavement, trying to secure them a record deal. But no record company wanted them. Still, he had such belief in their talents, and his enthusiasm never waned. He worked tirelessly on their behalf until he finally achieved his goal and secured the Beatles a recording deal with EMI.

Brian Epstein made the world pay attention to those four lads from Liverpool, and it saddens me that he has become a forgotten man in Beatles history.

The Fifth Beatle changes all that.

The Fifth Beatle captures Brian's love and dedication, his savvy business sense, and so many other traits that led to the Beatles' success. It finally gives Brian the credit that he so deserves. I only wish he were here to see that fifty years later, the legacy he left behind is as strong as ever, if not stronger.

Turn the page to meet Brian Epstein—my manager, mentor, and friend.

—**BILLY J. KRAMER**
New York, 2013

the beatles changed our lives, brian epstein changed theirs

he made it all possible, possible for us to be having this chat today,

brian told them who they could be and helped them become it.

we were not there on that new year's day of 1962 when the beatles auditioned for decca at their west hampstead studios.

we were not there when an a & r man, after turning down the band, chased brian out onto the street and told him that for a hundred quid he could knock the beatles into shape for another audition.

the humiliation, the pain . . . brian already had at least two social marks against him— he was jewish and gay.

christ, you know it ain't easy. dusty springfield was catholic and gay but she was able to sing her way through it.

brian had to stand in the wings and watch his lads twist and shout

but those wings became the wings of the world

from scunthorpe to shea stadium in three super fast, incredible singalong years the world was given a songbook it has never stopped singing and an idea as to what a life could be about.

brian persevered against all odds and got his lads a recording contract and that act changed all our lives for the better.

if brian had loved himself as much as he loved the beatles he may have still been with us today,

but we do have all that they did together . . .

andrew loog oldham
bogotá, mm13

DEDICATIONS

VIVEK J. TIWARY

for
Nandini Beharry Tiwary
and
Malka "Queenie" Epstein

ANDREW C. ROBINSON

for
Jim and Leah

Part I: Or I'll Dress You in Mourning

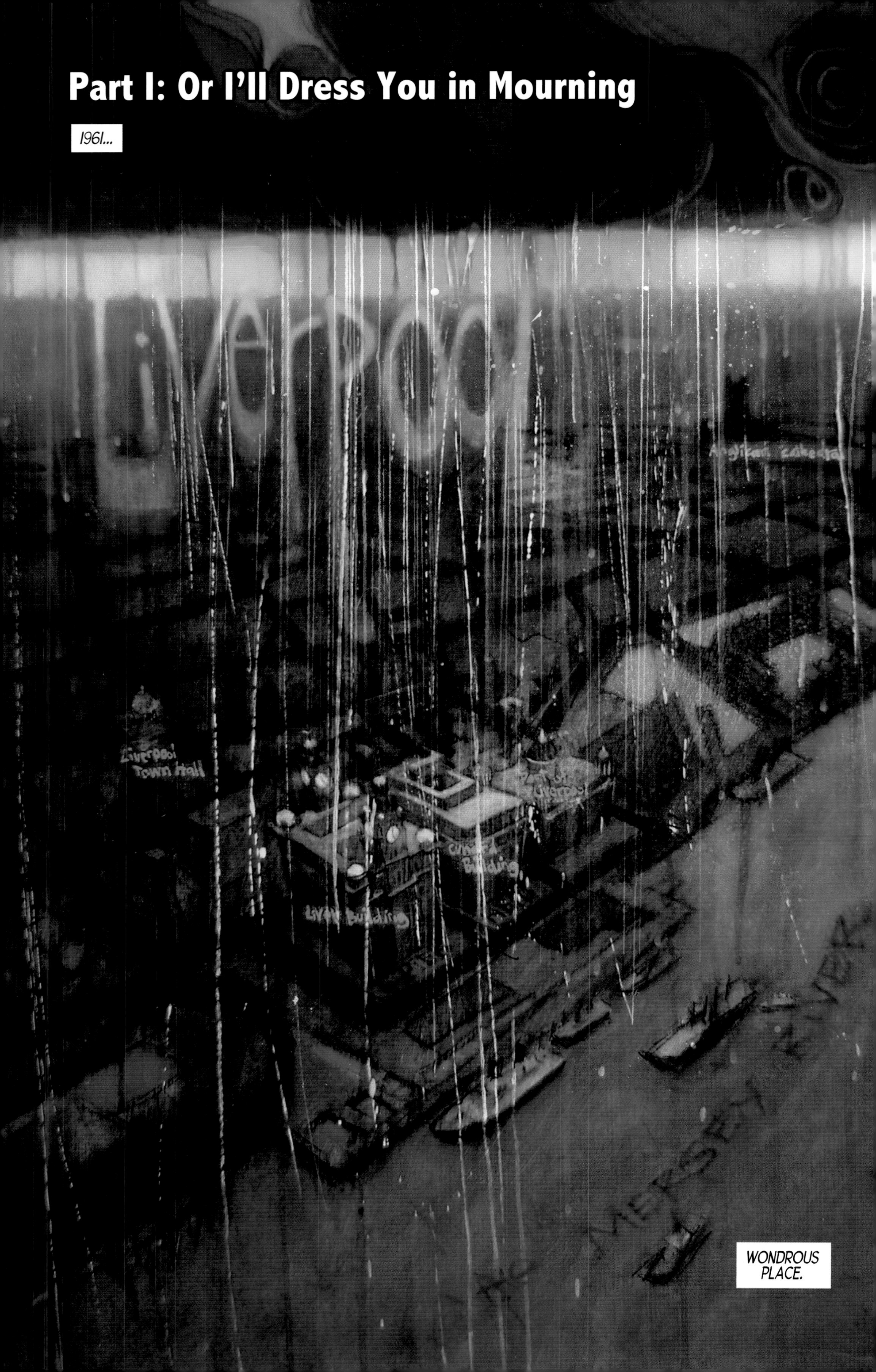
1961...
Liverpool
Liverpool Town Hall
Cunard Building
Liver Building
WONDROUS PLACE.

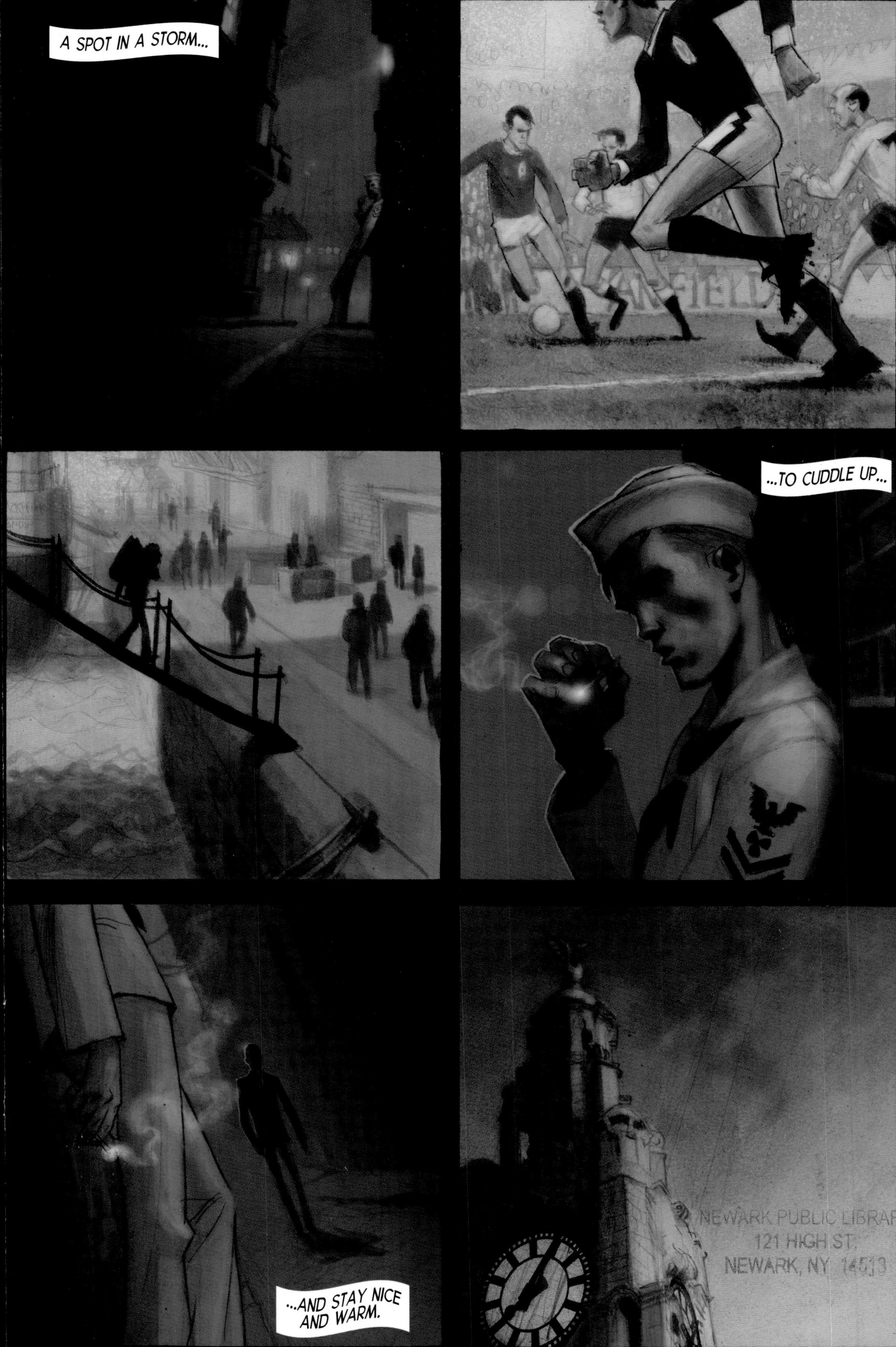
A SPOT IN A STORM...
...TO CUDDLE UP...
...AND STAY NICE AND WARM.

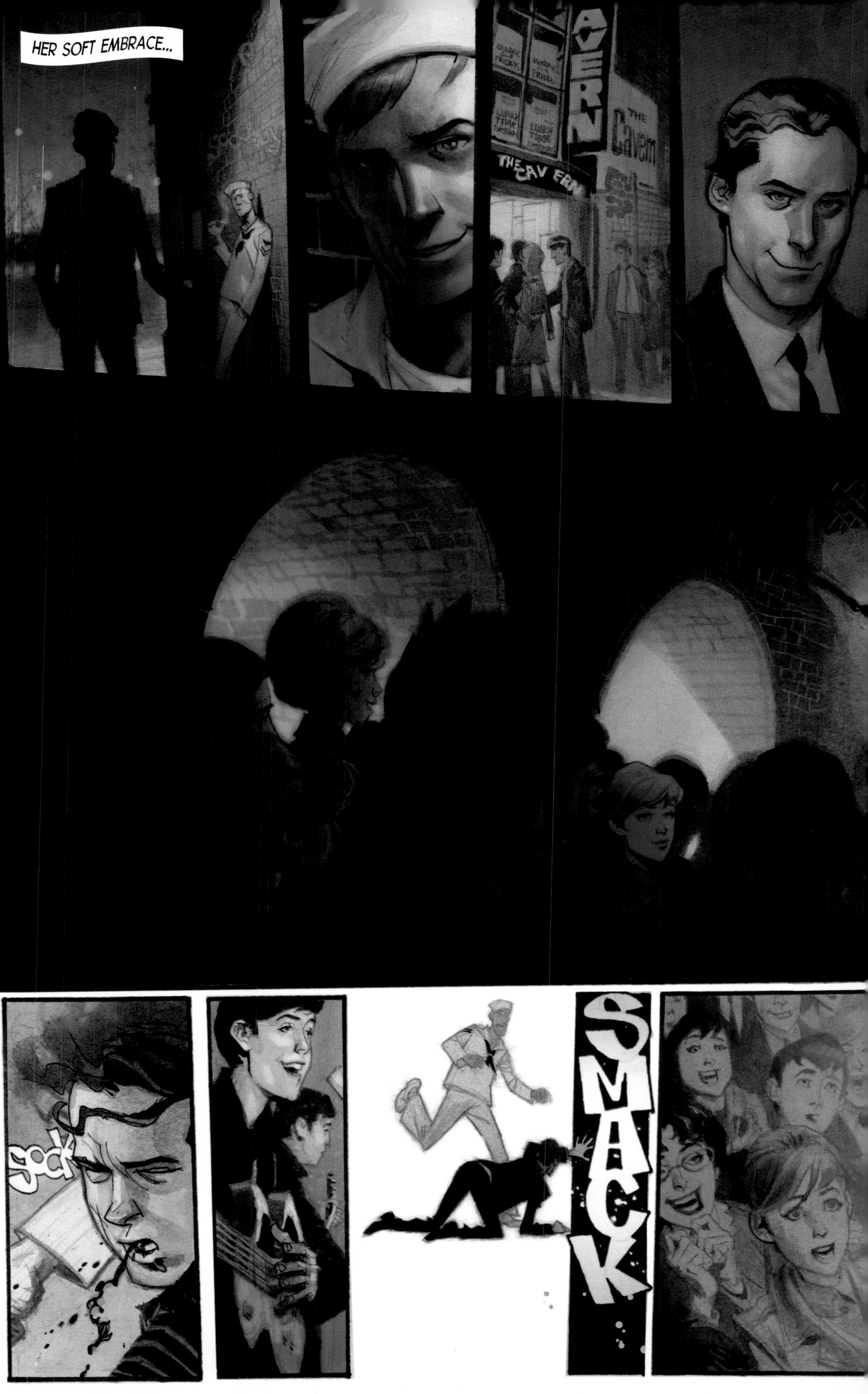

HER SOFT EMBRACE...
THE CAVERN
The Cavern
sock
SMACK

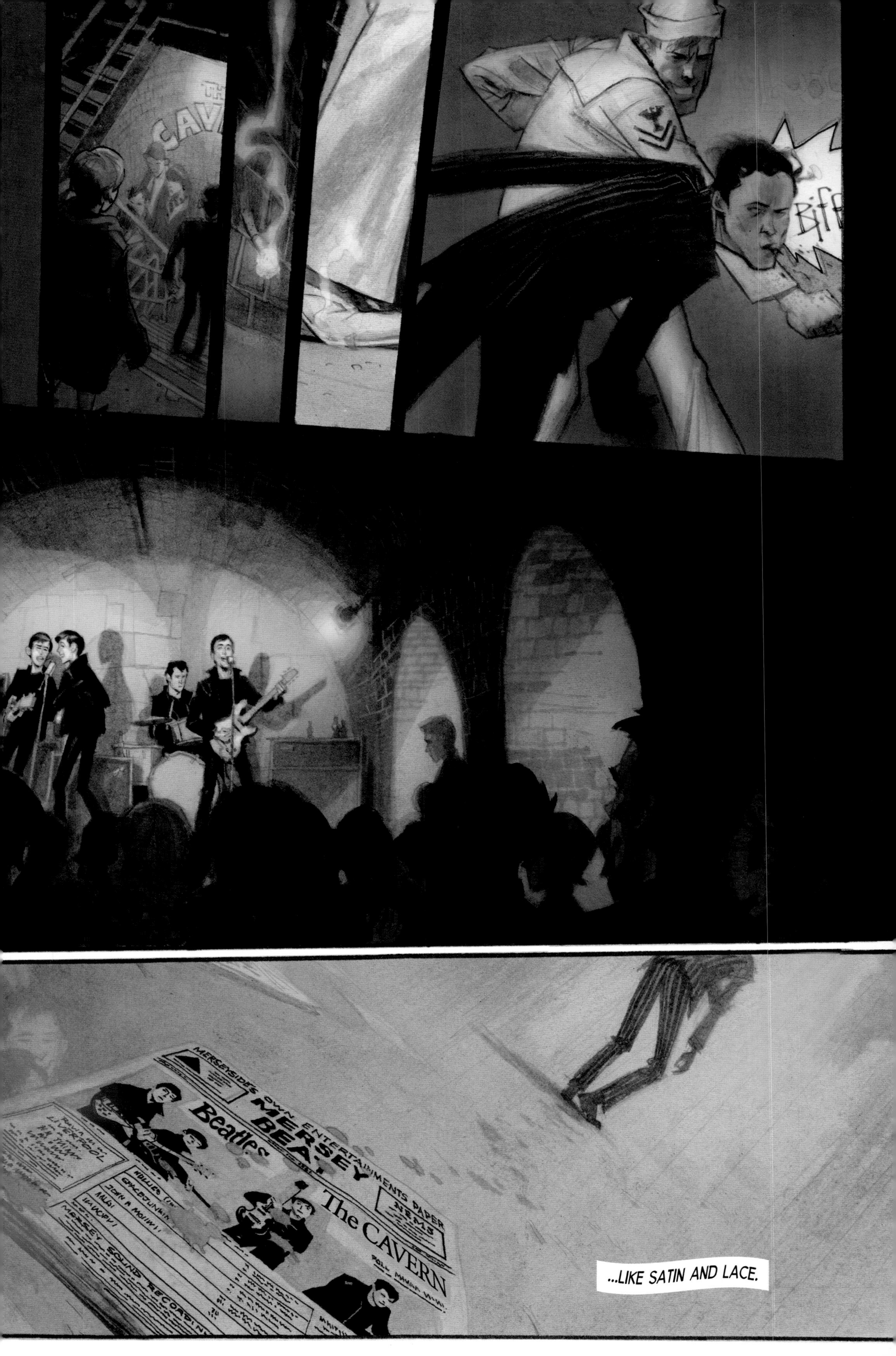
MERSEYSIDES OWN ENTERTAINMENTS PAPER
MERSEY BEAT
Beatles
The CAVERN
LIVERPOOL
...LIKE SATIN AND LACE.

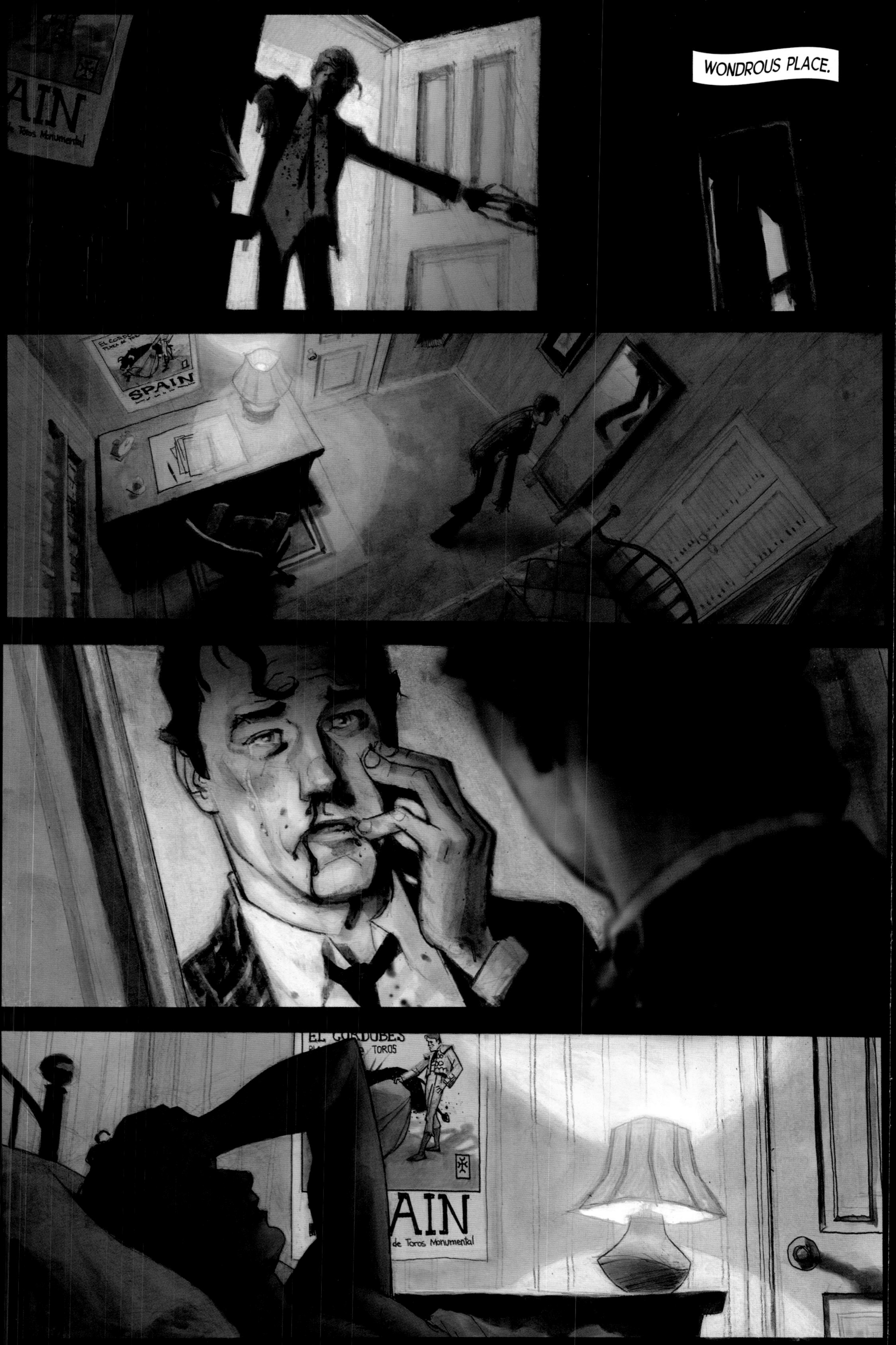
WONDROUS PLACE.
AIN
Toros Monumental
SPAIN
TOROS
AIN
de Toros Monumental

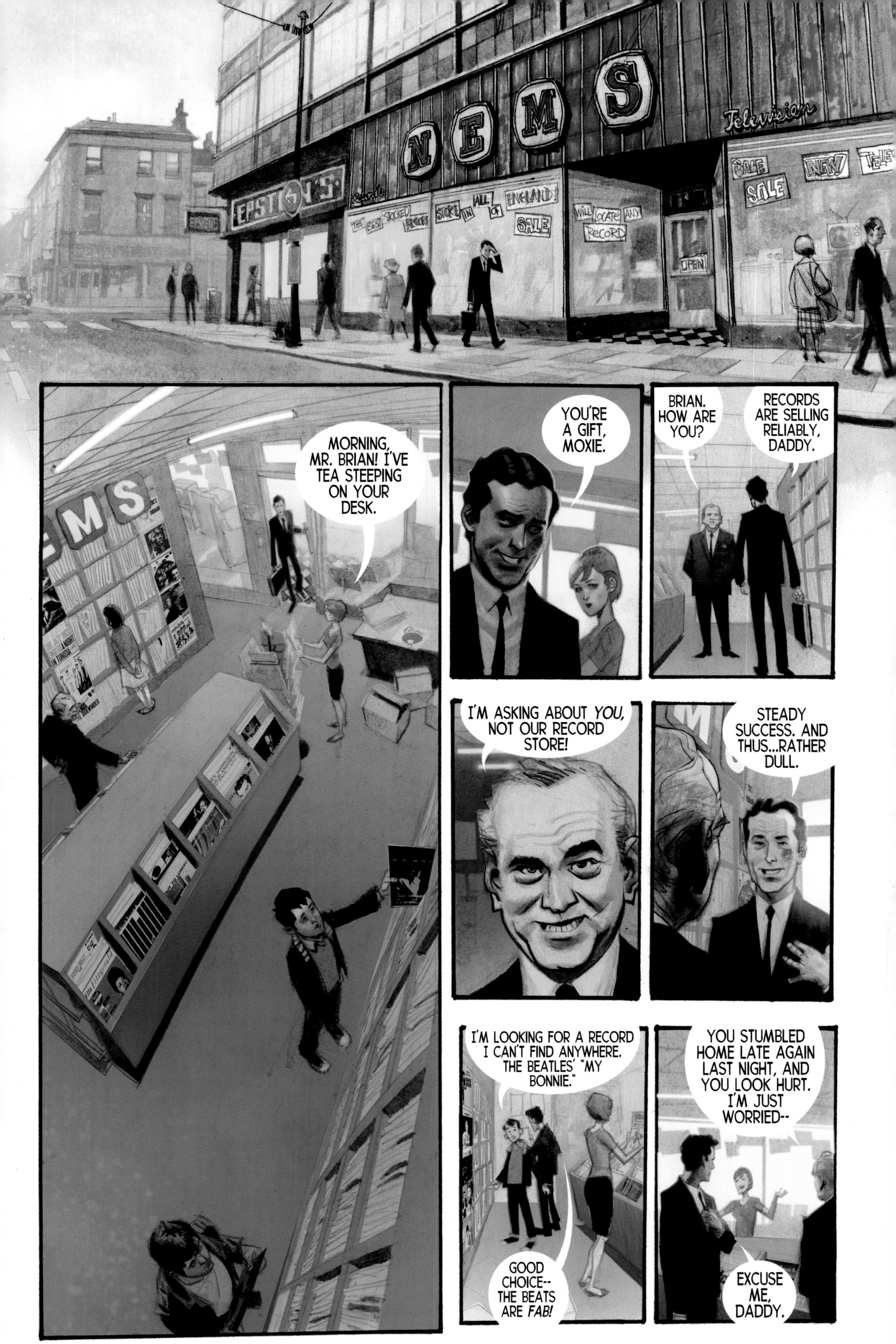
NEMS
EPSTEIN'S
Records
THE BEST STOCKED RECORD STORE IN ALL OF ENGLAND!
SALE
WILL LOCATE ANY RECORD
OPEN
Television
SALE
SALE
NEW
MORNING, MR. BRIAN! I'VE TEA STEEPING ON YOUR DESK.
YOU'RE A GIFT, MOXIE.
BRIAN. HOW ARE YOU?
RECORDS ARE SELLING RELIABLY, DADDY.
I'M ASKING ABOUT *YOU*, NOT OUR RECORD STORE!
STEADY SUCCESS. AND THUS...RATHER DULL.
I'M LOOKING FOR A RECORD I CAN'T FIND ANYWHERE. THE BEATLES' "MY BONNIE."
GOOD CHOICE-- THE BEATS ARE *FAB!*
YOU STUMBLED HOME LATE AGAIN LAST NIGHT, AND YOU LOOK HURT. I'M JUST WORRIED--
EXCUSE ME, DADDY.

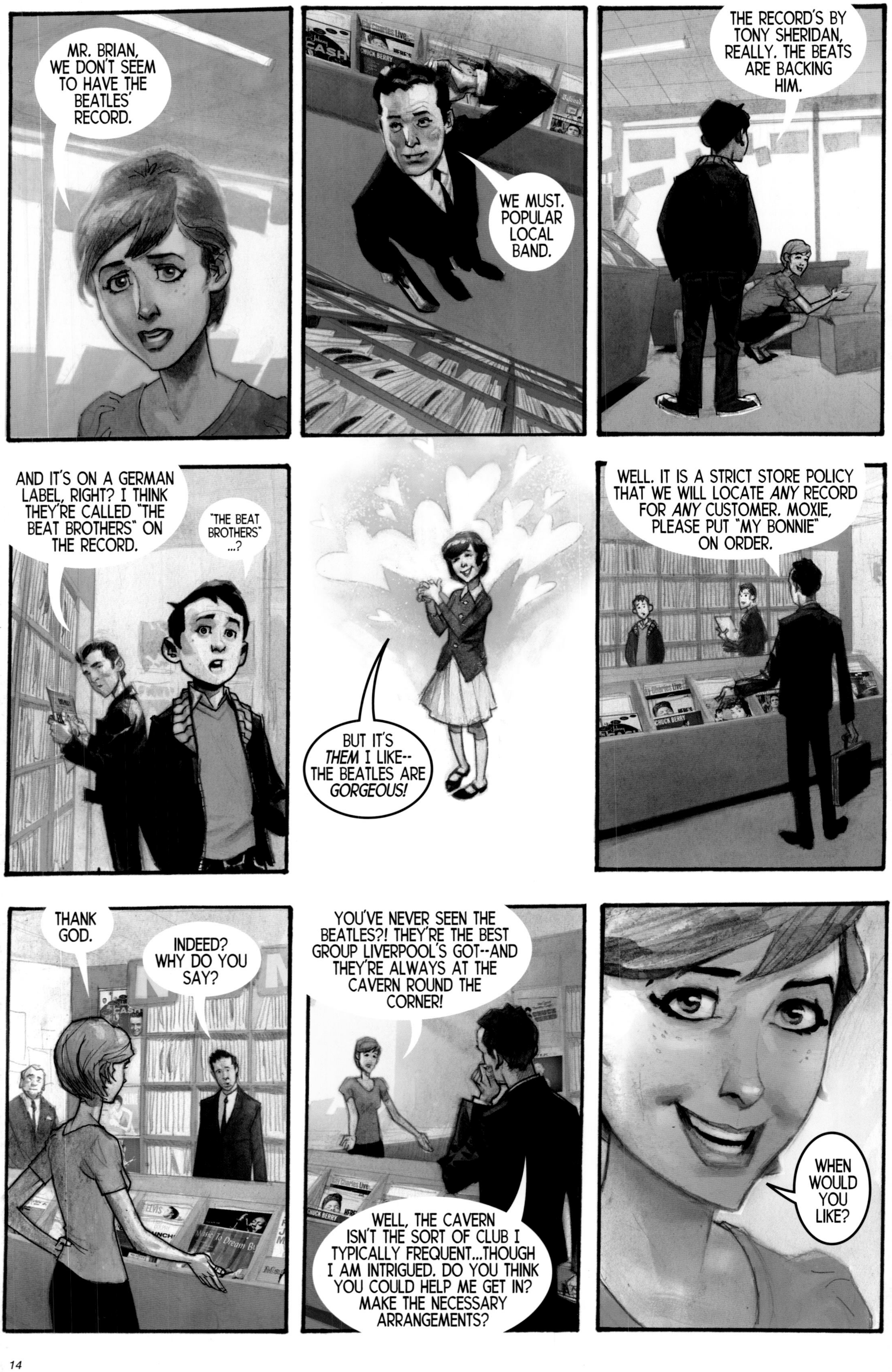
MR. BRIAN, WE DON'T SEEM TO HAVE THE BEATLES' RECORD.
WE MUST. POPULAR LOCAL BAND.
THE RECORD'S BY TONY SHERIDAN, REALLY. THE BEATS ARE BACKING HIM.
AND IT'S ON A GERMAN LABEL, RIGHT? I THINK THEY'RE CALLED "THE BEAT BROTHERS" ON THE RECORD.
"THE BEAT BROTHERS" ...?
BUT IT'S *THEM* I LIKE-- THE BEATLES ARE *GORGEOUS!*
WELL. IT IS A STRICT STORE POLICY THAT WE WILL LOCATE *ANY* RECORD FOR *ANY* CUSTOMER. MOXIE, PLEASE PUT "MY BONNIE" ON ORDER.
THANK GOD.
INDEED? WHY DO YOU SAY?
YOU'VE NEVER SEEN THE BEATLES?! THEY'RE THE BEST GROUP LIVERPOOL'S GOT--AND THEY'RE ALWAYS AT THE CAVERN ROUND THE CORNER!
WELL, THE CAVERN ISN'T THE SORT OF CLUB I TYPICALLY FREQUENT...THOUGH I AM INTRIGUED. DO YOU THINK YOU COULD HELP ME GET IN? MAKE THE NECESSARY ARRANGEMENTS?
WHEN WOULD YOU LIKE?

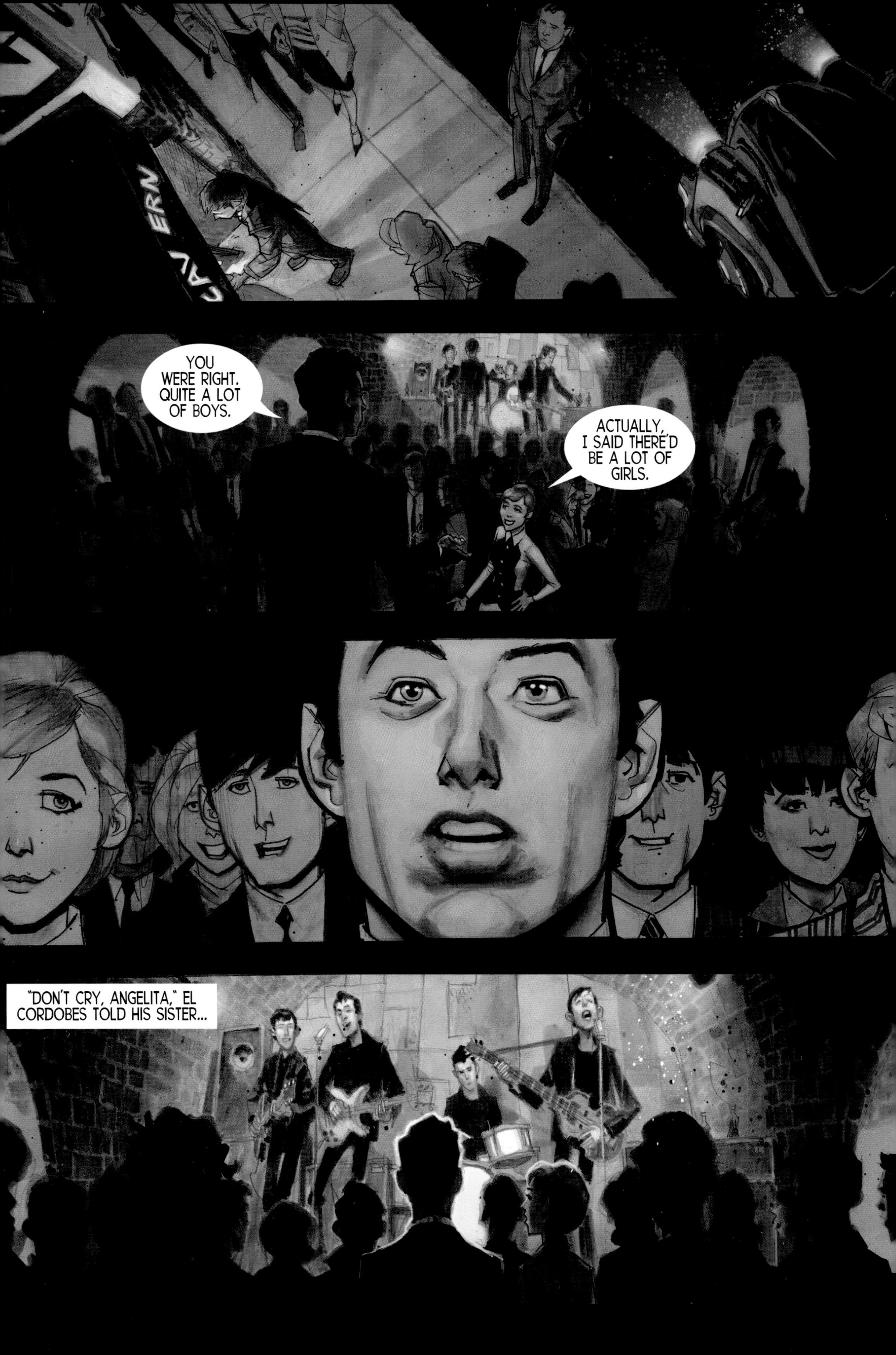
YOU WERE RIGHT. QUITE A LOT OF BOYS.
ACTUALLY, I SAID THERE'D BE A LOT OF GIRLS.
"DON'T CRY, ANGELITA," EL CORDOBES TOLD HIS SISTER...

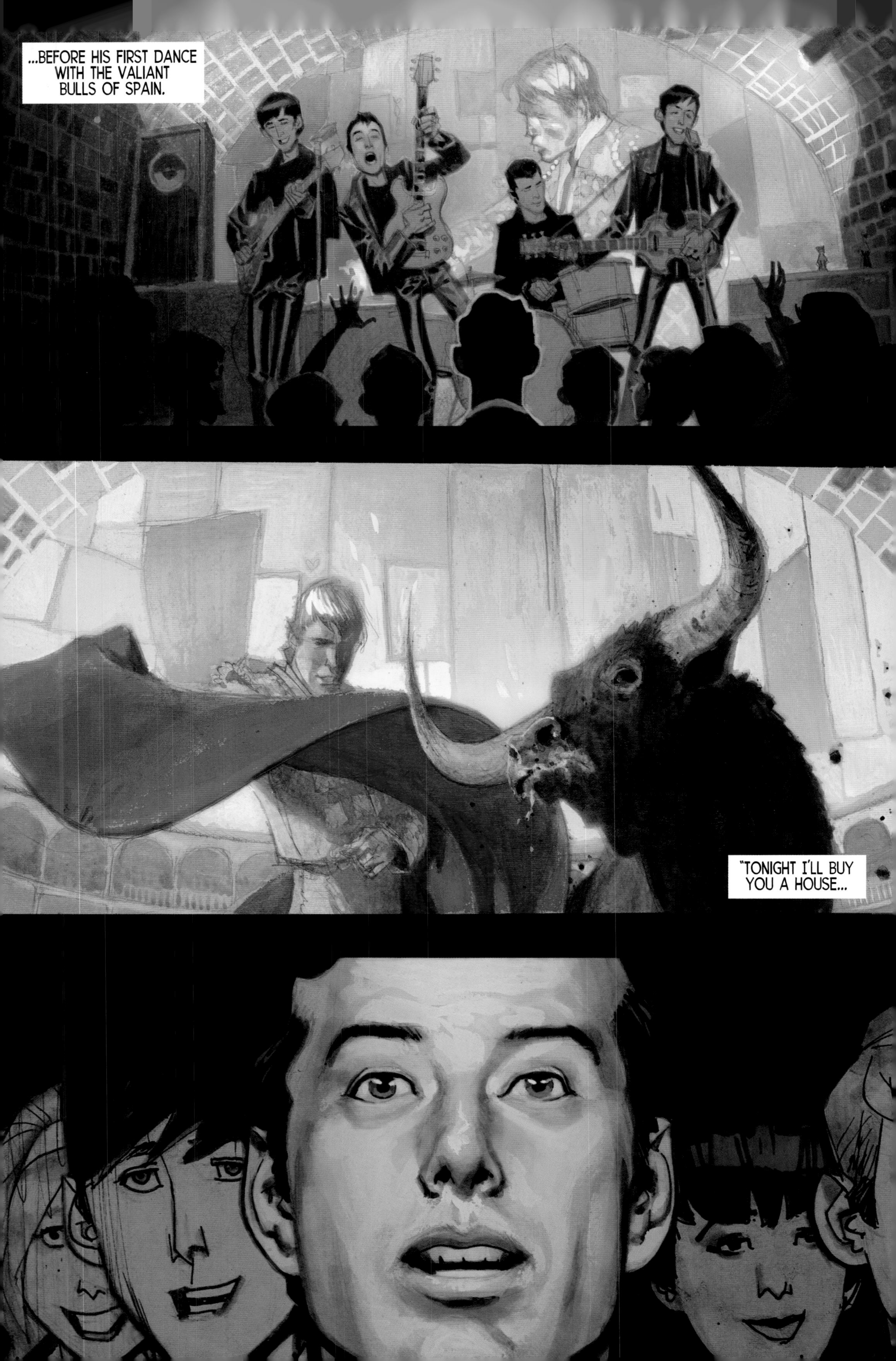
...BEFORE HIS FIRST DANCE WITH THE VALIANT BULLS OF SPAIN.
"TONIGHT I'LL BUY YOU A HOUSE...

"...OR I'LL DRESS YOU IN MOURNING."
OUR FAVORITE ROCK AND DOLE GROUP--THE BEATLES--IN THE BEST OF CELLARS, YOU CAVERN DWELLERS! AND WE'VE A MUSIC CELEBRITY OF A DIFFERENT SORT HERE TONIGHT--LET'S GIVE A HAND TO MR. BRIAN EPSTEIN OF NEMS!!

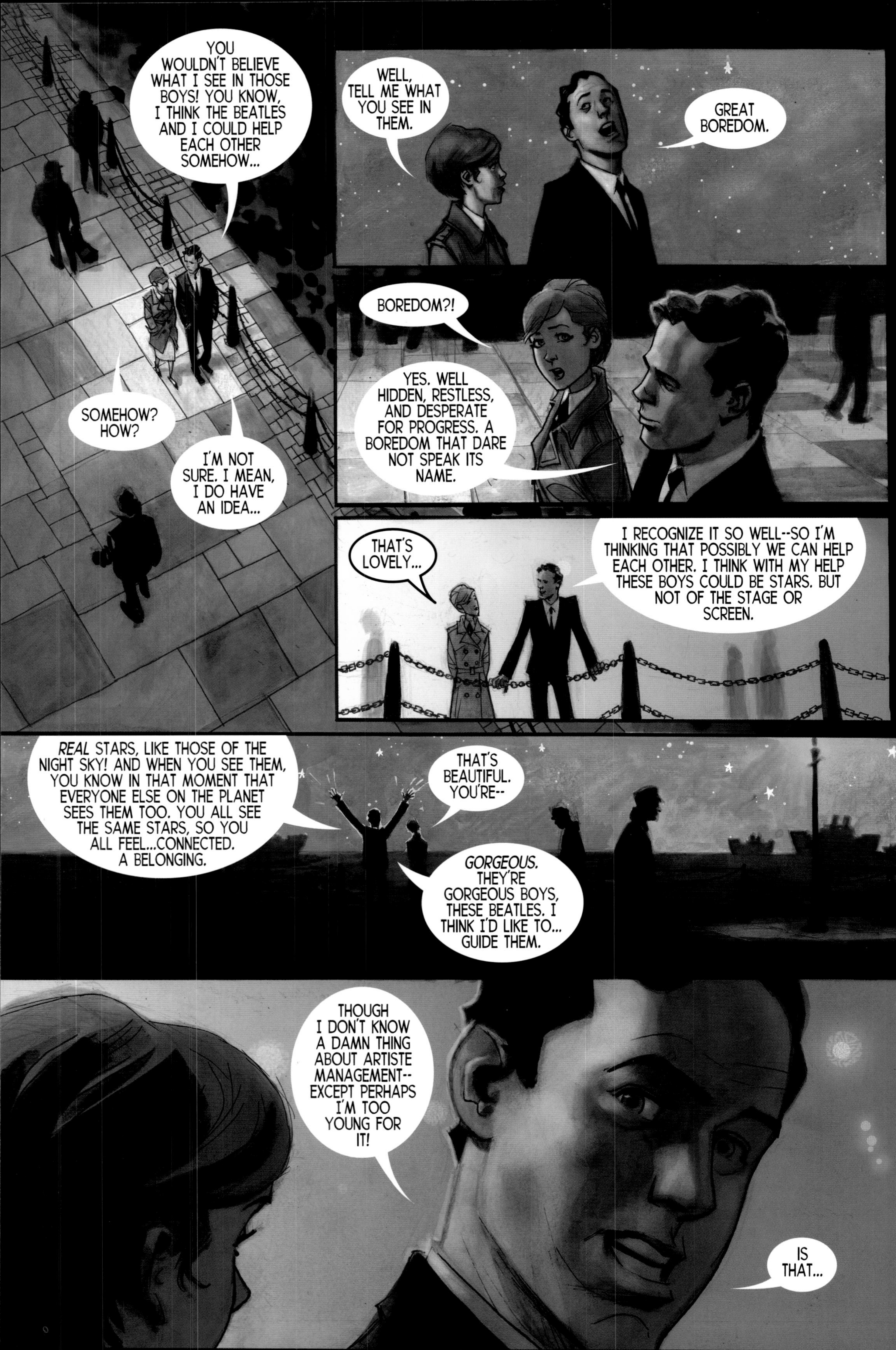
YOU WOULDN'T BELIEVE WHAT I SEE IN THOSE BOYS! YOU KNOW, I THINK THE BEATLES AND I COULD HELP EACH OTHER SOMEHOW...
SOMEHOW? HOW?
I'M NOT SURE. I MEAN, I DO HAVE AN IDEA...
WELL, TELL ME WHAT YOU SEE IN THEM.
GREAT BOREDOM.
BOREDOM?!
YES. WELL HIDDEN, RESTLESS, AND DESPERATE FOR PROGRESS. A BOREDOM THAT DARE NOT SPEAK ITS NAME.
THAT'S LOVELY...
I RECOGNIZE IT SO WELL--SO I'M THINKING THAT POSSIBLY WE CAN HELP EACH OTHER. I THINK WITH MY HELP THESE BOYS COULD BE STARS. BUT NOT OF THE STAGE OR SCREEN.
REAL STARS, LIKE THOSE OF THE NIGHT SKY! AND WHEN YOU SEE THEM, YOU KNOW IN THAT MOMENT THAT EVERYONE ELSE ON THE PLANET SEES THEM TOO. YOU ALL SEE THE SAME STARS, SO YOU ALL FEEL...CONNECTED. A BELONGING.
THAT'S BEAUTIFUL. YOU'RE--
GORGEOUS. THEY'RE GORGEOUS BOYS, THESE BEATLES. I THINK I'D LIKE TO... GUIDE THEM.
THOUGH I DON'T KNOW A DAMN THING ABOUT ARTISTE MANAGEMENT--EXCEPT PERHAPS I'M TOO YOUNG FOR IT!
IS THAT...

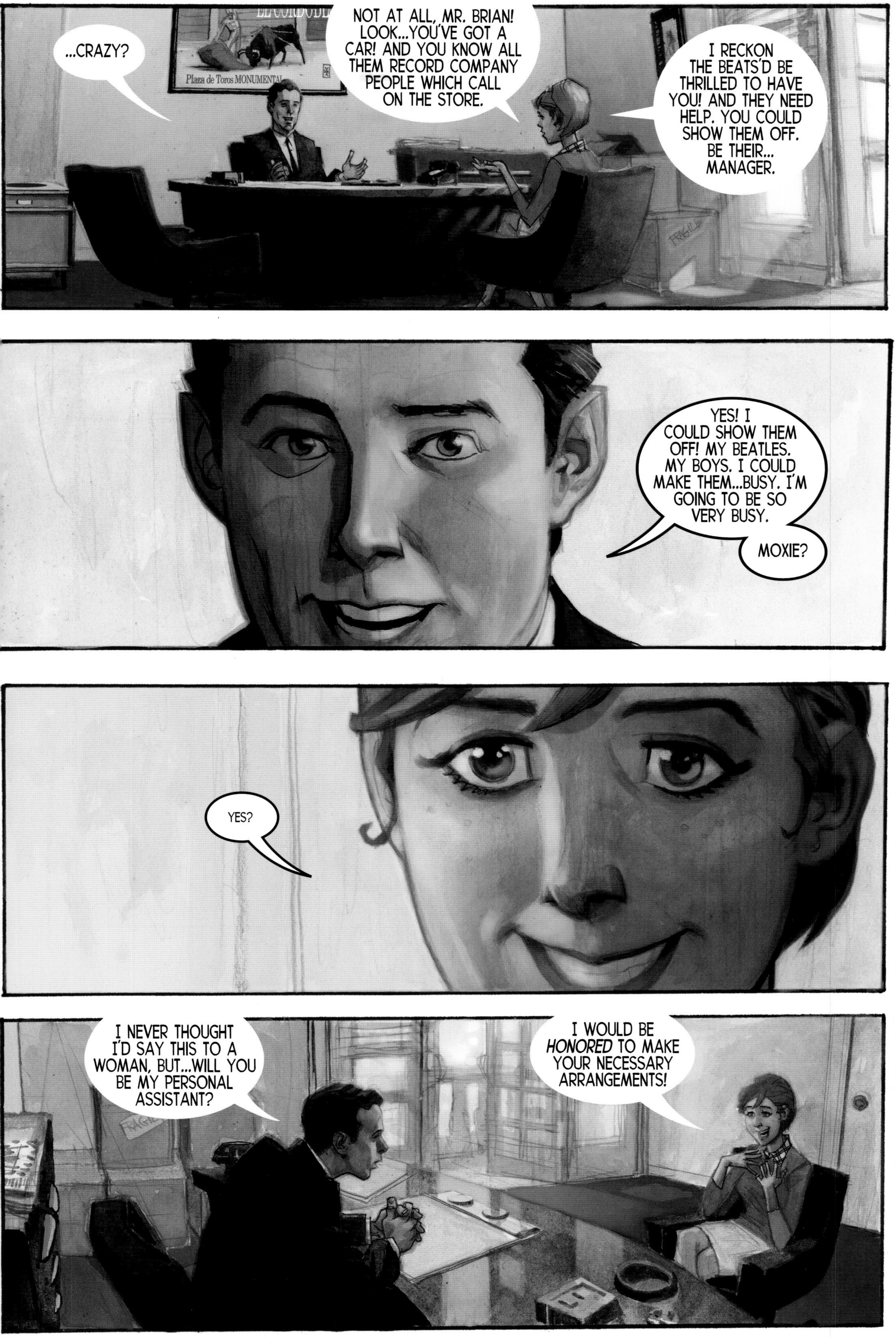
...CRAZY?
Plaza de Toros MONUMENTAL
NOT AT ALL, MR. BRIAN! LOOK...YOU'VE GOT A CAR! AND YOU KNOW ALL THEM RECORD COMPANY PEOPLE WHICH CALL ON THE STORE.
I RECKON THE BEATS'D BE THRILLED TO HAVE YOU! AND THEY NEED HELP. YOU COULD SHOW THEM OFF. BE THEIR... MANAGER.
YES! I COULD SHOW THEM OFF! MY BEATLES. MY BOYS. I COULD MAKE THEM...BUSY. I'M GOING TO BE SO VERY BUSY.
MOXIE?
YES?
I NEVER THOUGHT I'D SAY THIS TO A WOMAN, BUT...WILL YOU BE MY PERSONAL ASSISTANT?
I WOULD BE *HONORED* TO MAKE YOUR NECESSARY ARRANGEMENTS!

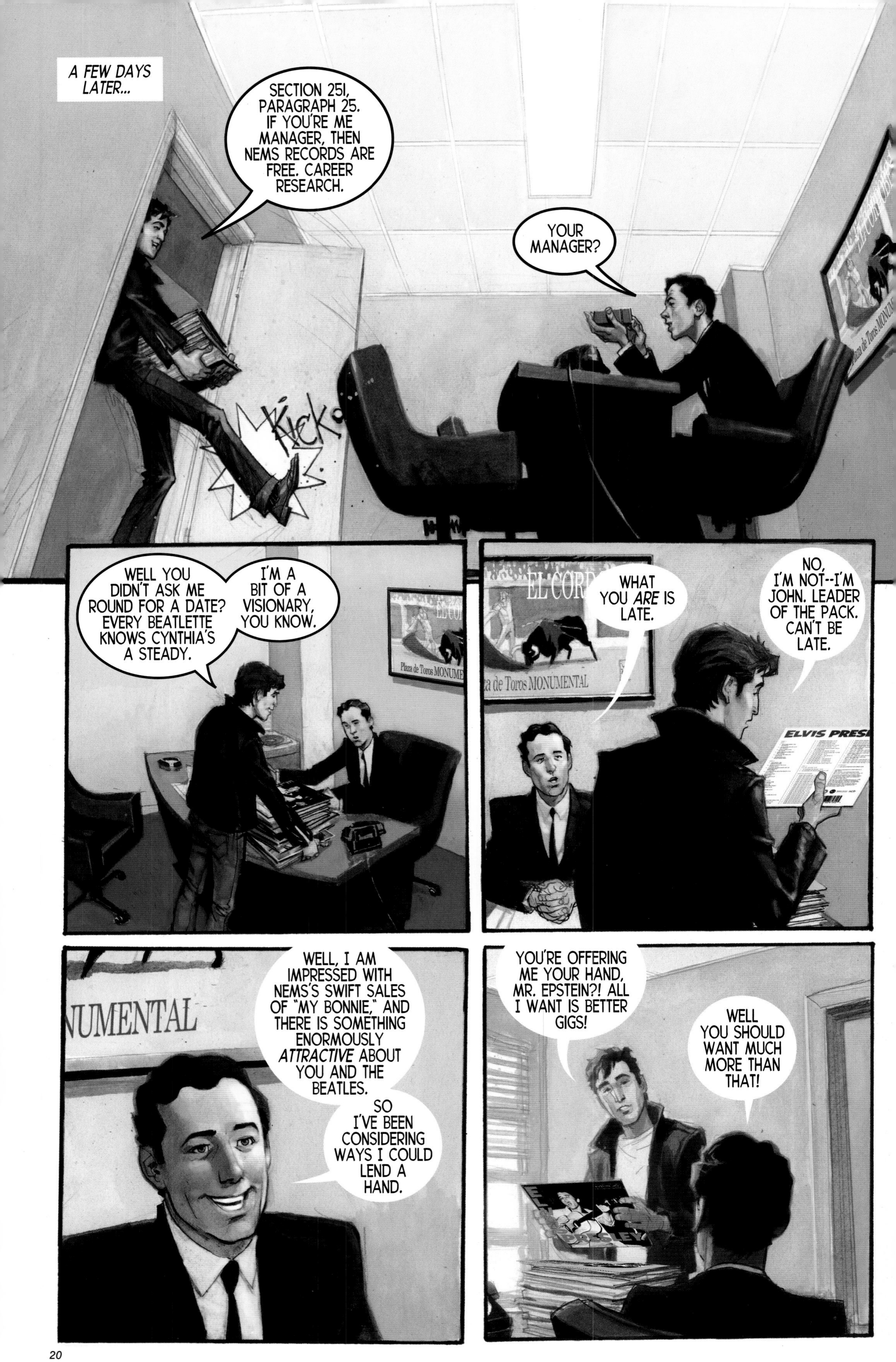
A FEW DAYS LATER...
SECTION 251, PARAGRAPH 25. IF YOU'RE ME MANAGER, THEN NEMS RECORDS ARE FREE. CAREER RESEARCH.
YOUR MANAGER?
KICK
WELL YOU DIDN'T ASK ME ROUND FOR A DATE? EVERY BEATLETTE KNOWS CYNTHIA'S A STEADY.
I'M A BIT OF A VISIONARY, YOU KNOW.
Plaza de Toros MONUMENTAL
WHAT YOU *ARE* IS LATE.
NO, I'M NOT--I'M JOHN. LEADER OF THE PACK. CAN'T BE LATE.
ELVIS PRES
NUMENTAL
WELL, I AM IMPRESSED WITH NEMS'S SWIFT SALES OF "MY BONNIE," AND THERE IS SOMETHING ENORMOUSLY *ATTRACTIVE* ABOUT YOU AND THE BEATLES.
SO I'VE BEEN CONSIDERING WAYS I COULD LEND A HAND.
YOU'RE OFFERING ME YOUR HAND, MR. EPSTEIN?! ALL I WANT IS BETTER GIGS!
WELL YOU SHOULD WANT MUCH MORE THAN THAT!

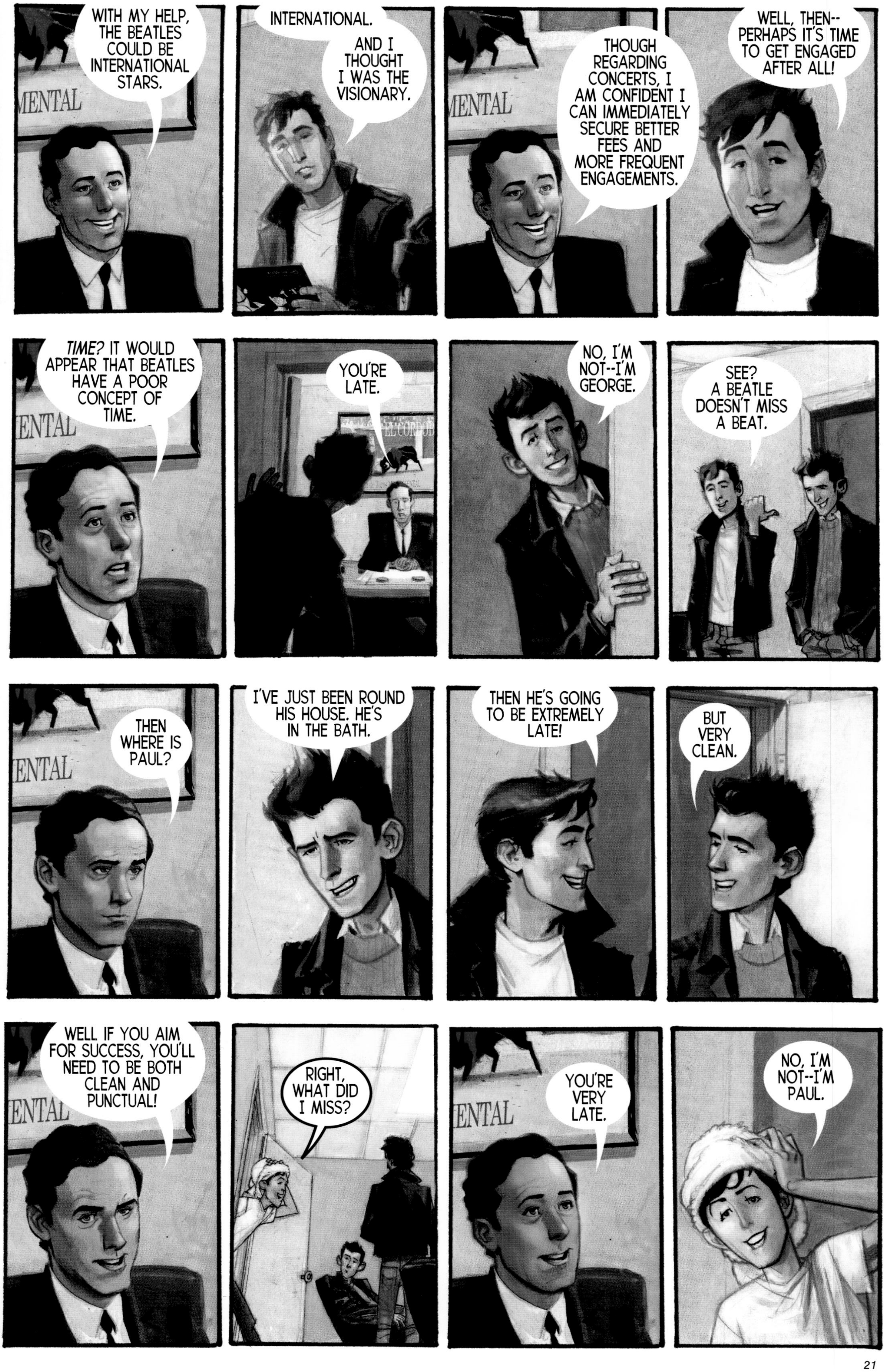
WITH MY HELP, THE BEATLES COULD BE INTERNATIONAL STARS.
INTERNATIONAL.
AND I THOUGHT I WAS THE VISIONARY.
THOUGH REGARDING CONCERTS, I AM CONFIDENT I CAN IMMEDIATELY SECURE BETTER FEES AND MORE FREQUENT ENGAGEMENTS.
WELL, THEN-- PERHAPS IT'S TIME TO GET ENGAGED AFTER ALL!
TIME? IT WOULD APPEAR THAT BEATLES HAVE A POOR CONCEPT OF TIME.
YOU'RE LATE.
NO, I'M NOT--I'M GEORGE.
SEE? A BEATLE DOESN'T MISS A BEAT.
THEN WHERE IS PAUL?
I'VE JUST BEEN ROUND HIS HOUSE. HE'S IN THE BATH.
THEN HE'S GOING TO BE EXTREMELY LATE!
BUT VERY CLEAN.
WELL IF YOU AIM FOR SUCCESS, YOU'LL NEED TO BE BOTH CLEAN AND PUNCTUAL!
RIGHT, WHAT DID I MISS?
YOU'RE VERY LATE.
NO, I'M NOT--I'M PAUL.

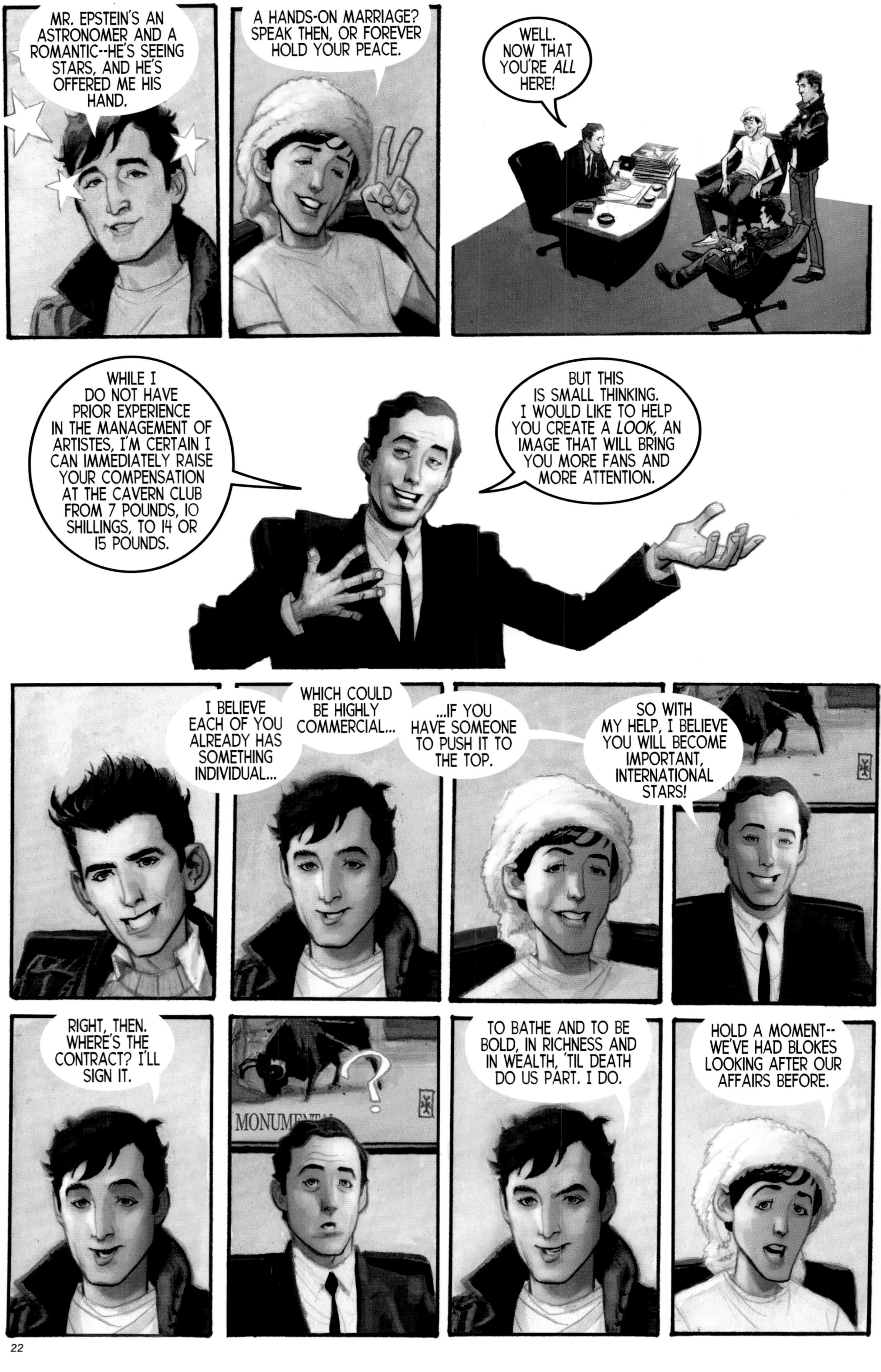
MR. EPSTEIN'S AN ASTRONOMER AND A ROMANTIC--HE'S SEEING STARS, AND HE'S OFFERED ME HIS HAND.
A HANDS-ON MARRIAGE? SPEAK THEN, OR FOREVER HOLD YOUR PEACE.
WELL. NOW THAT YOU'RE *ALL* HERE!
WHILE I DO NOT HAVE PRIOR EXPERIENCE IN THE MANAGEMENT OF ARTISTES, I'M CERTAIN I CAN IMMEDIATELY RAISE YOUR COMPENSATION AT THE CAVERN CLUB FROM 7 POUNDS, 10 SHILLINGS, TO 14 OR 15 POUNDS.
BUT THIS IS SMALL THINKING. I WOULD LIKE TO HELP YOU CREATE A *LOOK,* AN IMAGE THAT WILL BRING YOU MORE FANS AND MORE ATTENTION.
I BELIEVE EACH OF YOU ALREADY HAS SOMETHING INDIVIDUAL...
WHICH COULD BE HIGHLY COMMERCIAL...
...IF YOU HAVE SOMEONE TO PUSH IT TO THE TOP.
SO WITH MY HELP, I BELIEVE YOU WILL BECOME IMPORTANT, INTERNATIONAL STARS!
RIGHT, THEN. WHERE'S THE CONTRACT? I'LL SIGN IT.
?
MONUMENTAL
TO BATHE AND TO BE BOLD, IN RICHNESS AND IN WEALTH, 'TIL DEATH DO US PART. I DO.
HOLD A MOMENT--WE'VE HAD BLOKES LOOKING AFTER OUR AFFAIRS BEFORE.

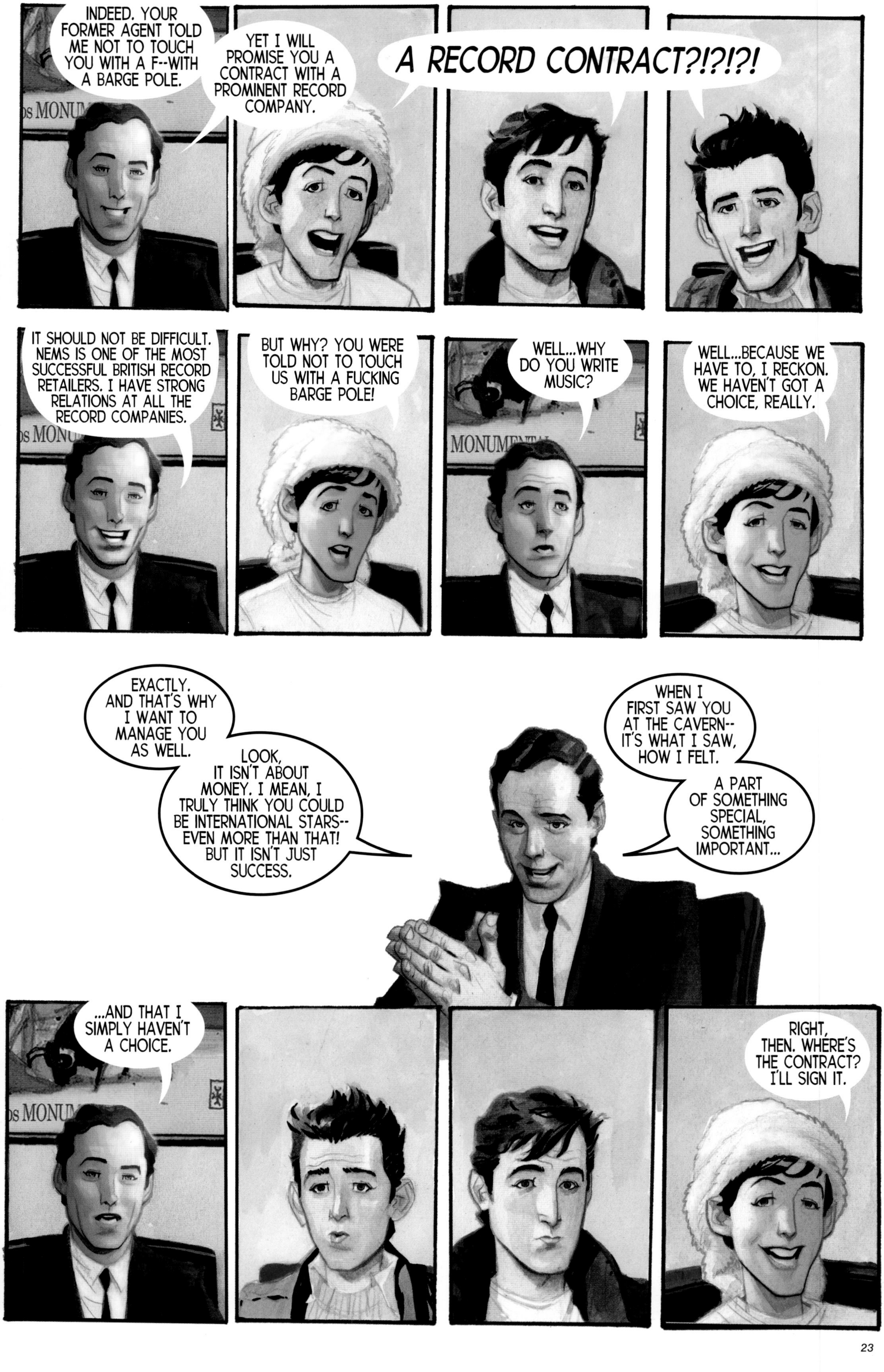
INDEED. YOUR FORMER AGENT TOLD ME NOT TO TOUCH YOU WITH A F--WITH A BARGE POLE.
YET I WILL PROMISE YOU A CONTRACT WITH A PROMINENT RECORD COMPANY.
A RECORD CONTRACT?!?!?!
IT SHOULD NOT BE DIFFICULT. NEMS IS ONE OF THE MOST SUCCESSFUL BRITISH RECORD RETAILERS. I HAVE STRONG RELATIONS AT ALL THE RECORD COMPANIES.
BUT WHY? YOU WERE TOLD NOT TO TOUCH US WITH A FUCKING BARGE POLE!
WELL...WHY DO YOU WRITE MUSIC?
WELL...BECAUSE WE HAVE TO, I RECKON. WE HAVEN'T GOT A CHOICE, REALLY.
EXACTLY. AND THAT'S WHY I WANT TO MANAGE YOU AS WELL.
LOOK, IT ISN'T ABOUT MONEY. I MEAN, I TRULY THINK YOU COULD BE INTERNATIONAL STARS-- EVEN MORE THAN THAT! BUT IT ISN'T JUST SUCCESS.
WHEN I FIRST SAW YOU AT THE CAVERN-- IT'S WHAT I SAW, HOW I FELT.
A PART OF SOMETHING SPECIAL, SOMETHING IMPORTANT...
...AND THAT I SIMPLY HAVEN'T A CHOICE.
RIGHT, THEN. WHERE'S THE CONTRACT? I'LL SIGN IT.

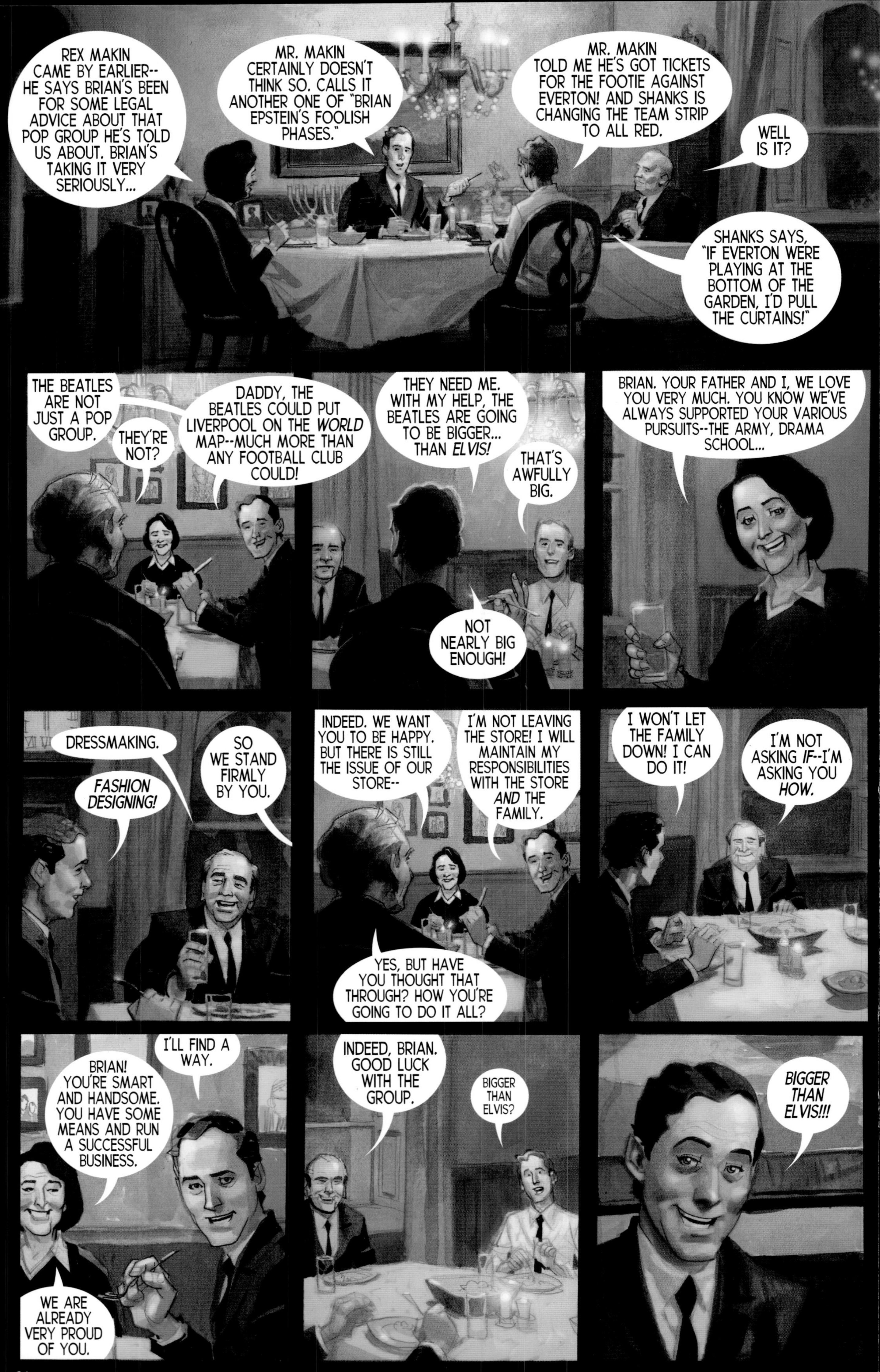
REX MAKIN CAME BY EARLIER-- HE SAYS BRIAN'S BEEN FOR SOME LEGAL ADVICE ABOUT THAT POP GROUP HE'S TOLD US ABOUT. BRIAN'S TAKING IT VERY SERIOUSLY...
MR. MAKIN CERTAINLY DOESN'T THINK SO. CALLS IT ANOTHER ONE OF "BRIAN EPSTEIN'S FOOLISH PHASES."
MR. MAKIN TOLD ME HE'S GOT TICKETS FOR THE FOOTIE AGAINST EVERTON! AND SHANKS IS CHANGING THE TEAM STRIP TO ALL RED.
WELL IS IT?
SHANKS SAYS, "IF EVERTON WERE PLAYING AT THE BOTTOM OF THE GARDEN, I'D PULL THE CURTAINS!"
THE BEATLES ARE NOT JUST A POP GROUP.
THEY'RE NOT?
DADDY, THE BEATLES COULD PUT LIVERPOOL ON THE *WORLD* MAP--MUCH MORE THAN ANY FOOTBALL CLUB COULD!
THEY NEED ME. WITH MY HELP, THE BEATLES ARE GOING TO BE BIGGER... THAN *ELVIS!*
THAT'S AWFULLY BIG.
NOT NEARLY BIG ENOUGH!
BRIAN. YOUR FATHER AND I, WE LOVE YOU VERY MUCH. YOU KNOW WE'VE ALWAYS SUPPORTED YOUR VARIOUS PURSUITS--THE ARMY, DRAMA SCHOOL...
DRESSMAKING.
FASHION DESIGNING!
SO WE STAND FIRMLY BY YOU.
INDEED. WE WANT YOU TO BE HAPPY. BUT THERE IS STILL THE ISSUE OF OUR STORE--
I'M NOT LEAVING THE STORE! I WILL MAINTAIN MY RESPONSIBILITIES WITH THE STORE *AND* THE FAMILY.
YES, BUT HAVE YOU THOUGHT THAT THROUGH? HOW YOU'RE GOING TO DO IT ALL?
I WON'T LET THE FAMILY DOWN! I CAN DO IT!
I'M NOT ASKING *IF*--I'M ASKING YOU *HOW.*
BRIAN! YOU'RE SMART AND HANDSOME. YOU HAVE SOME MEANS AND RUN A SUCCESSFUL BUSINESS.
I'LL FIND A WAY.
WE ARE ALREADY VERY PROUD OF YOU.
INDEED, BRIAN. GOOD LUCK WITH THE GROUP.
BIGGER THAN ELVIS?
BIGGER THAN ELVIS!!!

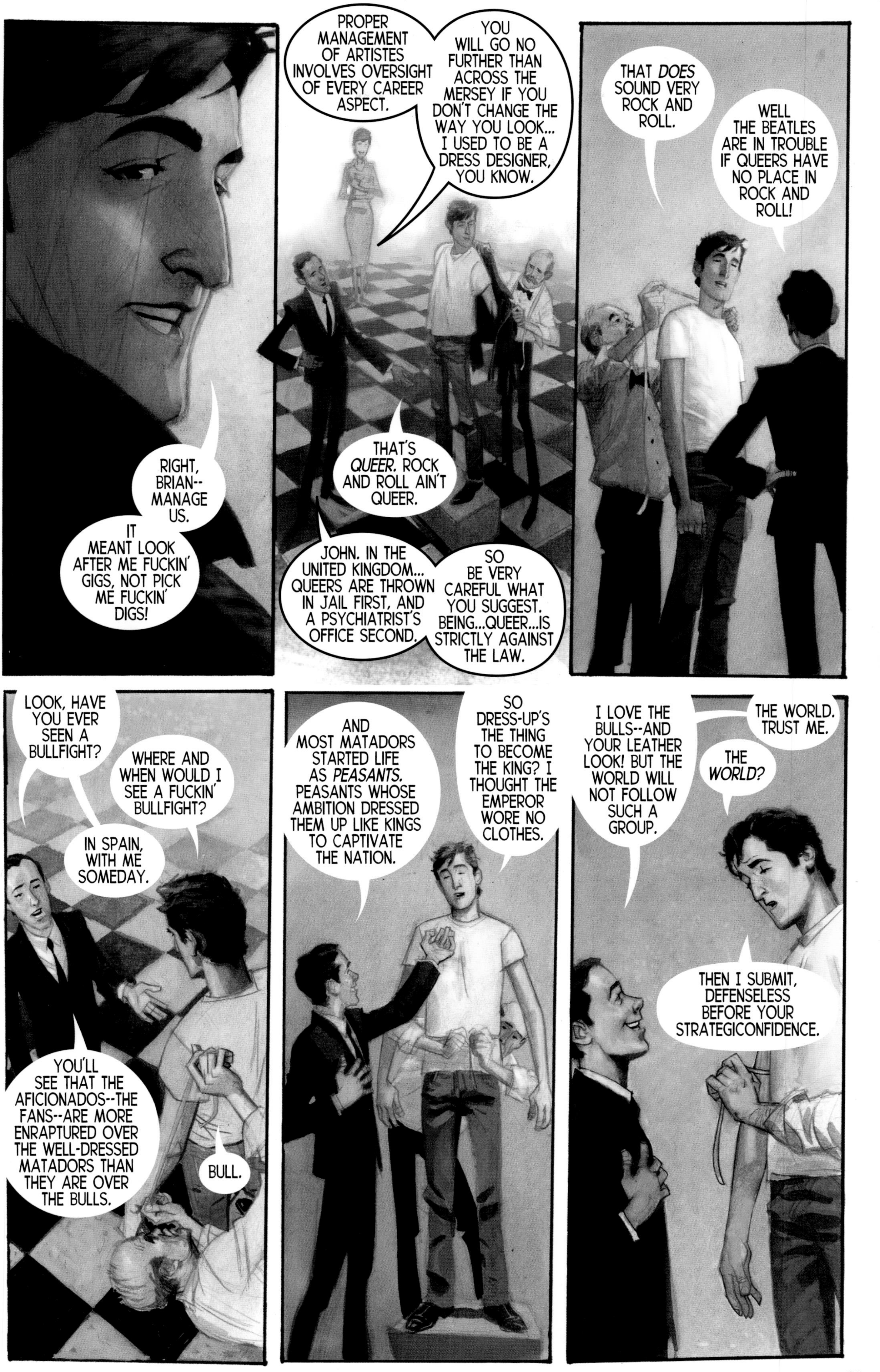
RIGHT, BRIAN--MANAGE US.
IT MEANT LOOK AFTER ME FUCKIN' GIGS, NOT PICK ME FUCKIN' DIGS!
PROPER MANAGEMENT OF ARTISTES INVOLVES OVERSIGHT OF EVERY CAREER ASPECT.
YOU WILL GO NO FURTHER THAN ACROSS THE MERSEY IF YOU DON'T CHANGE THE WAY YOU LOOK... I USED TO BE A DRESS DESIGNER, YOU KNOW.
THAT'S *QUEER.* ROCK AND ROLL AIN'T QUEER.
JOHN. IN THE UNITED KINGDOM... QUEERS ARE THROWN IN JAIL FIRST, AND A PSYCHIATRIST'S OFFICE SECOND.
SO BE VERY CAREFUL WHAT YOU SUGGEST. BEING...QUEER...IS STRICTLY AGAINST THE LAW.
THAT *DOES* SOUND VERY ROCK AND ROLL.
WELL THE BEATLES ARE IN TROUBLE IF QUEERS HAVE NO PLACE IN ROCK AND ROLL!
LOOK, HAVE YOU EVER SEEN A BULLFIGHT?
WHERE AND WHEN WOULD I SEE A FUCKIN' BULLFIGHT?
IN SPAIN, WITH ME SOMEDAY.
YOU'LL SEE THAT THE AFICIONADOS--THE FANS--ARE MORE ENRAPTURED OVER THE WELL-DRESSED MATADORS THAN THEY ARE OVER THE BULLS.
BULL.
AND MOST MATADORS STARTED LIFE AS *PEASANTS.* PEASANTS WHOSE AMBITION DRESSED THEM UP LIKE KINGS TO CAPTIVATE THE NATION.
SO DRESS-UP'S THE THING TO BECOME THE KING? I THOUGHT THE EMPEROR WORE NO CLOTHES.
I LOVE THE BULLS--AND YOUR LEATHER LOOK! BUT THE WORLD WILL NOT FOLLOW SUCH A GROUP.
THE WORLD. TRUST ME.
THE *WORLD?*
THEN I SUBMIT, DEFENSELESS BEFORE YOUR STRATEGICONFIDENCE.

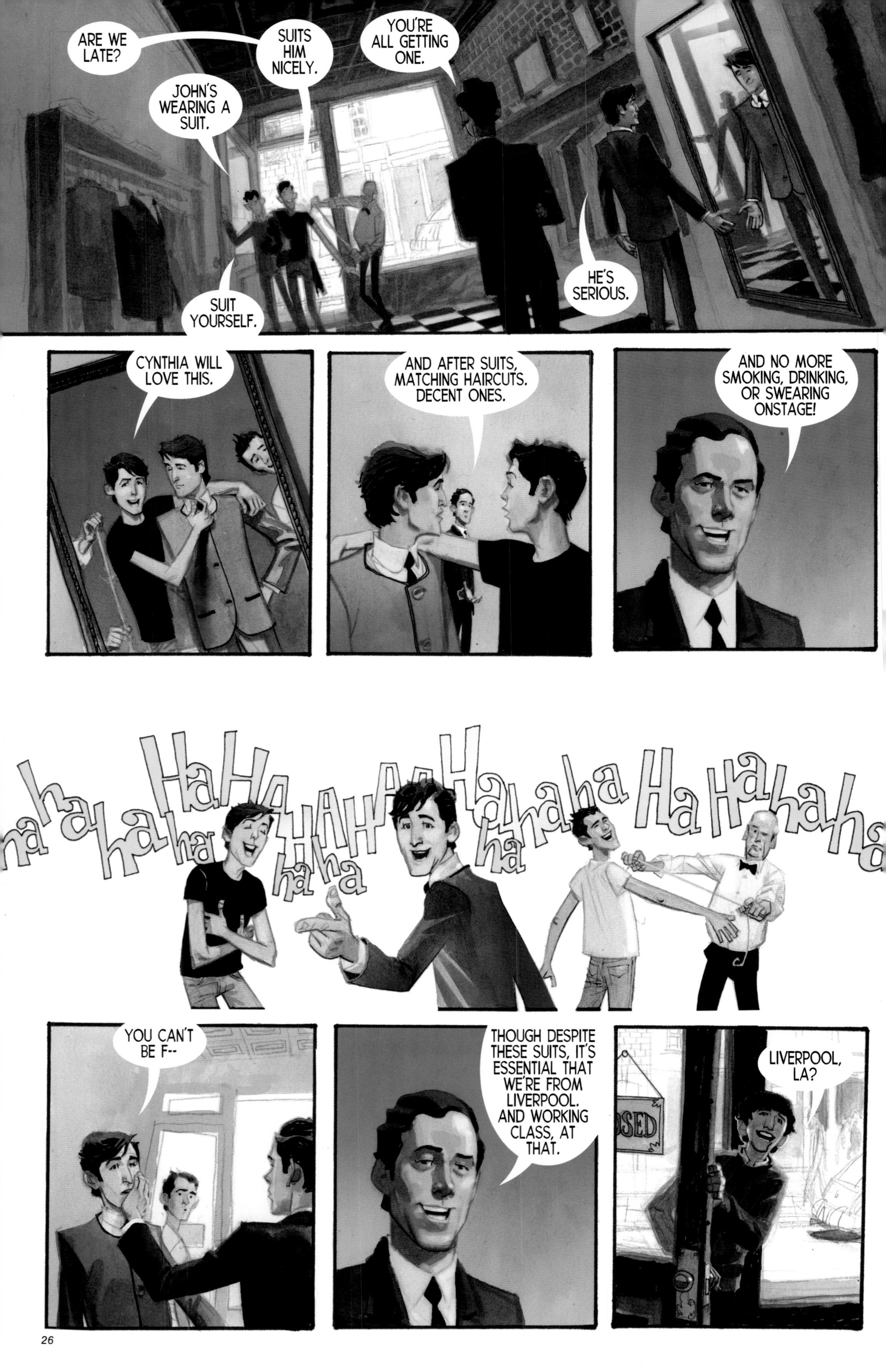
ARE WE LATE?
SUITS HIM NICELY.
YOU'RE ALL GETTING ONE.
JOHN'S WEARING A SUIT.
HE'S SERIOUS.
SUIT YOURSELF.
CYNTHIA WILL LOVE THIS.
AND AFTER SUITS, MATCHING HAIRCUTS. DECENT ONES.
AND NO MORE SMOKING, DRINKING, OR SWEARING ONSTAGE!
ha ha ha ha Ha HA HAHA ha ha HA Ha ha haha Ha Ha ha ha
YOU CAN'T BE F--
THOUGH DESPITE THESE SUITS, IT'S ESSENTIAL THAT WE'RE FROM LIVERPOOL. AND WORKING CLASS, AT THAT.
LIVERPOOL, LA?

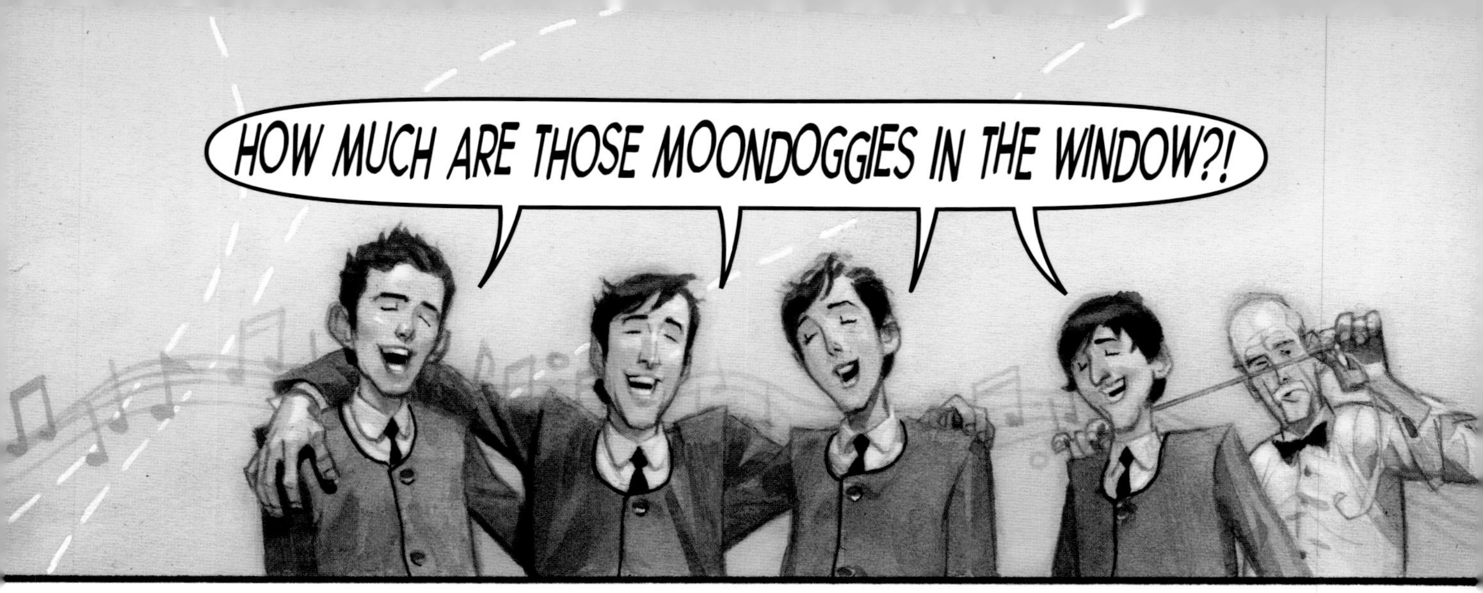
HOW MUCH ARE THOSE MOONDOGGIES IN THE WINDOW?!

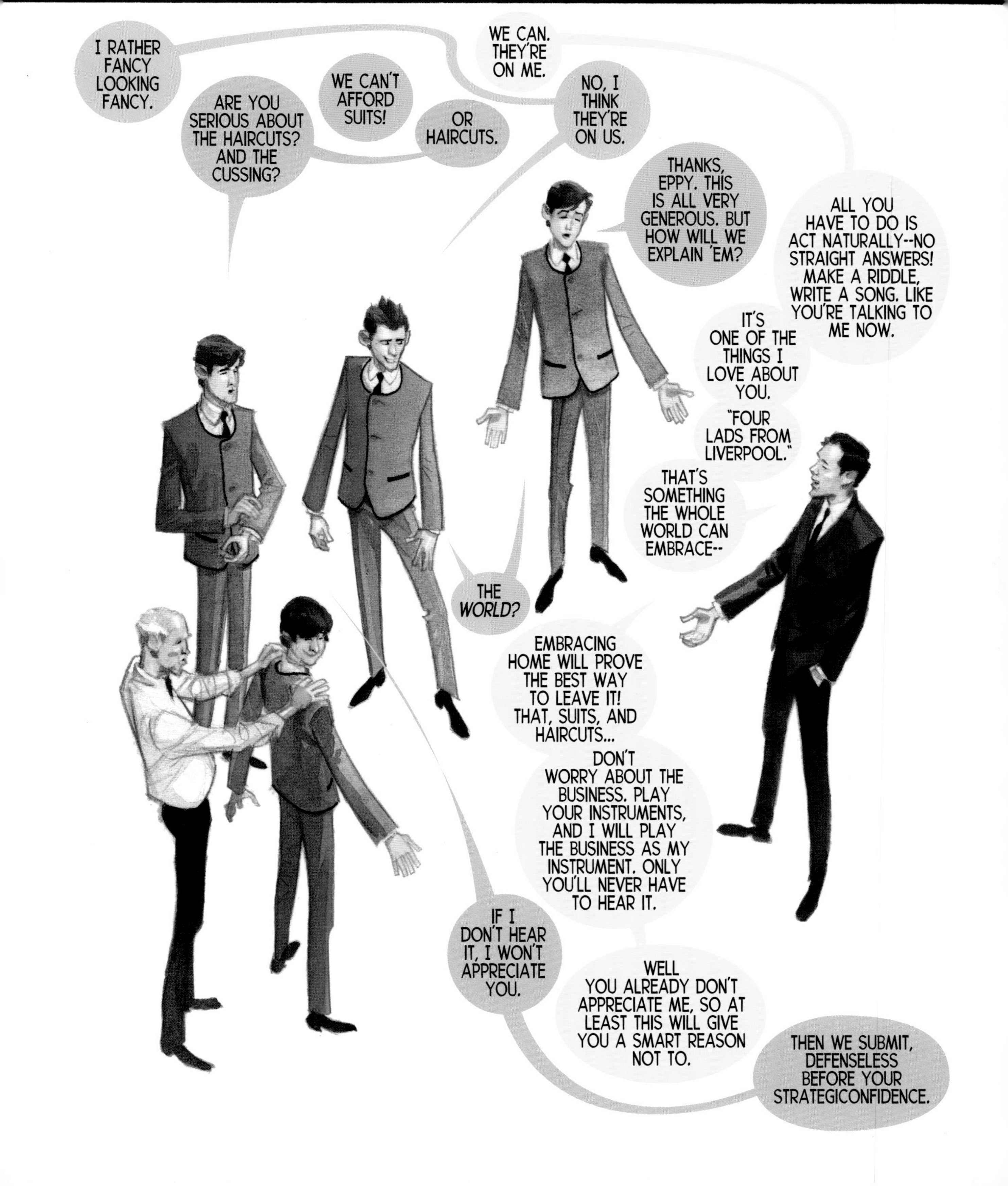
I RATHER FANCY LOOKING FANCY.
WE CAN. THEY'RE ON ME.
ARE YOU SERIOUS ABOUT THE HAIRCUTS? AND THE CUSSING?
WE CAN'T AFFORD SUITS!
OR HAIRCUTS.
NO, I THINK THEY'RE ON US.
THANKS, EPPY. THIS IS ALL VERY GENEROUS. BUT HOW WILL WE EXPLAIN 'EM?
ALL YOU HAVE TO DO IS ACT NATURALLY--NO STRAIGHT ANSWERS! MAKE A RIDDLE, WRITE A SONG. LIKE YOU'RE TALKING TO ME NOW.
IT'S ONE OF THE THINGS I LOVE ABOUT YOU.
"FOUR LADS FROM LIVERPOOL."
THAT'S SOMETHING THE WHOLE WORLD CAN EMBRACE--
THE *WORLD?*
EMBRACING HOME WILL PROVE THE BEST WAY TO LEAVE IT! THAT, SUITS, AND HAIRCUTS...
DON'T WORRY ABOUT THE BUSINESS. PLAY YOUR INSTRUMENTS, AND I WILL PLAY THE BUSINESS AS MY INSTRUMENT. ONLY YOU'LL NEVER HAVE TO HEAR IT.
IF I DON'T HEAR IT, I WON'T APPRECIATE YOU.
WELL YOU ALREADY DON'T APPRECIATE ME, SO AT LEAST THIS WILL GIVE YOU A SMART REASON NOT TO.
THEN WE SUBMIT, DEFENSELESS BEFORE YOUR STRATEGICONFIDENCE.

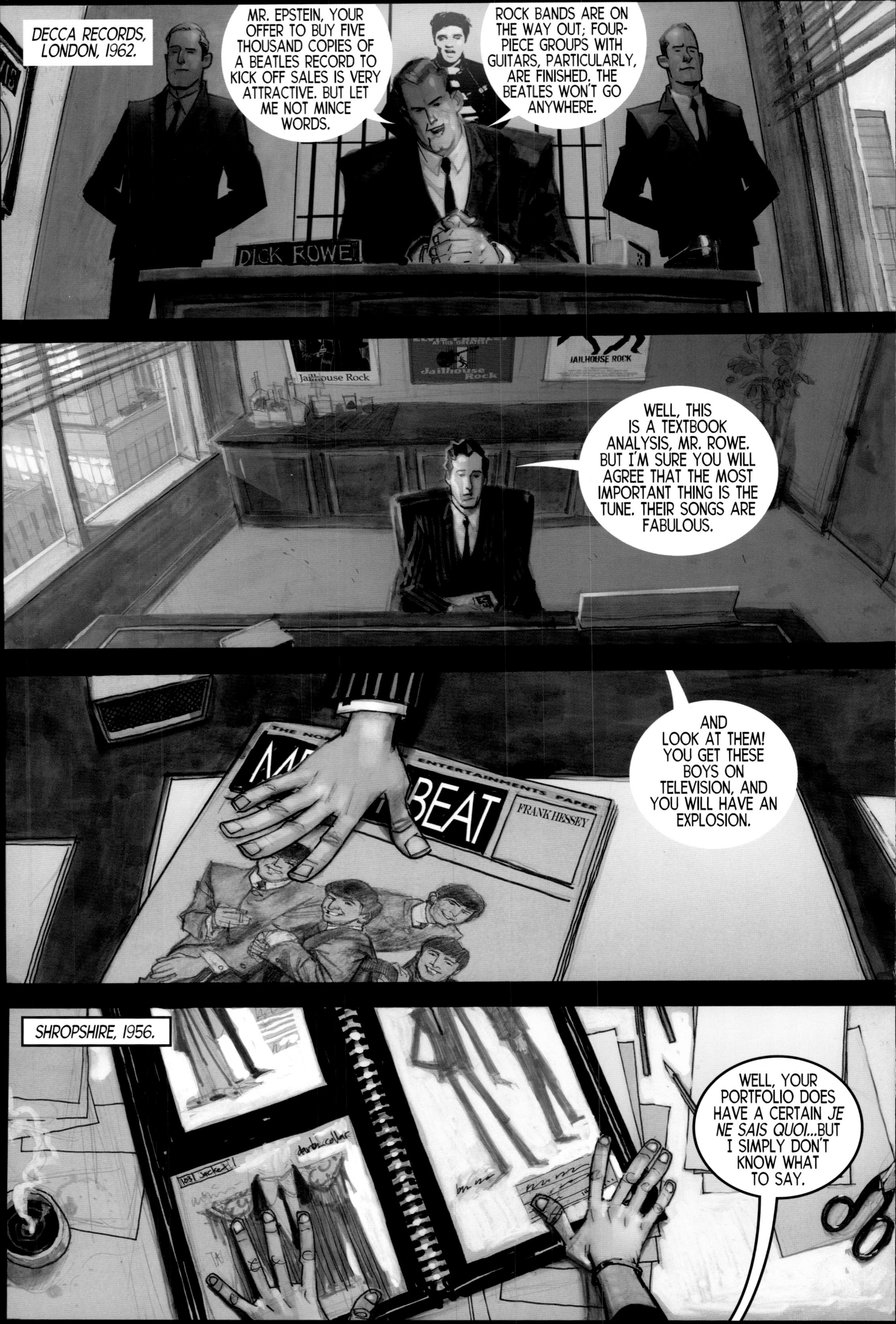
DECCA RECORDS, LONDON, 1962.
MR. EPSTEIN, YOUR OFFER TO BUY FIVE THOUSAND COPIES OF A BEATLES RECORD TO KICK OFF SALES IS VERY ATTRACTIVE. BUT LET ME NOT MINCE WORDS.
ROCK BANDS ARE ON THE WAY OUT; FOUR-PIECE GROUPS WITH GUITARS, PARTICULARLY, ARE FINISHED. THE BEATLES WON'T GO ANYWHERE.
DICK ROWE
Jailhouse Rock
Jailhouse Rock
JAILHOUSE ROCK
WELL, THIS IS A TEXTBOOK ANALYSIS, MR. ROWE. BUT I'M SURE YOU WILL AGREE THAT THE MOST IMPORTANT THING IS THE TUNE. THEIR SONGS ARE FABULOUS.
ENTERTAINMENTS PAPER
BEAT
FRANK HESSEY
AND LOOK AT THEM! YOU GET THESE BOYS ON TELEVISION, AND YOU WILL HAVE AN EXPLOSION.
SHROPSHIRE, 1956.
WELL, YOUR PORTFOLIO DOES HAVE A CERTAIN *JE NE SAIS QUOI*...BUT I SIMPLY DON'T KNOW WHAT TO SAY.

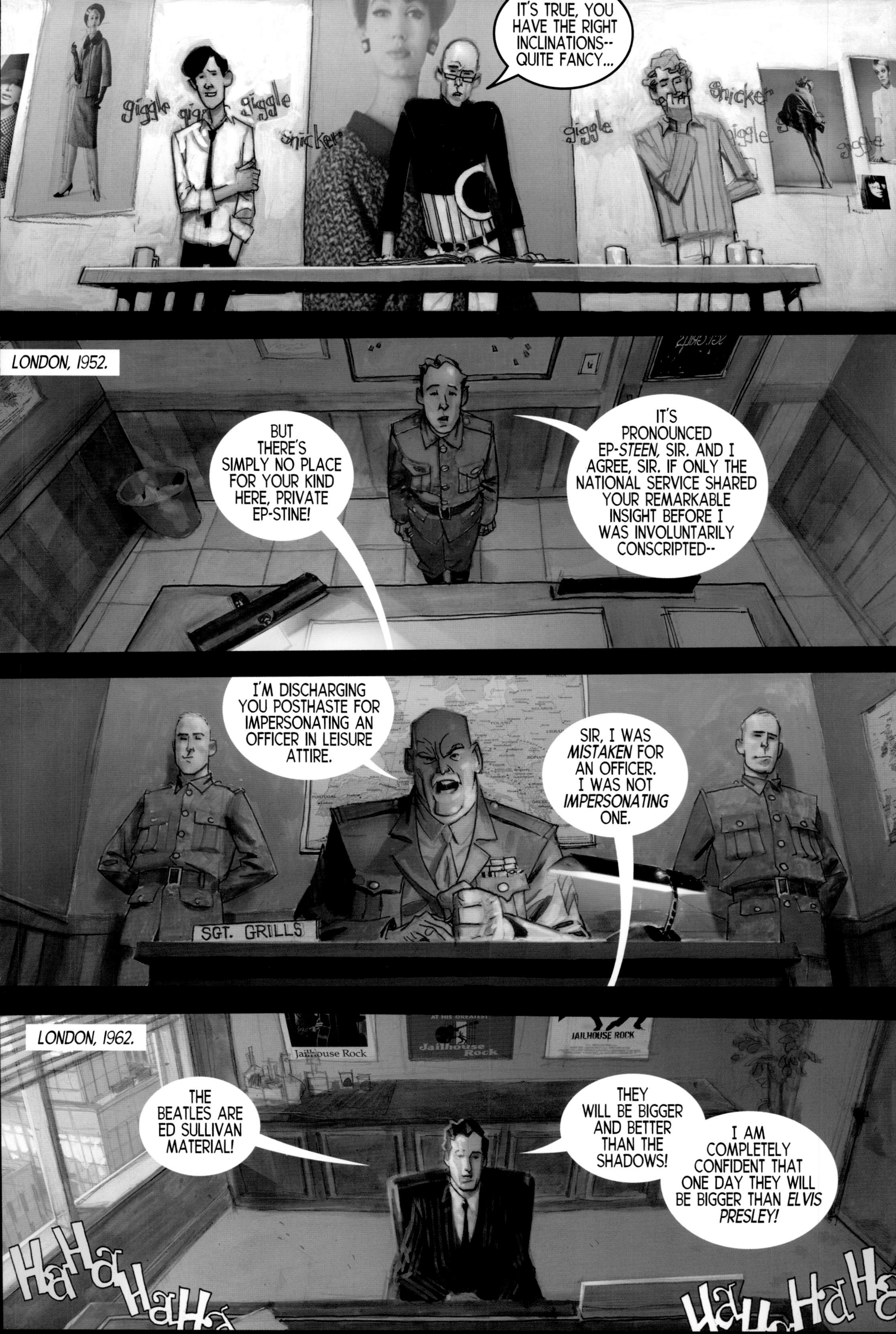
IT'S TRUE, YOU HAVE THE RIGHT INCLINATIONS-- QUITE FANCY...
giggle
giggle
snicker
giggle
snicker
giggle
LONDON, 1952.
BUT THERE'S SIMPLY NO PLACE FOR YOUR KIND HERE, PRIVATE EP-STINE!
IT'S PRONOUNCED EP-*STEEN*, SIR. AND I AGREE, SIR. IF ONLY THE NATIONAL SERVICE SHARED YOUR REMARKABLE INSIGHT BEFORE I WAS INVOLUNTARILY CONSCRIPTED--
I'M DISCHARGING YOU POSTHASTE FOR IMPERSONATING AN OFFICER IN LEISURE ATTIRE.
SIR, I WAS *MISTAKEN* FOR AN OFFICER. I WAS NOT *IMPERSONATING* ONE.
SGT. GRILLS
LONDON, 1962.
Jailhouse Rock
Jailhouse Rock
JAILHOUSE ROCK
THE BEATLES ARE ED SULLIVAN MATERIAL!
THEY WILL BE BIGGER AND BETTER THAN THE SHADOWS!
I AM COMPLETELY CONFIDENT THAT ONE DAY THEY WILL BE BIGGER THAN *ELVIS PRESLEY!*
HaHaHaHa
HaHaHaHa

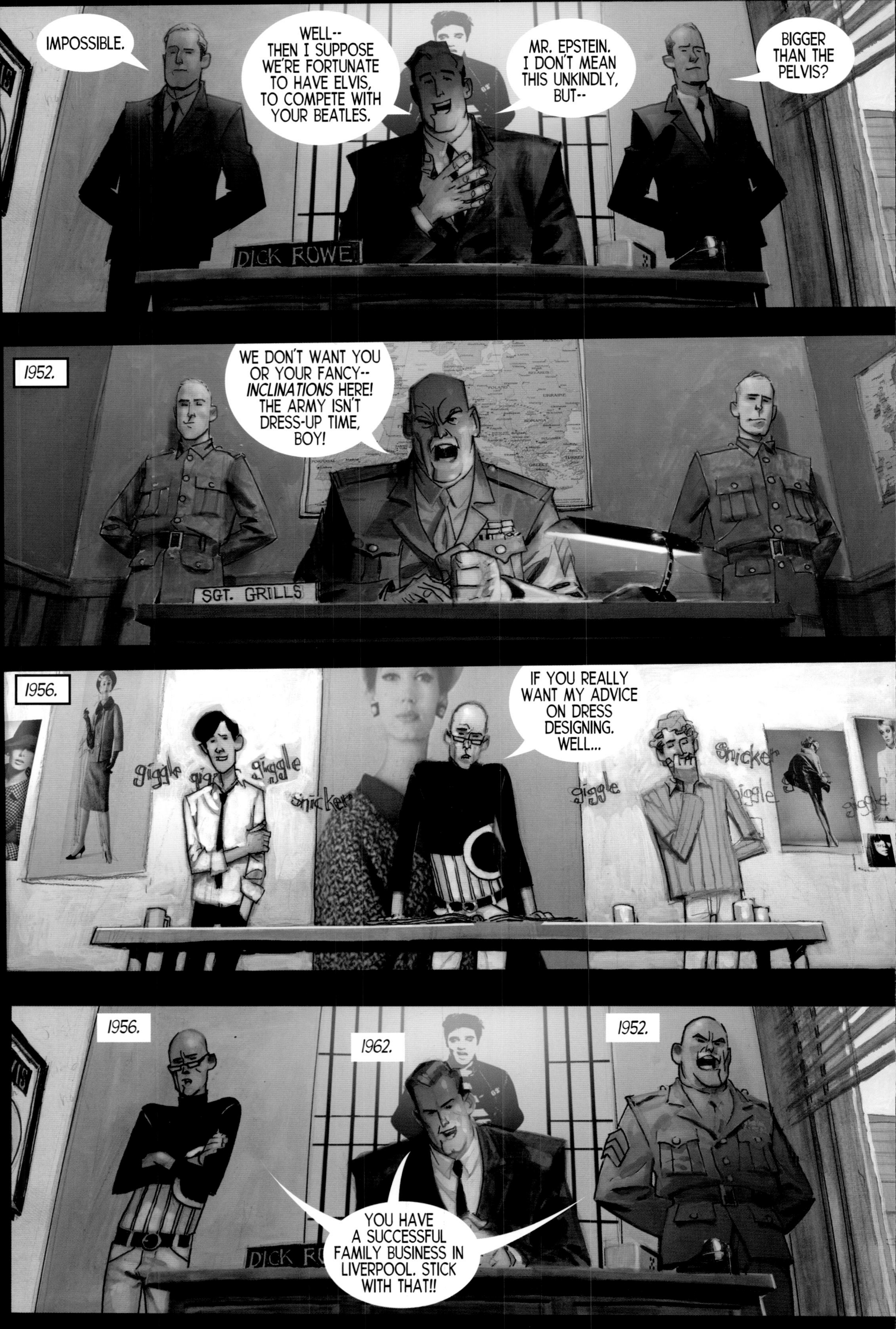
IMPOSSIBLE.
WELL-- THEN I SUPPOSE WE'RE FORTUNATE TO HAVE ELVIS, TO COMPETE WITH YOUR BEATLES.
MR. EPSTEIN. I DON'T MEAN THIS UNKINDLY, BUT--
BIGGER THAN THE PELVIS?
DICK ROWE
1952.
WE DON'T WANT YOU OR YOUR FANCY-- *INCLINATIONS* HERE! THE ARMY ISN'T DRESS-UP TIME, BOY!
SGT. GRILLS
1956.
giggle giggle giggle
snicker
IF YOU REALLY WANT MY ADVICE ON DRESS DESIGNING. WELL...
giggle
snicker
giggle
giggle
1956.
1962.
1952.
YOU HAVE A SUCCESSFUL FAMILY BUSINESS IN LIVERPOOL. STICK WITH THAT!!

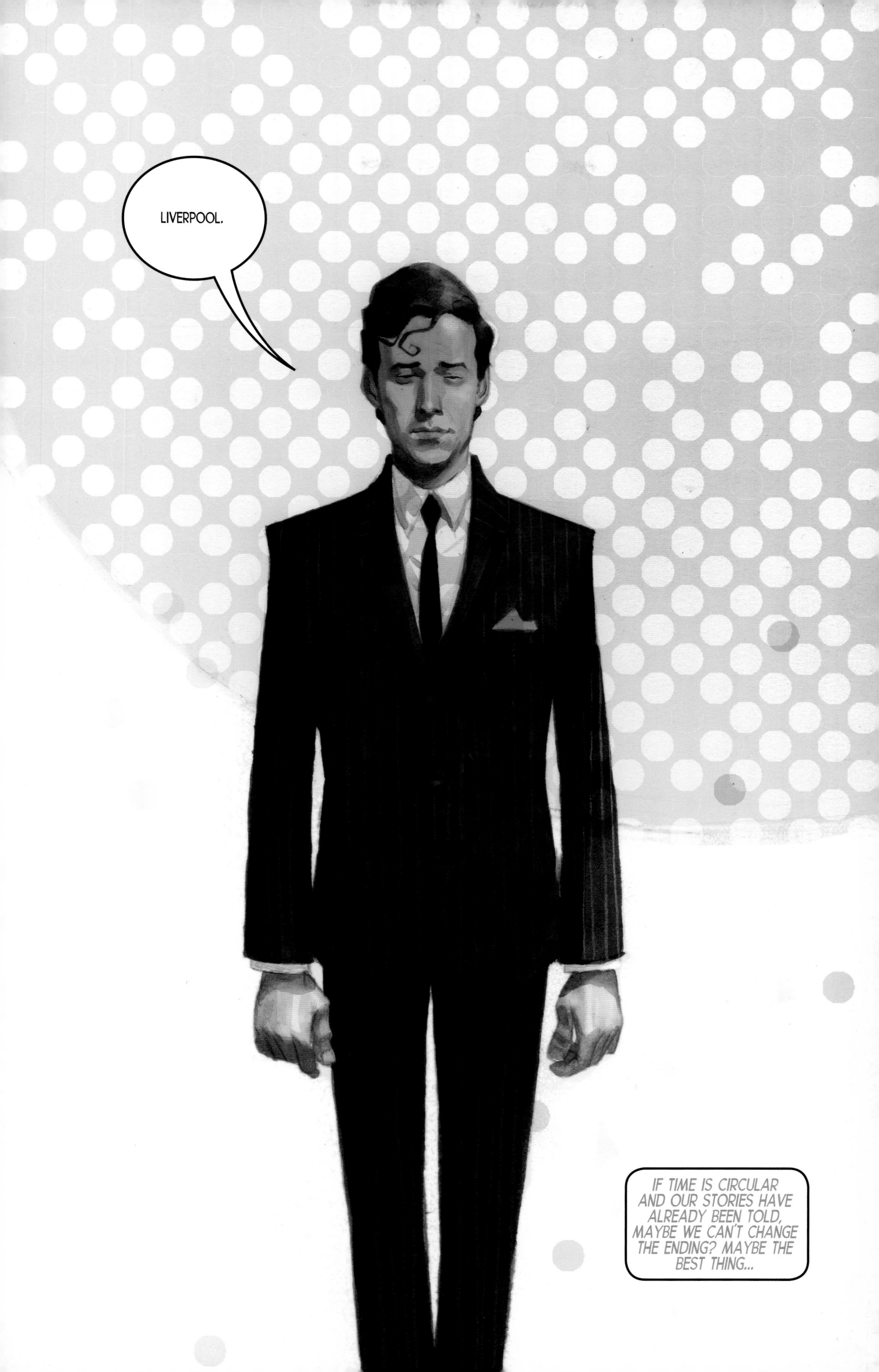
LIVERPOOL.
IF TIME IS CIRCULAR AND OUR STORIES HAVE ALREADY BEEN TOLD, MAYBE WE CAN'T CHANGE THE ENDING? MAYBE THE BEST THING...

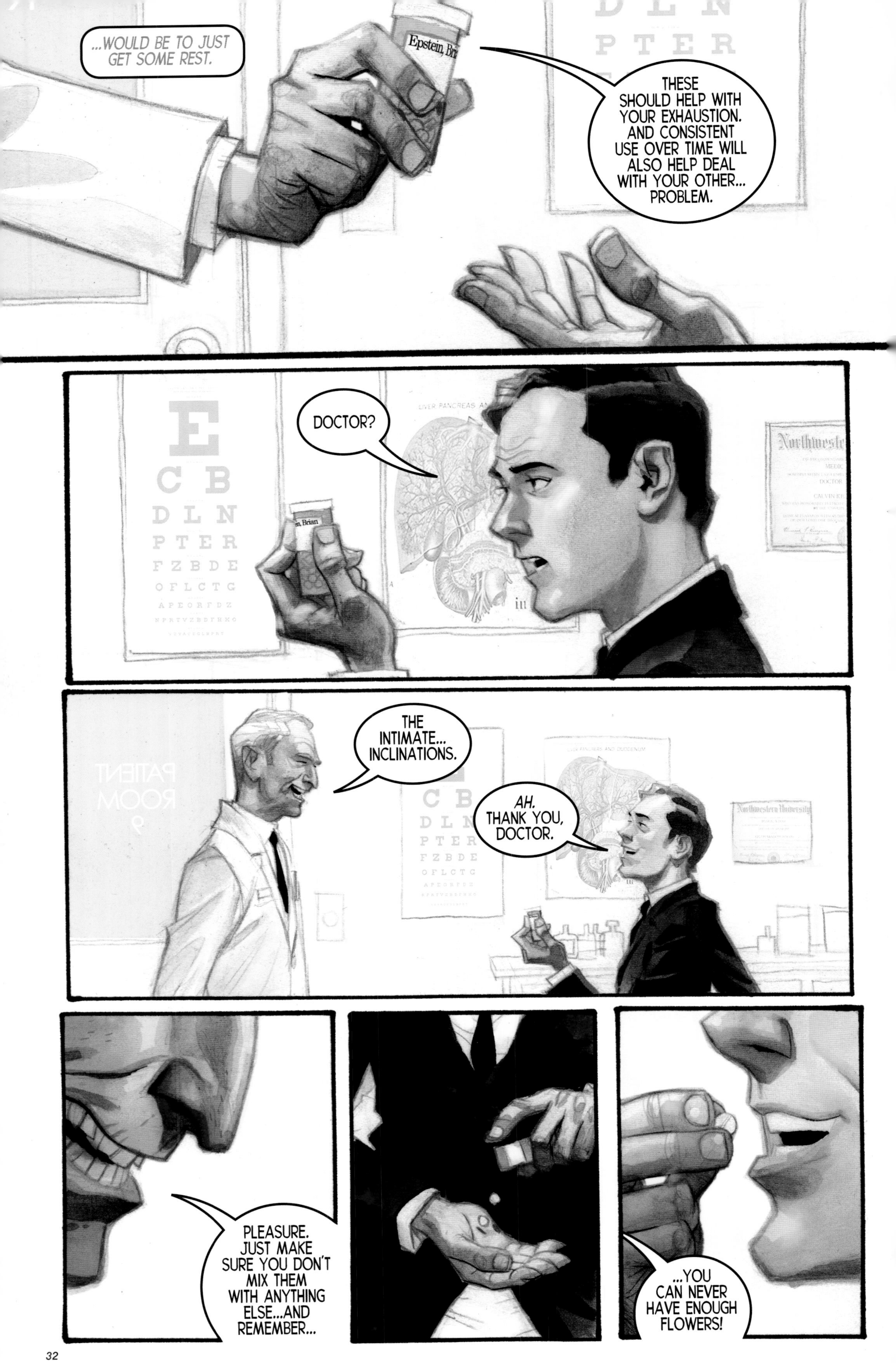
...WOULD BE TO JUST GET SOME REST.
Epstein, Bri
THESE SHOULD HELP WITH YOUR EXHAUSTION. AND CONSISTENT USE OVER TIME WILL ALSO HELP DEAL WITH YOUR OTHER... PROBLEM.
DOCTOR?
THE INTIMATE... INCLINATIONS.
AH. THANK YOU, DOCTOR.
PLEASURE. JUST MAKE SURE YOU DON'T MIX THEM WITH ANYTHING ELSE...AND REMEMBER...
...YOU CAN NEVER HAVE ENOUGH FLOWERS!

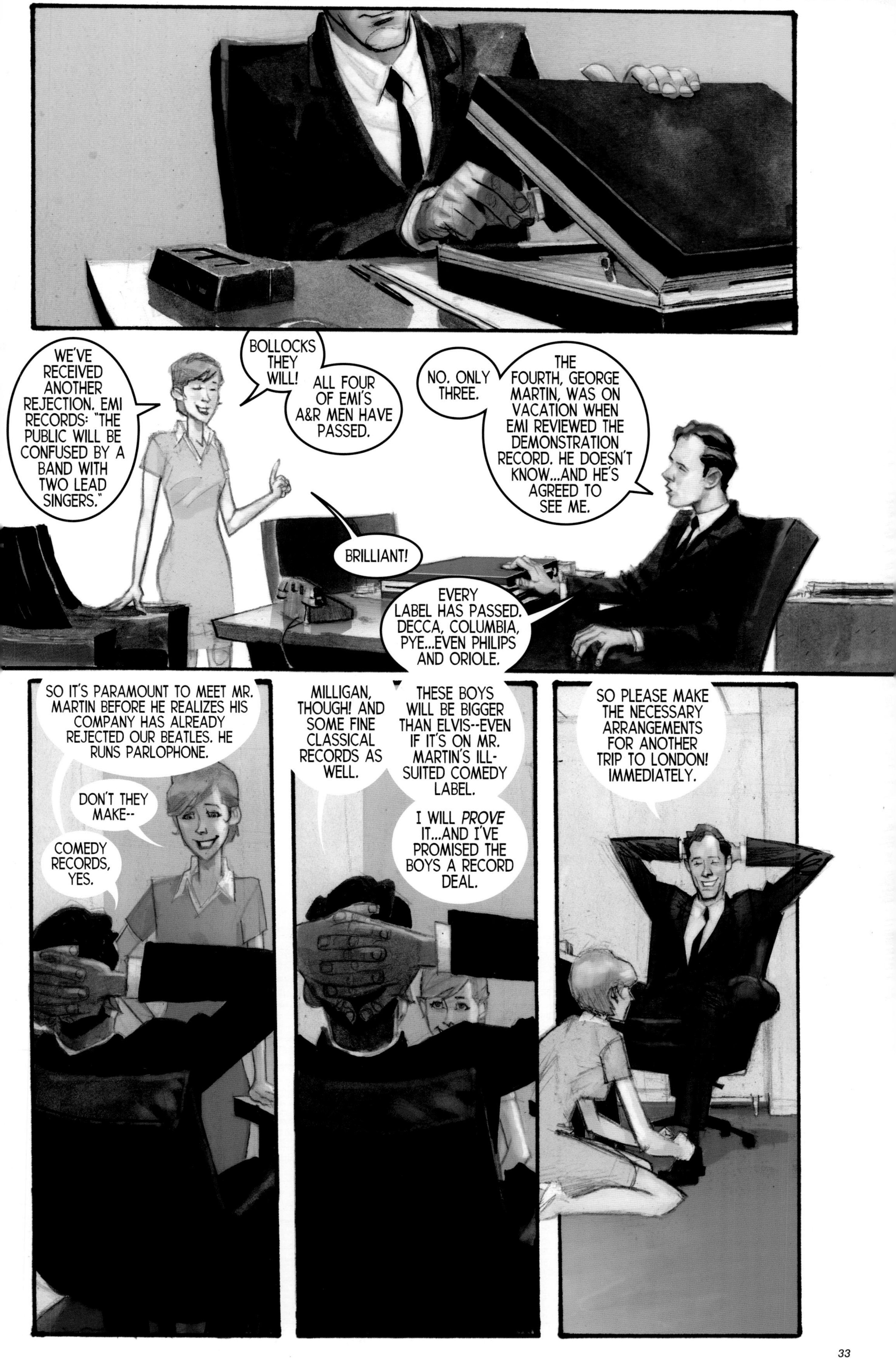
WE'VE RECEIVED ANOTHER REJECTION. EMI RECORDS: "THE PUBLIC WILL BE CONFUSED BY A BAND WITH TWO LEAD SINGERS."
BOLLOCKS THEY WILL!
ALL FOUR OF EMI'S A&R MEN HAVE PASSED.
NO. ONLY THREE.
THE FOURTH, GEORGE MARTIN, WAS ON VACATION WHEN EMI REVIEWED THE DEMONSTRATION RECORD. HE DOESN'T KNOW...AND HE'S AGREED TO SEE ME.
BRILLIANT!
EVERY LABEL HAS PASSED. DECCA, COLUMBIA, PYE...EVEN PHILIPS AND ORIOLE.
SO IT'S PARAMOUNT TO MEET MR. MARTIN BEFORE HE REALIZES HIS COMPANY HAS ALREADY REJECTED OUR BEATLES. HE RUNS PARLOPHONE.
DON'T THEY MAKE--
COMEDY RECORDS, YES.
MILLIGAN, THOUGH! AND SOME FINE CLASSICAL RECORDS AS WELL.
THESE BOYS WILL BE BIGGER THAN ELVIS--EVEN IF IT'S ON MR. MARTIN'S ILL-SUITED COMEDY LABEL.
I WILL *PROVE* IT...AND I'VE PROMISED THE BOYS A RECORD DEAL.
SO PLEASE MAKE THE NECESSARY ARRANGEMENTS FOR ANOTHER TRIP TO LONDON! IMMEDIATELY.

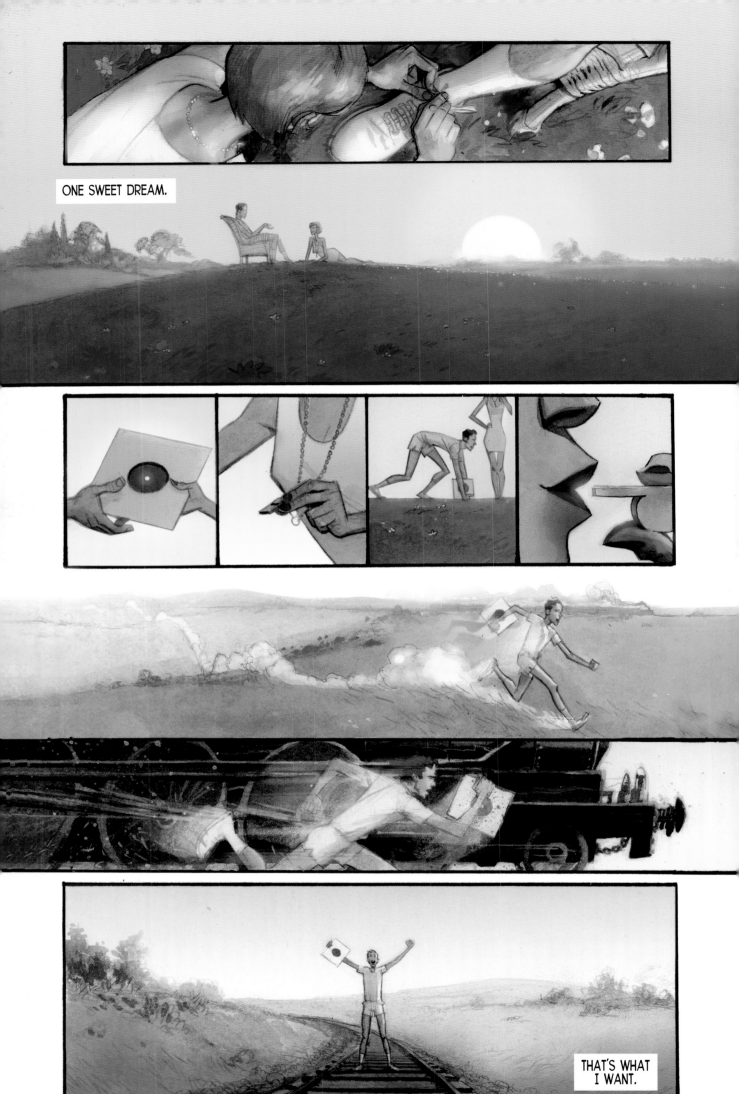

ONE SWEET DREAM.

THAT'S WHAT I WANT.

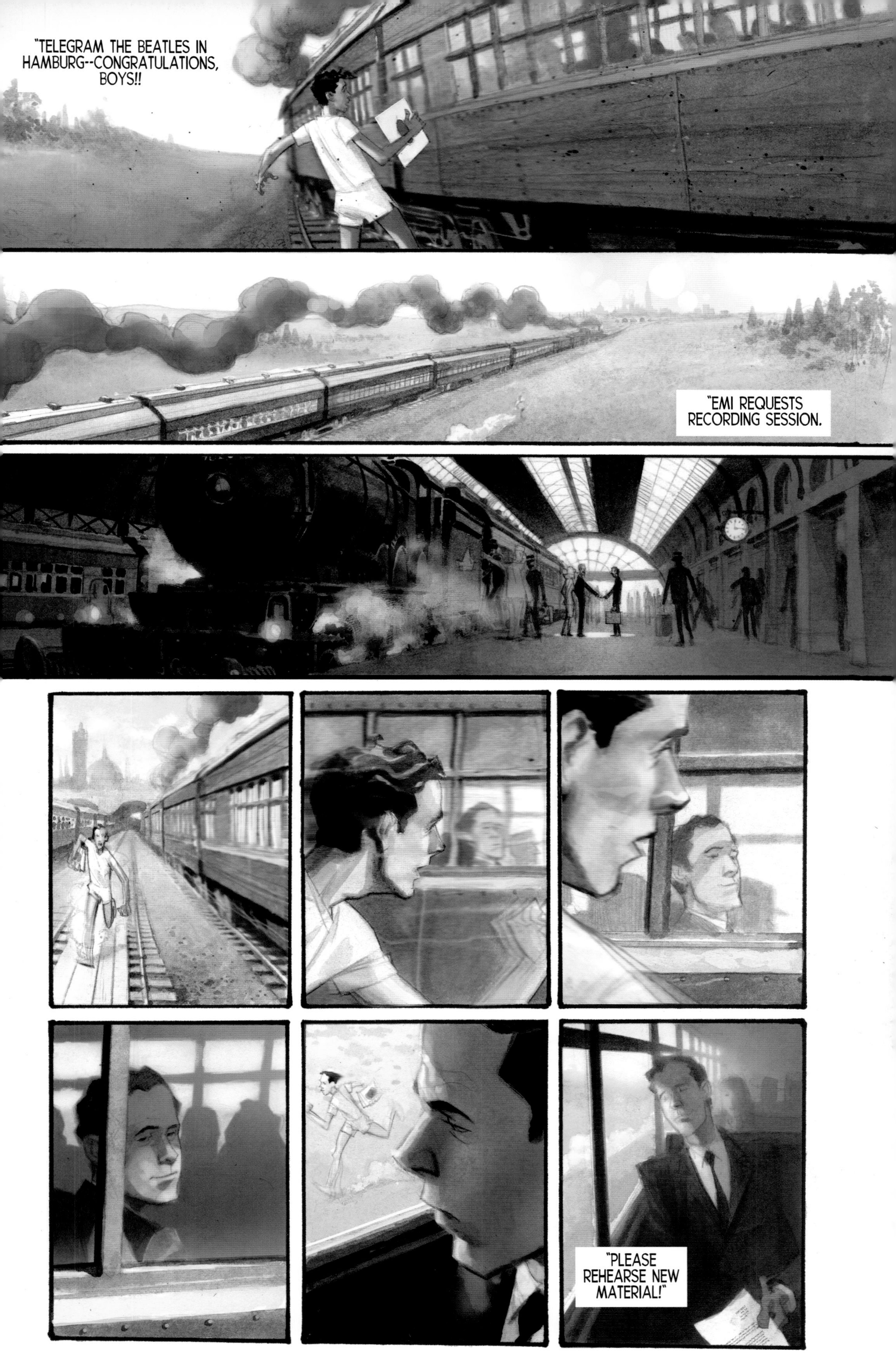
"TELEGRAM THE BEATLES IN HAMBURG--CONGRATULATIONS, BOYS!!
"EMI REQUESTS RECORDING SESSION.
"PLEASE REHEARSE NEW MATERIAL!"

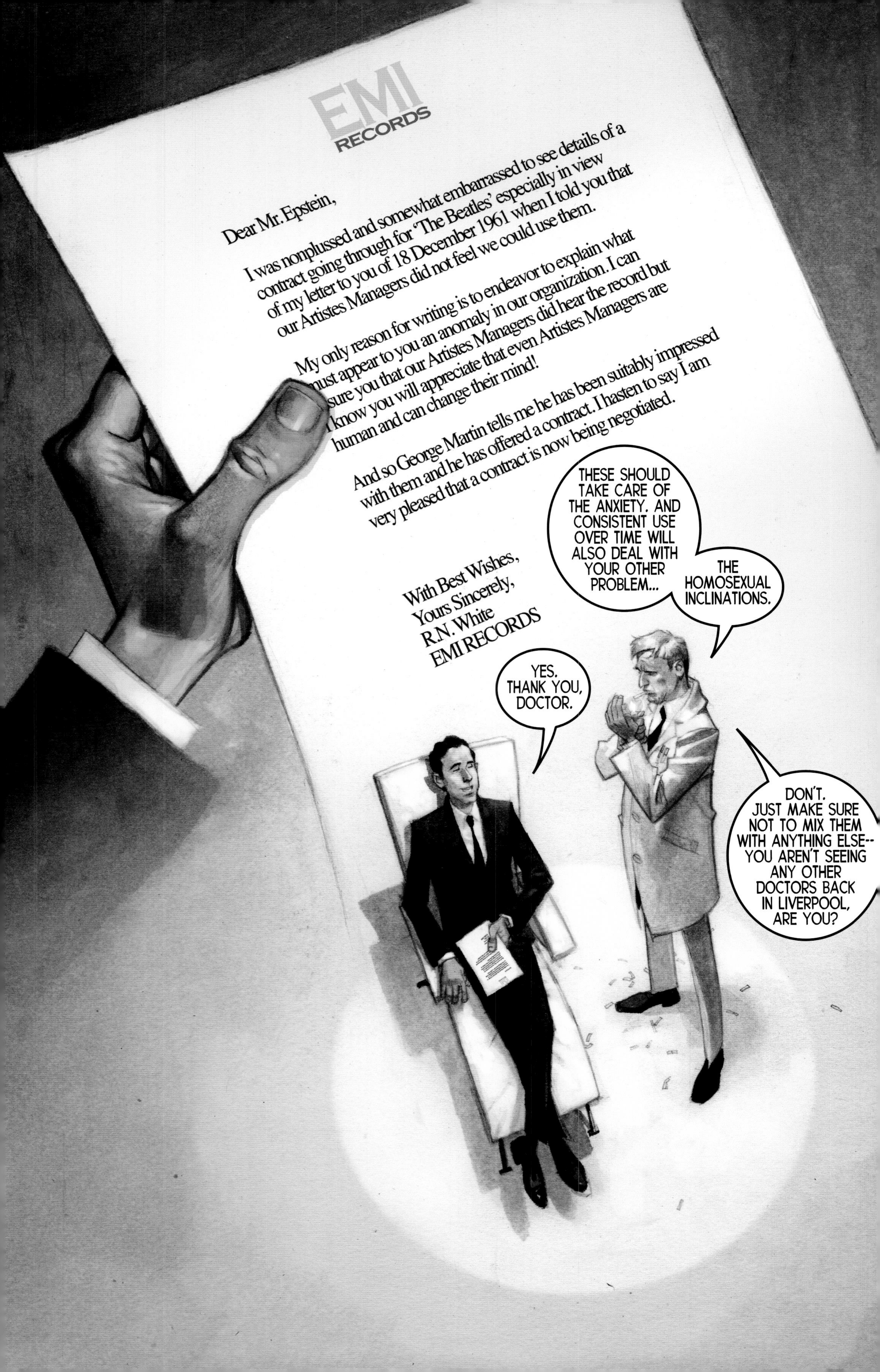
EMI RECORDS
Dear Mr. Epstein,
I was nonplussed and somewhat embarrassed to see details of a contract going through for 'The Beatles' especially in view of my letter to you of 18 December 1961 when I told you that our Artistes Managers did not feel we could use them.
My only reason for writing is to endeavor to explain what must appear to you an anomaly in our organization. I can assure you that our Artistes Managers did hear the record but I know you will appreciate that even Artistes Managers are human and can change their mind!
And so George Martin tells me he has been suitably impressed with them and he has offered a contract. I hasten to say I am very pleased that a contract is now being negotiated.
With Best Wishes,
Yours Sincerely,
R.N. White
EMI RECORDS
THESE SHOULD TAKE CARE OF THE ANXIETY. AND CONSISTENT USE OVER TIME WILL ALSO DEAL WITH YOUR OTHER PROBLEM...
THE HOMOSEXUAL INCLINATIONS.
YES. THANK YOU, DOCTOR.
DON'T. JUST MAKE SURE NOT TO MIX THEM WITH ANYTHING ELSE-- YOU AREN'T SEEING ANY OTHER DOCTORS BACK IN LIVERPOOL, ARE YOU?

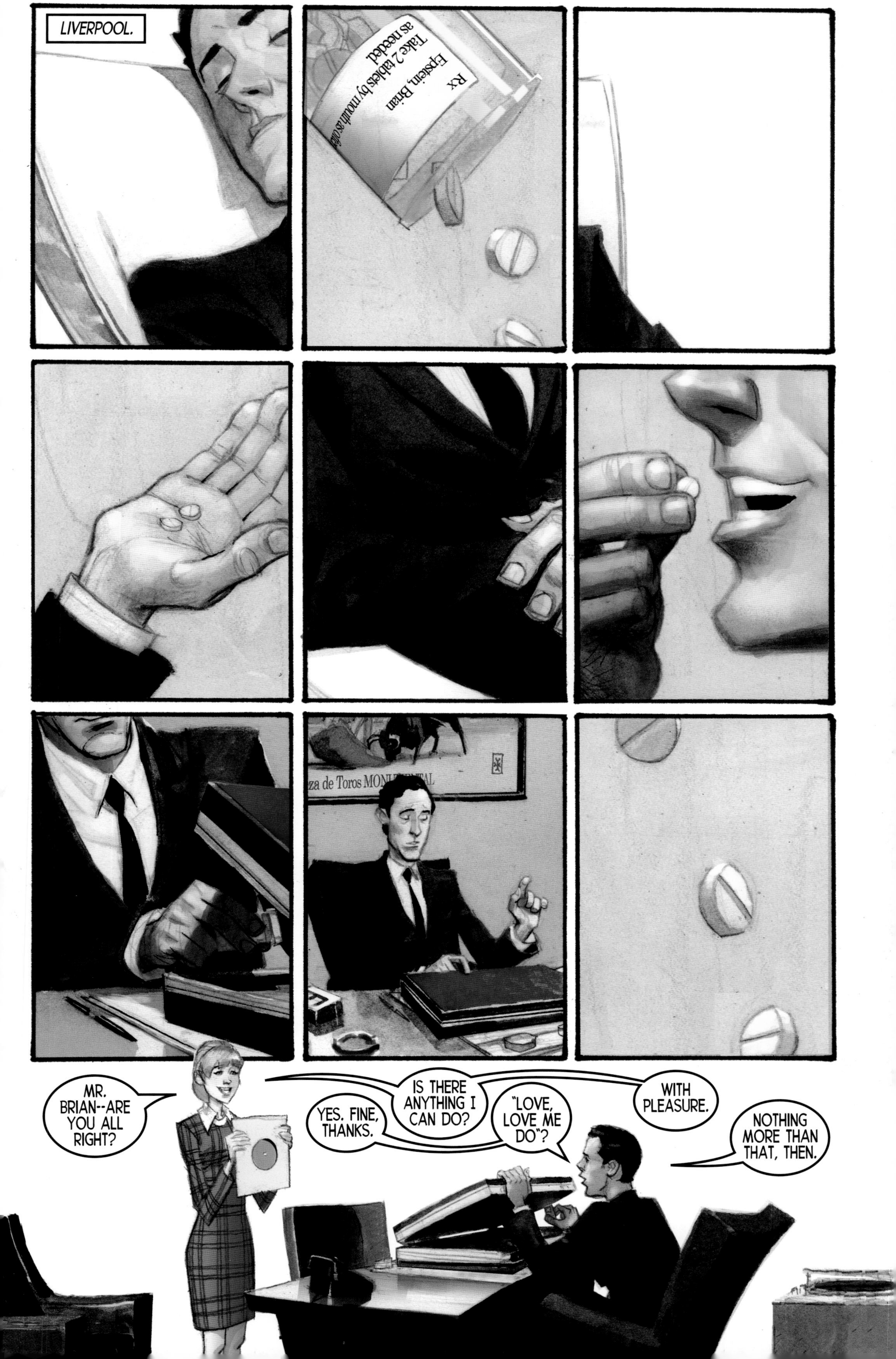
LIVERPOOL.
MR. BRIAN--ARE YOU ALL RIGHT?
YES. FINE, THANKS.
IS THERE ANYTHING I CAN DO?
"LOVE, LOVE ME DO"?
WITH PLEASURE.
NOTHING MORE THAN THAT, THEN.

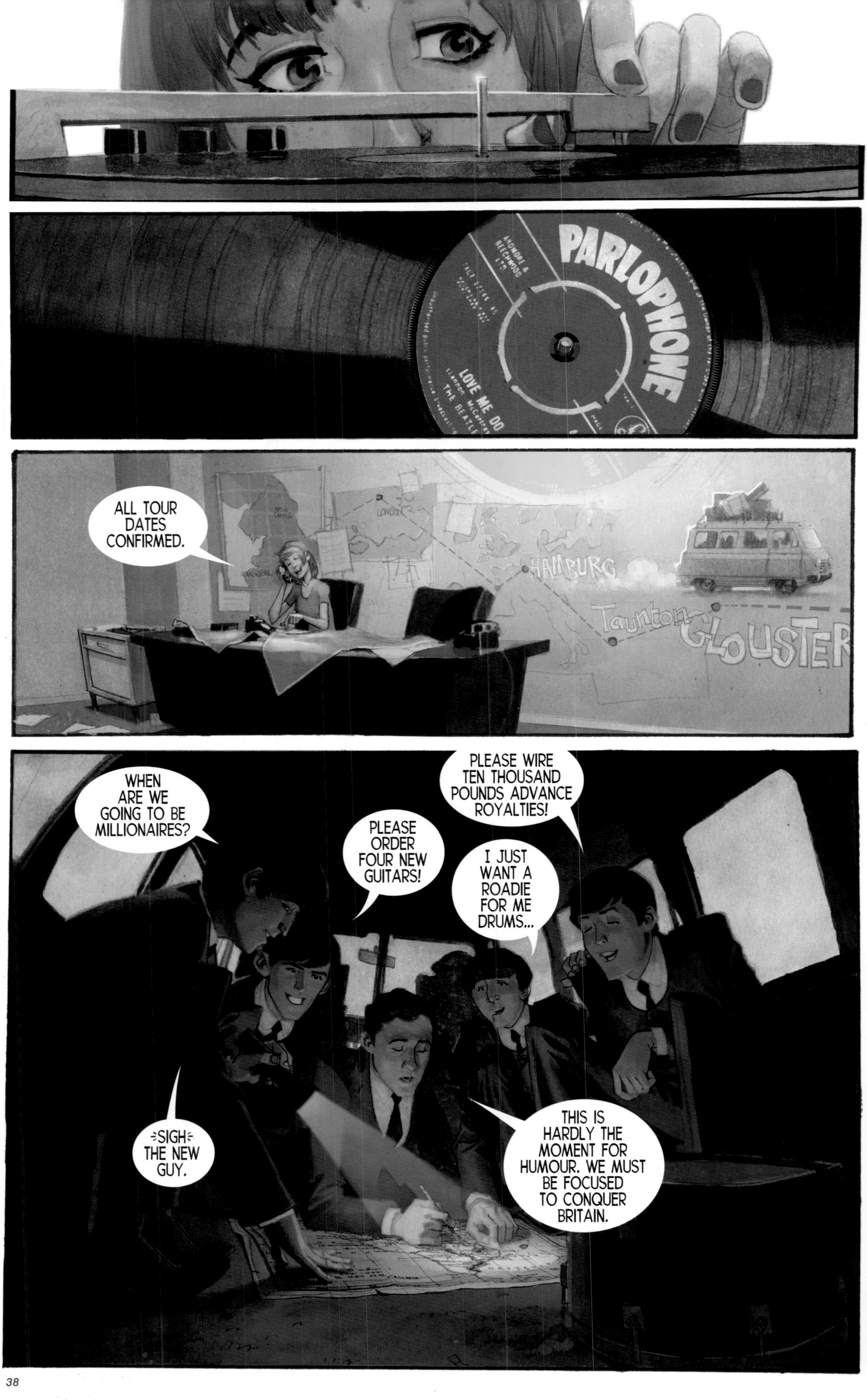
PARLOPHONE
LOVE ME DO
THE BEATLES
ALL TOUR DATES CONFIRMED.
HAMBURG
Taunton
GLOUSTER
WHEN ARE WE GOING TO BE MILLIONAIRES?
PLEASE ORDER FOUR NEW GUITARS!
PLEASE WIRE TEN THOUSAND POUNDS ADVANCE ROYALTIES!
I JUST WANT A ROADIE FOR ME DRUMS...
SIGH THE NEW GUY.
THIS IS HARDLY THE MOMENT FOR HUMOUR. WE MUST BE FOCUSED TO CONQUER BRITAIN.

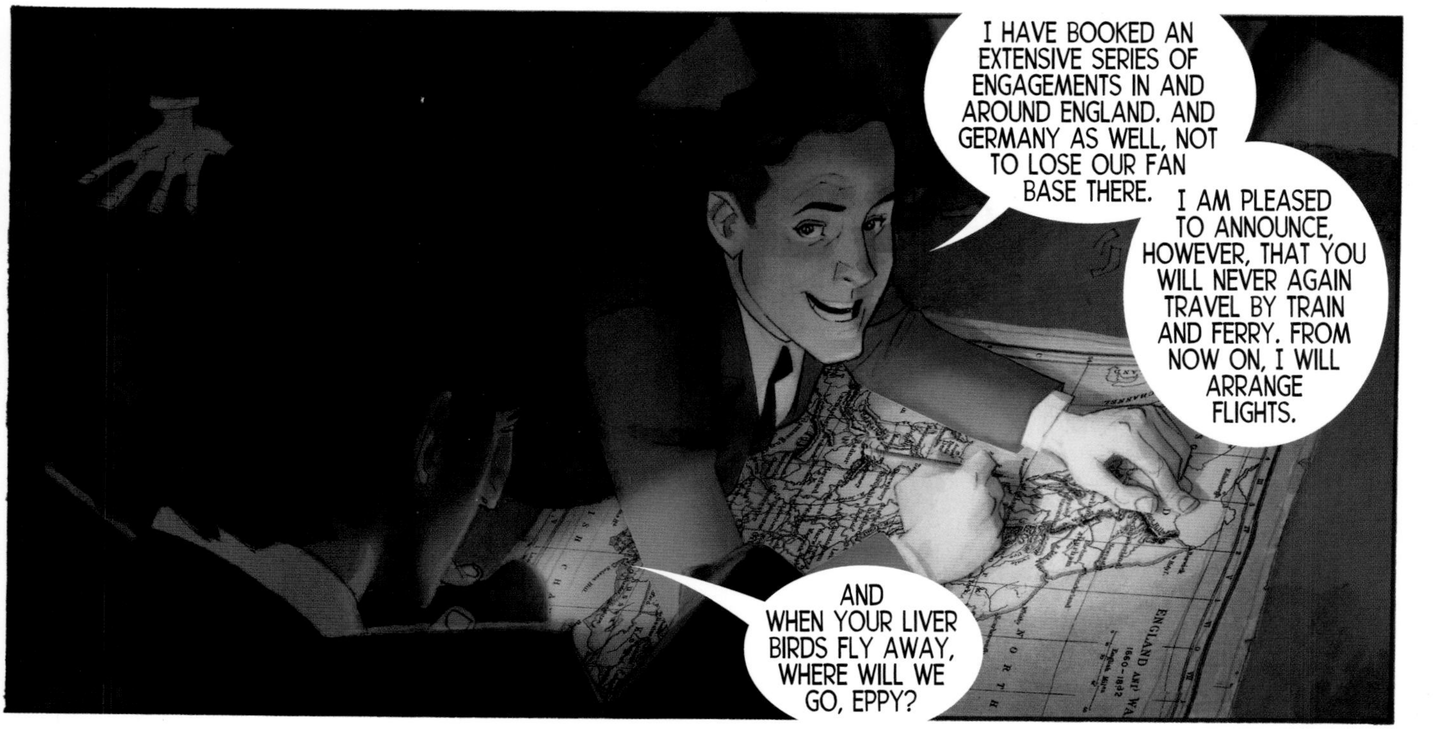
I HAVE BOOKED AN EXTENSIVE SERIES OF ENGAGEMENTS IN AND AROUND ENGLAND. AND GERMANY AS WELL, NOT TO LOSE OUR FAN BASE THERE.
I AM PLEASED TO ANNOUNCE, HOWEVER, THAT YOU WILL NEVER AGAIN TRAVEL BY TRAIN AND FERRY. FROM NOW ON, I WILL ARRANGE FLIGHTS.
AND WHEN YOUR LIVER BIRDS FLY AWAY, WHERE WILL WE GO, EPPY?

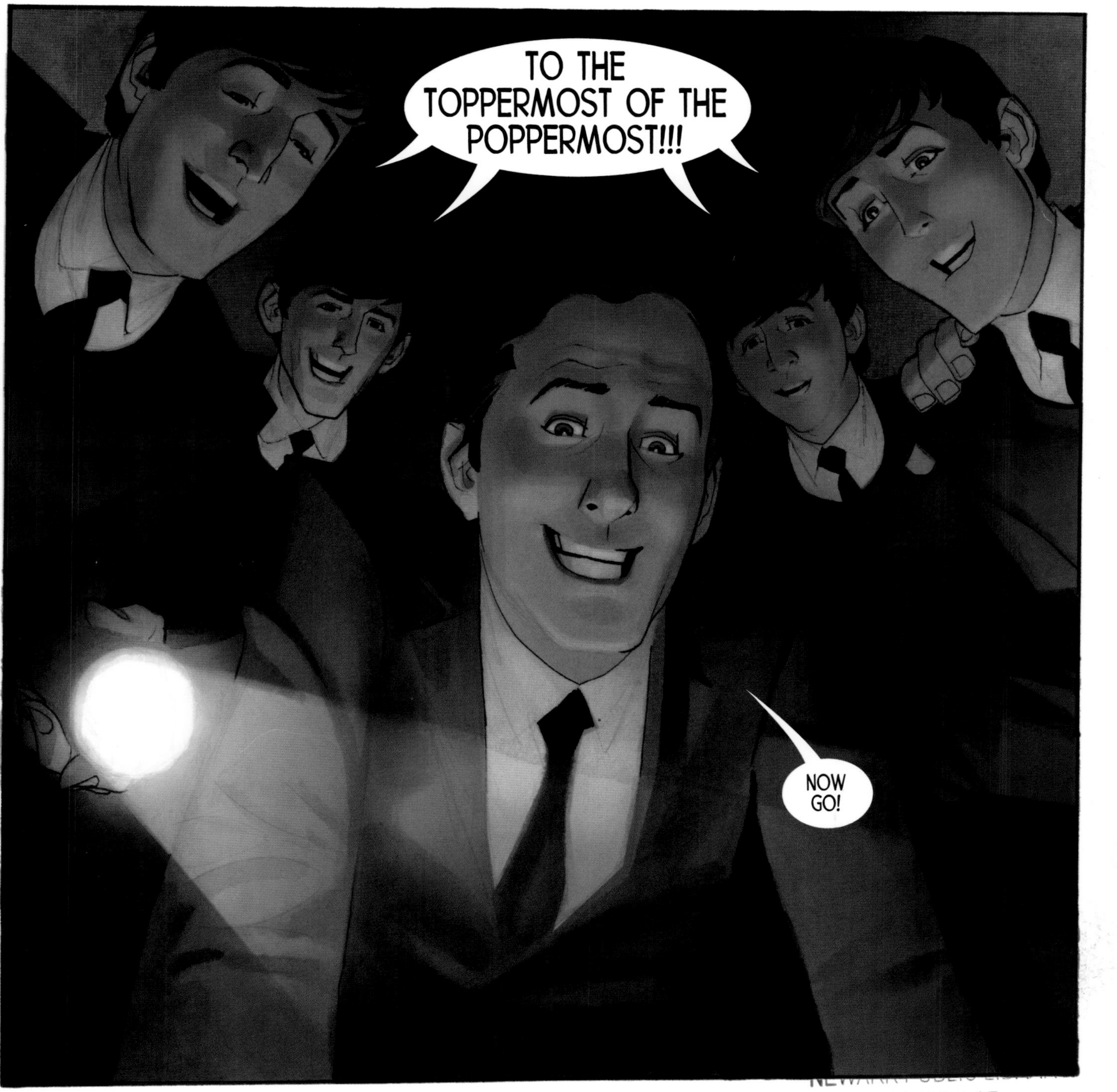
TO THE TOPPERMOST OF THE POPPERMOST!!!
NOW GO!

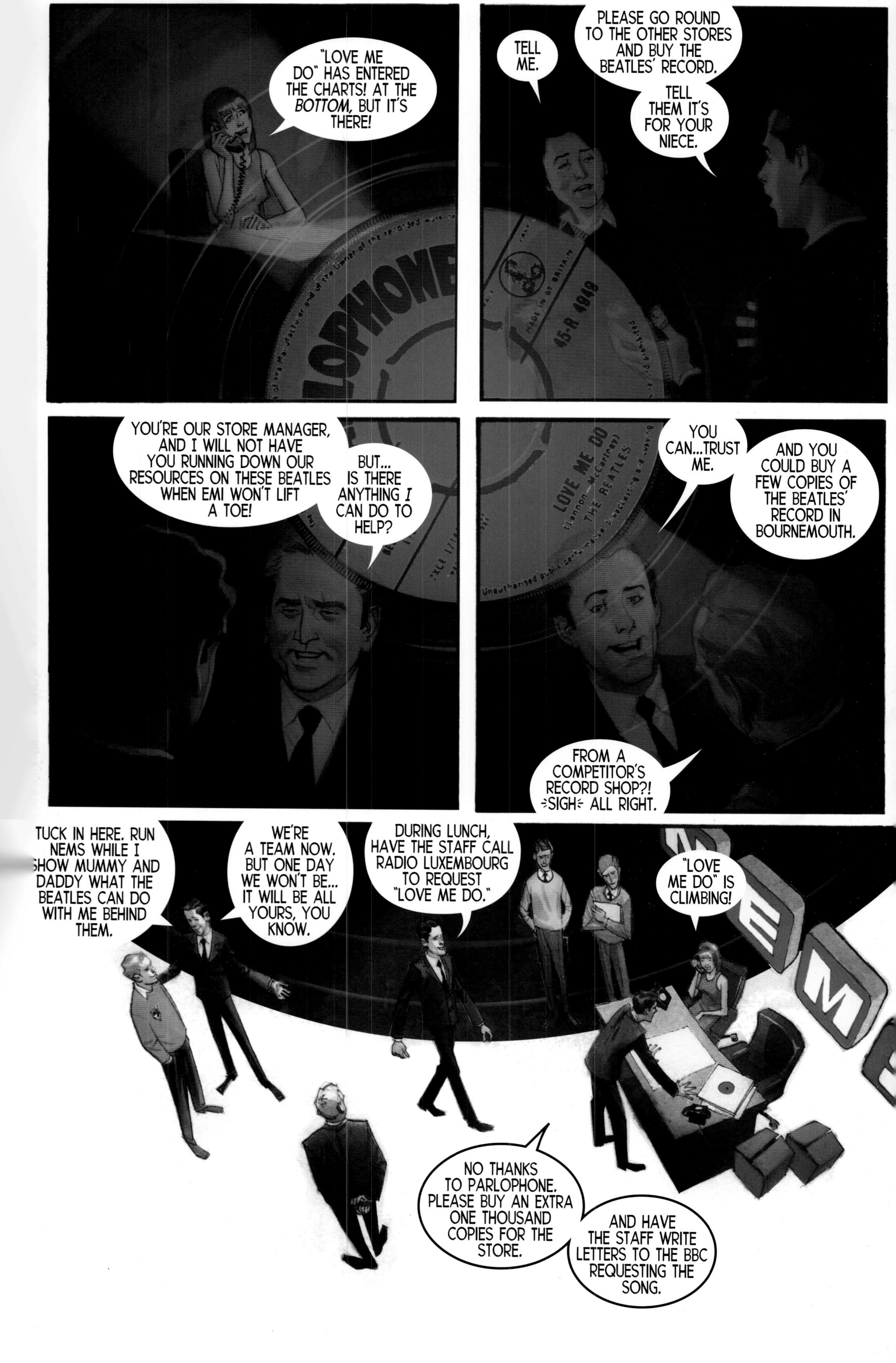
"LOVE ME DO" HAS ENTERED THE CHARTS! AT THE *BOTTOM,* BUT IT'S THERE!
TELL ME.
PLEASE GO ROUND TO THE OTHER STORES AND BUY THE BEATLES' RECORD.
TELL THEM IT'S FOR YOUR NIECE.
YOU'RE OUR STORE MANAGER, AND I WILL NOT HAVE YOU RUNNING DOWN OUR RESOURCES ON THESE BEATLES WHEN EMI WON'T LIFT A TOE!
BUT... IS THERE ANYTHING *I* CAN DO TO HELP?
YOU CAN...TRUST ME.
AND YOU COULD BUY A FEW COPIES OF THE BEATLES' RECORD IN BOURNEMOUTH.
FROM A COMPETITOR'S RECORD SHOP?! ⇒SIGH⇐ ALL RIGHT.
TUCK IN HERE. RUN NEMS WHILE I SHOW MUMMY AND DADDY WHAT THE BEATLES CAN DO WITH ME BEHIND THEM.
WE'RE A TEAM NOW. BUT ONE DAY WE WON'T BE... IT WILL BE ALL YOURS, YOU KNOW.
DURING LUNCH, HAVE THE STAFF CALL RADIO LUXEMBOURG TO REQUEST "LOVE ME DO."
"LOVE ME DO" IS CLIMBING!
NO THANKS TO PARLOPHONE. PLEASE BUY AN EXTRA ONE THOUSAND COPIES FOR THE STORE.
AND HAVE THE STAFF WRITE LETTERS TO THE BBC REQUESTING THE SONG.

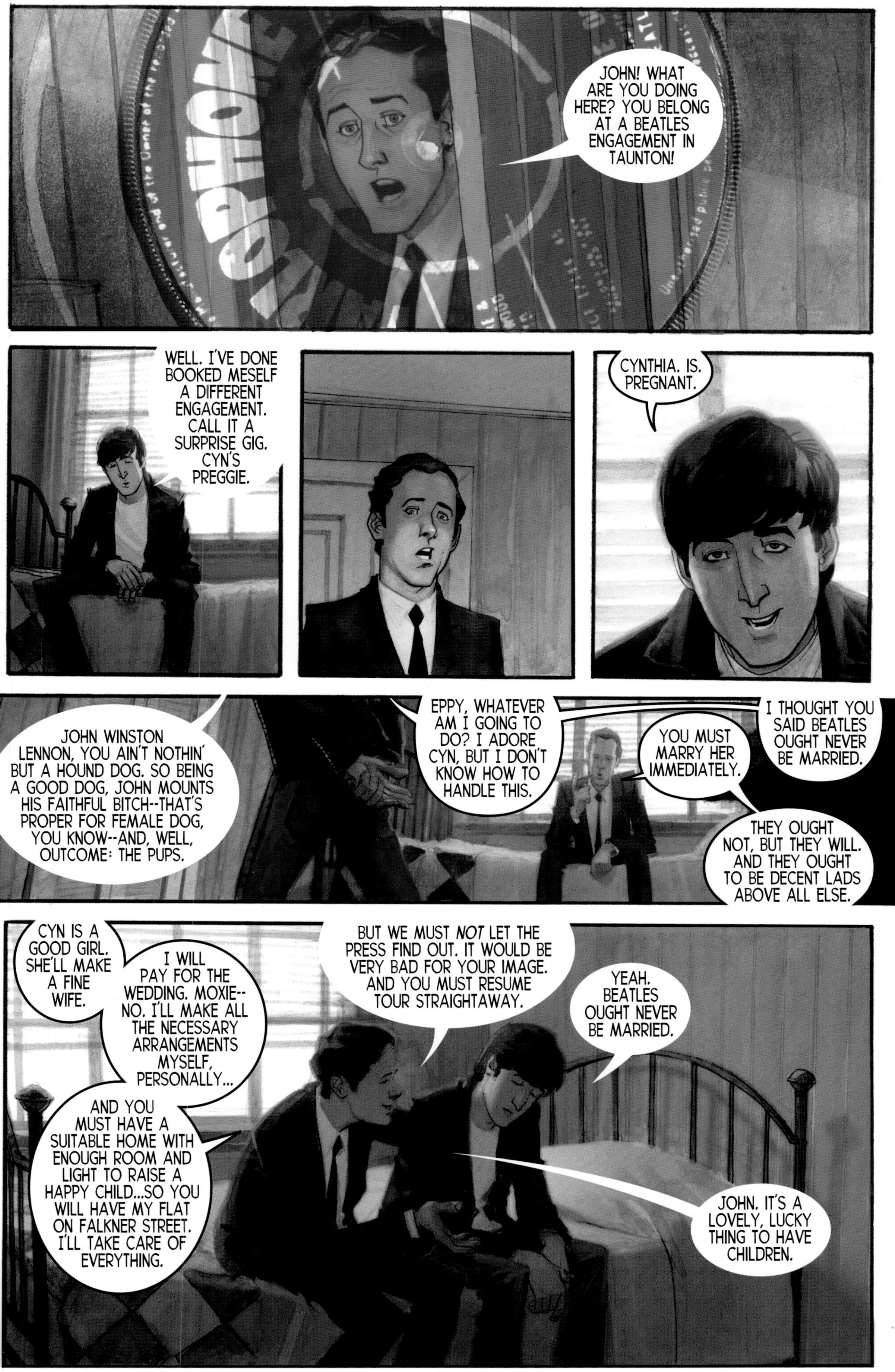
JOHN! WHAT ARE YOU DOING HERE? YOU BELONG AT A BEATLES ENGAGEMENT IN TAUNTON!
WELL. I'VE DONE BOOKED MESELF A DIFFERENT ENGAGEMENT. CALL IT A SURPRISE GIG. CYN'S PREGGIE.
CYNTHIA. IS. PREGNANT.
JOHN WINSTON LENNON, YOU AIN'T NOTHIN' BUT A HOUND DOG. SO BEING A GOOD DOG, JOHN MOUNTS HIS FAITHFUL BITCH--THAT'S PROPER FOR FEMALE DOG, YOU KNOW--AND, WELL, OUTCOME: THE PUPS.
EPPY, WHATEVER AM I GOING TO DO? I ADORE CYN, BUT I DON'T KNOW HOW TO HANDLE THIS.
I THOUGHT YOU SAID BEATLES OUGHT NEVER BE MARRIED.
YOU MUST MARRY HER IMMEDIATELY.
THEY OUGHT NOT, BUT THEY WILL. AND THEY OUGHT TO BE DECENT LADS ABOVE ALL ELSE.
CYN IS A GOOD GIRL. SHE'LL MAKE A FINE WIFE.
I WILL PAY FOR THE WEDDING. MOXIE--NO. I'LL MAKE ALL THE NECESSARY ARRANGEMENTS MYSELF, PERSONALLY...
AND YOU MUST HAVE A SUITABLE HOME WITH ENOUGH ROOM AND LIGHT TO RAISE A HAPPY CHILD...SO YOU WILL HAVE MY FLAT ON FALKNER STREET. I'LL TAKE CARE OF EVERYTHING.
BUT WE MUST *NOT* LET THE PRESS FIND OUT. IT WOULD BE VERY BAD FOR YOUR IMAGE. AND YOU MUST RESUME TOUR STRAIGHTAWAY.
YEAH. BEATLES OUGHT NEVER BE MARRIED.
JOHN. IT'S A LOVELY, LUCKY THING TO HAVE CHILDREN.

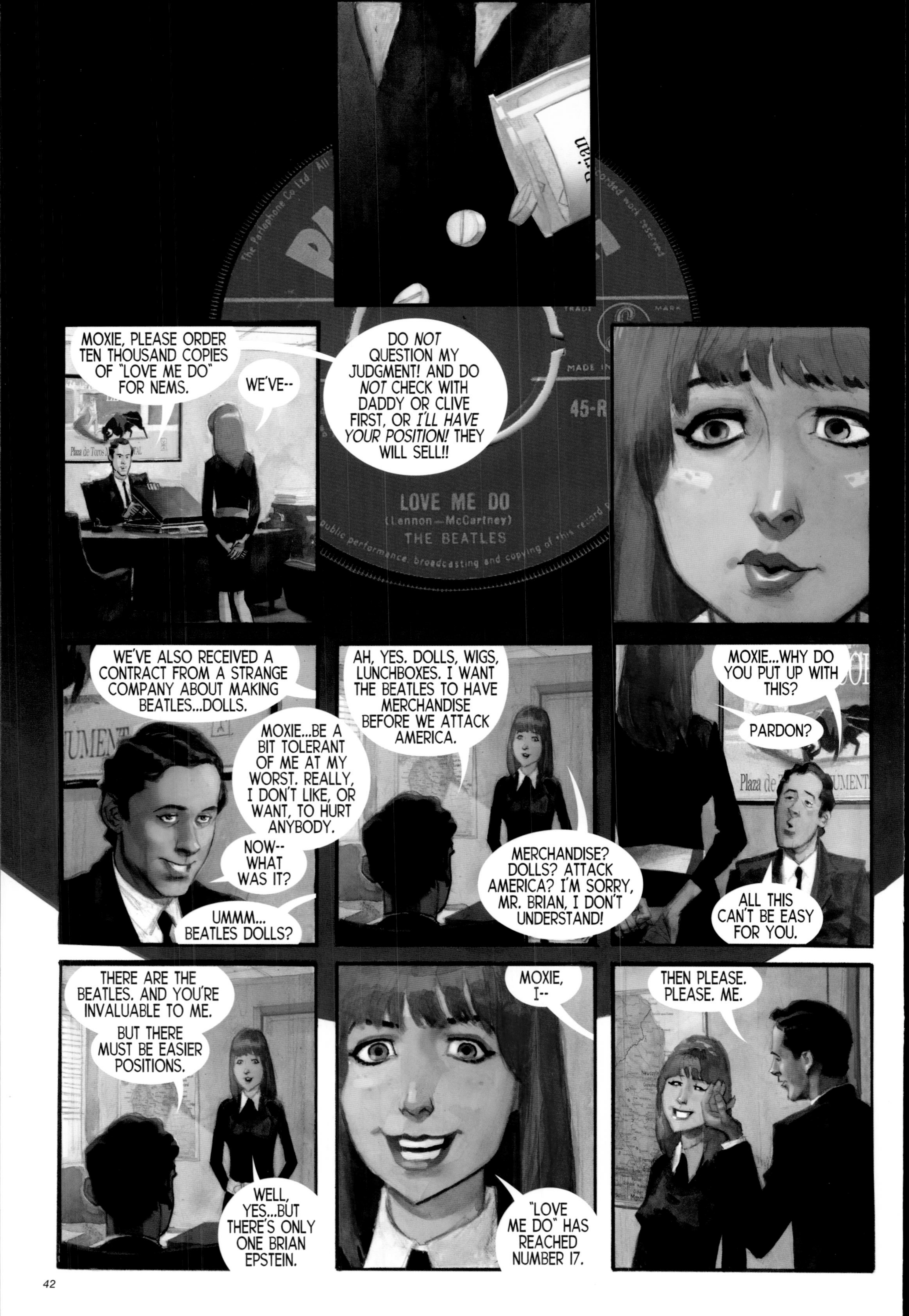
Brian
The Parlophone Co Ltd
All
recorded work reserved
TRADE MARK
MADE IN
45-R
LOVE ME DO
(Lennon–McCartney)
THE BEATLES
public performance, broadcasting and copying of this record
MOXIE, PLEASE ORDER TEN THOUSAND COPIES OF "LOVE ME DO" FOR NEMS.
WE'VE--
DO *NOT* QUESTION MY JUDGMENT! AND DO *NOT* CHECK WITH DADDY OR CLIVE FIRST, OR *I'LL HAVE YOUR POSITION!* THEY WILL SELL!!
WE'VE ALSO RECEIVED A CONTRACT FROM A STRANGE COMPANY ABOUT MAKING BEATLES...DOLLS.
MOXIE...BE A BIT TOLERANT OF ME AT MY WORST. REALLY, I DON'T LIKE, OR WANT, TO HURT ANYBODY.
NOW-- WHAT WAS IT?
UMMM... BEATLES DOLLS?
AH, YES. DOLLS, WIGS, LUNCHBOXES. I WANT THE BEATLES TO HAVE MERCHANDISE BEFORE WE ATTACK AMERICA.
MERCHANDISE? DOLLS? ATTACK AMERICA? I'M SORRY, MR. BRIAN, I DON'T UNDERSTAND!
MOXIE...WHY DO YOU PUT UP WITH THIS?
PARDON?
ALL THIS CAN'T BE EASY FOR YOU.
THERE ARE THE BEATLES. AND YOU'RE INVALUABLE TO ME.
BUT THERE MUST BE EASIER POSITIONS.
WELL, YES...BUT THERE'S ONLY ONE BRIAN EPSTEIN.
MOXIE, I--
"LOVE ME DO" HAS REACHED NUMBER 17.
THEN PLEASE. PLEASE. ME.

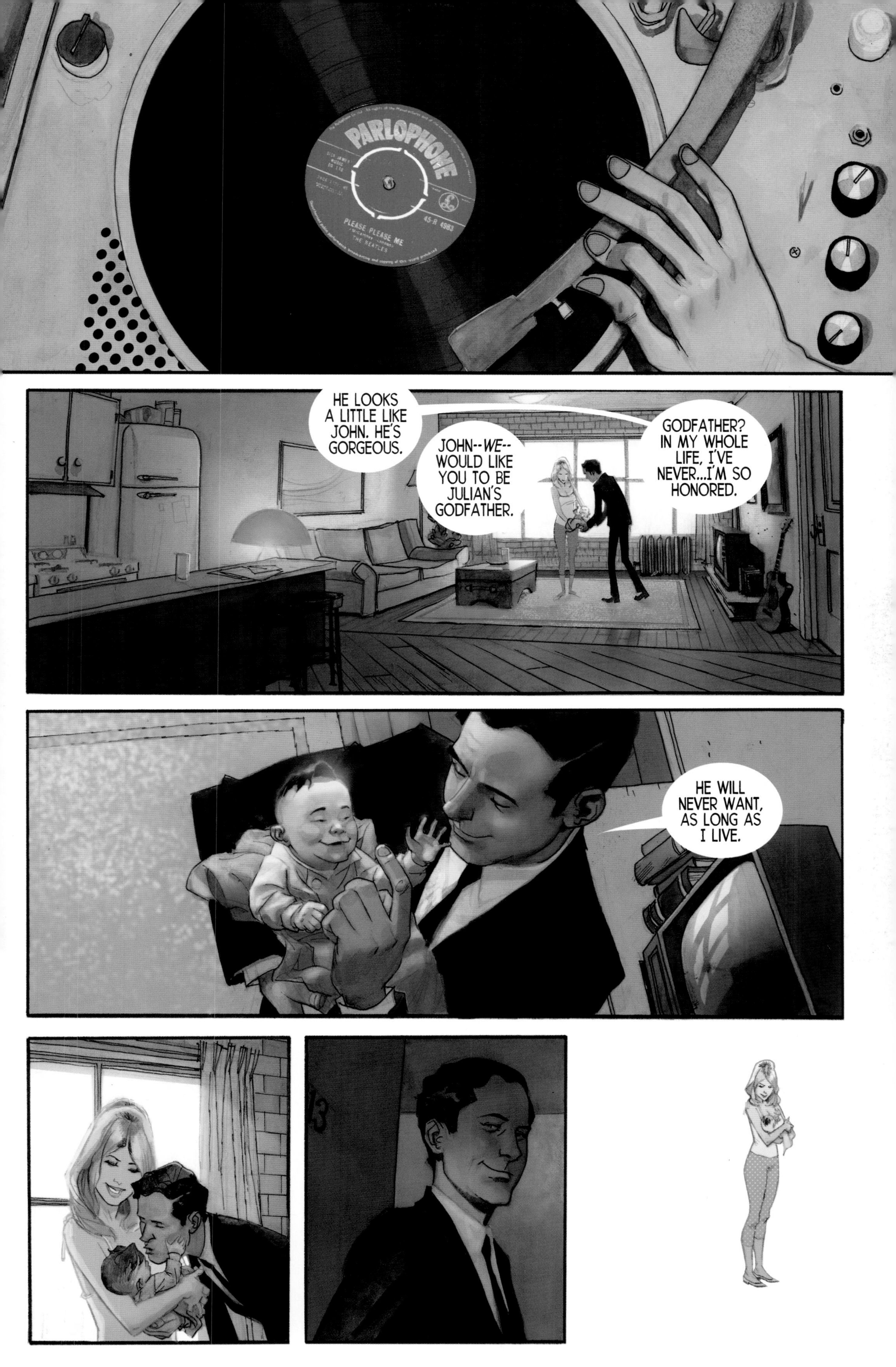

PARLOPHONE
PLEASE PLEASE ME
THE BEATLES
45-R 4983
HE LOOKS A LITTLE LIKE JOHN. HE'S GORGEOUS.
JOHN--*WE*--WOULD LIKE YOU TO BE JULIAN'S GODFATHER.
GODFATHER? IN MY WHOLE LIFE, I'VE NEVER...I'M SO HONORED.
HE WILL NEVER WANT, AS LONG AS I LIVE.

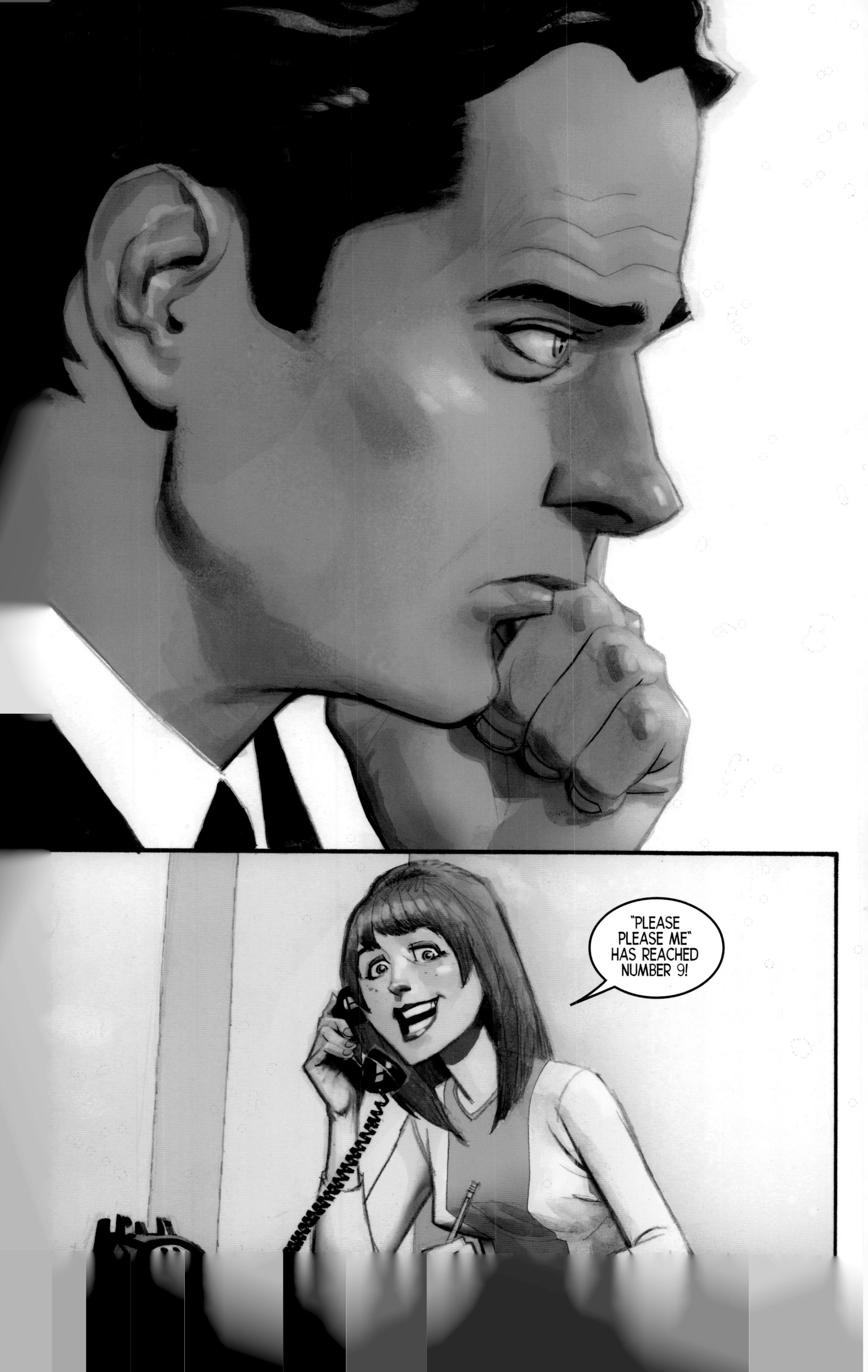
"PLEASE PLEASE ME" HAS REACHED NUMBER 9!

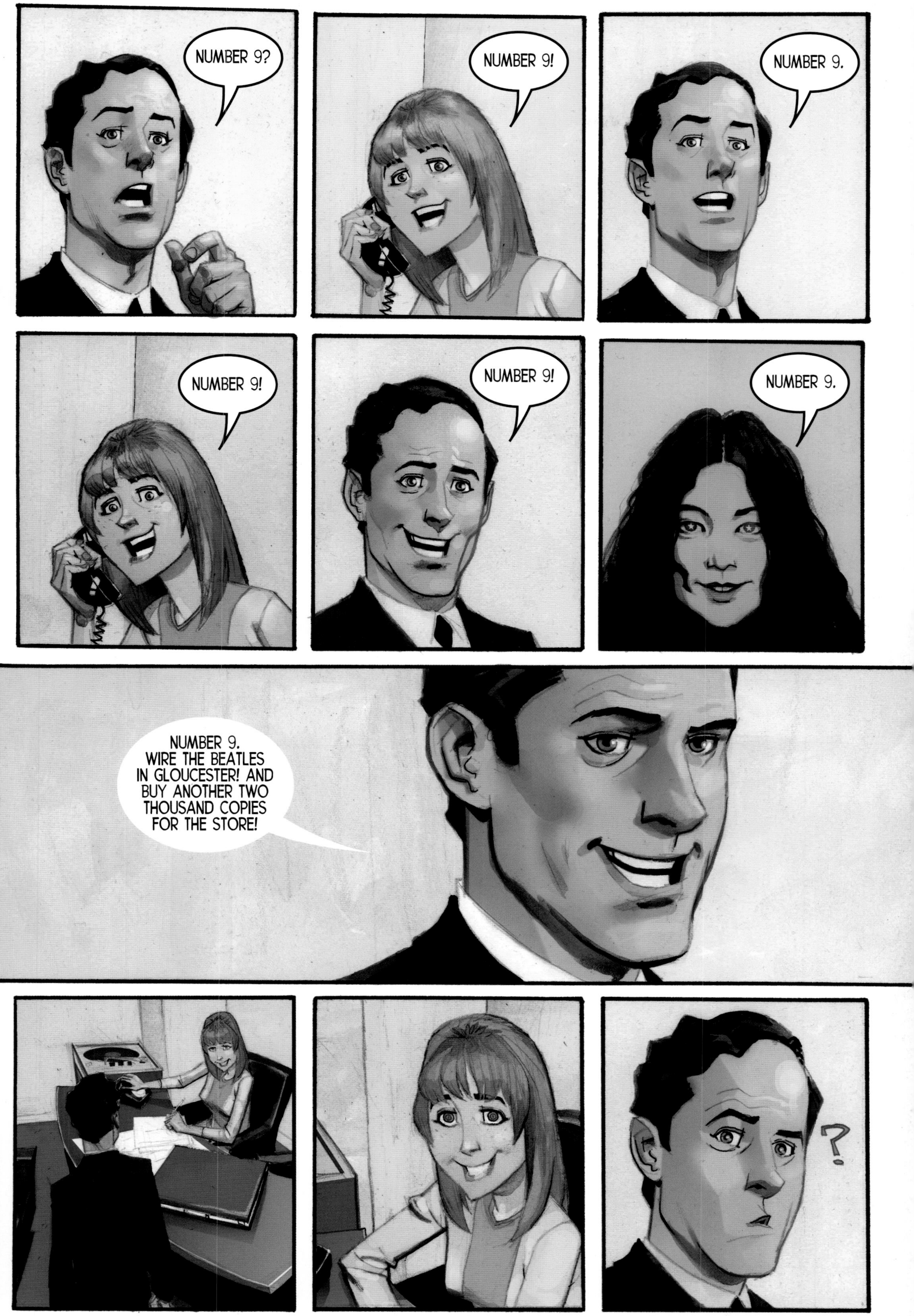
NUMBER 9?
NUMBER 9!
NUMBER 9.
NUMBER 9!
NUMBER 9!
NUMBER 9.
NUMBER 9. WIRE THE BEATLES IN GLOUCESTER! AND BUY ANOTHER TWO THOUSAND COPIES FOR THE STORE!
?

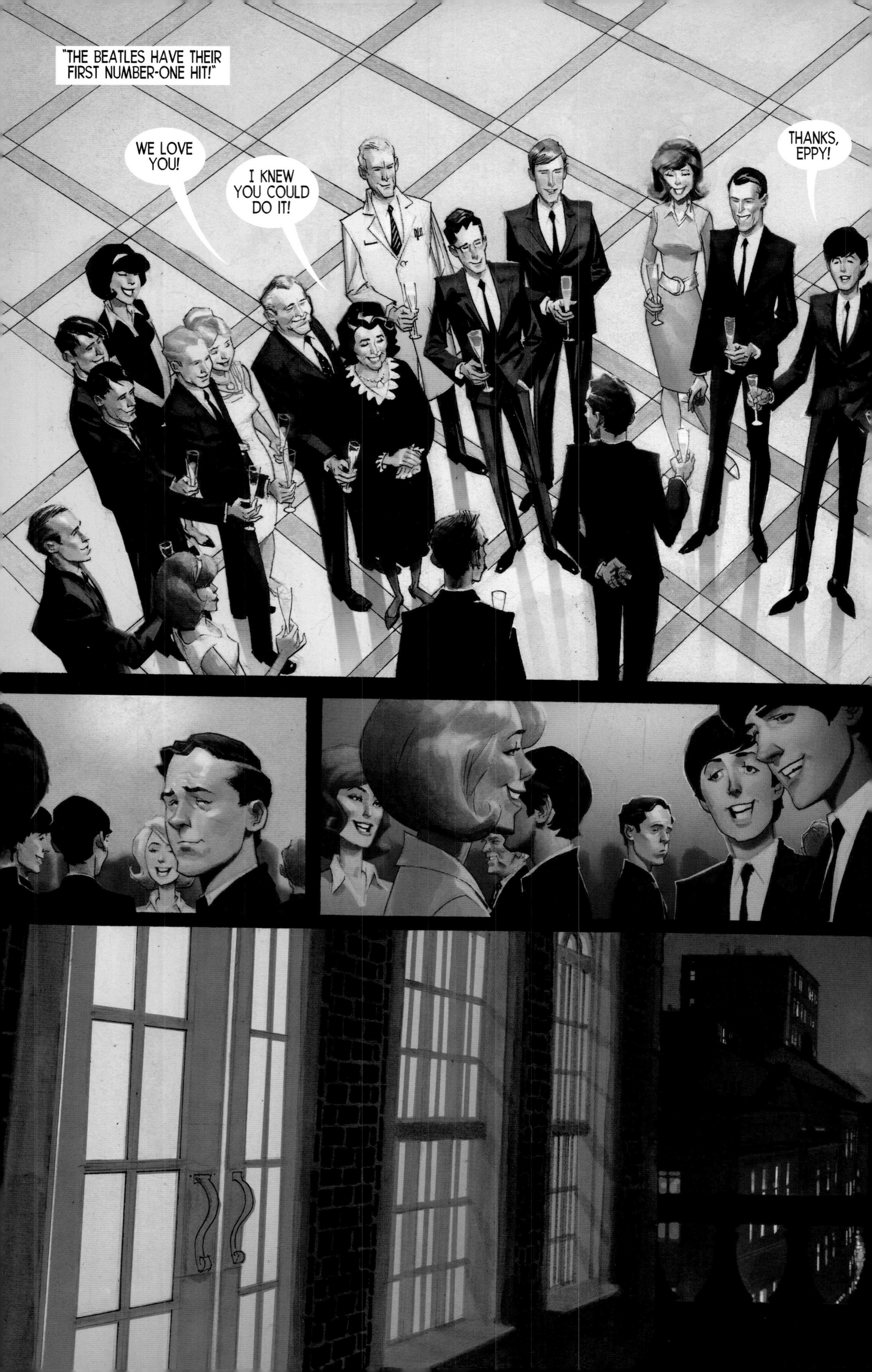
"THE BEATLES HAVE THEIR FIRST NUMBER-ONE HIT!"
WE LOVE YOU!
I KNEW YOU COULD DO IT!
THANKS, EPPY!

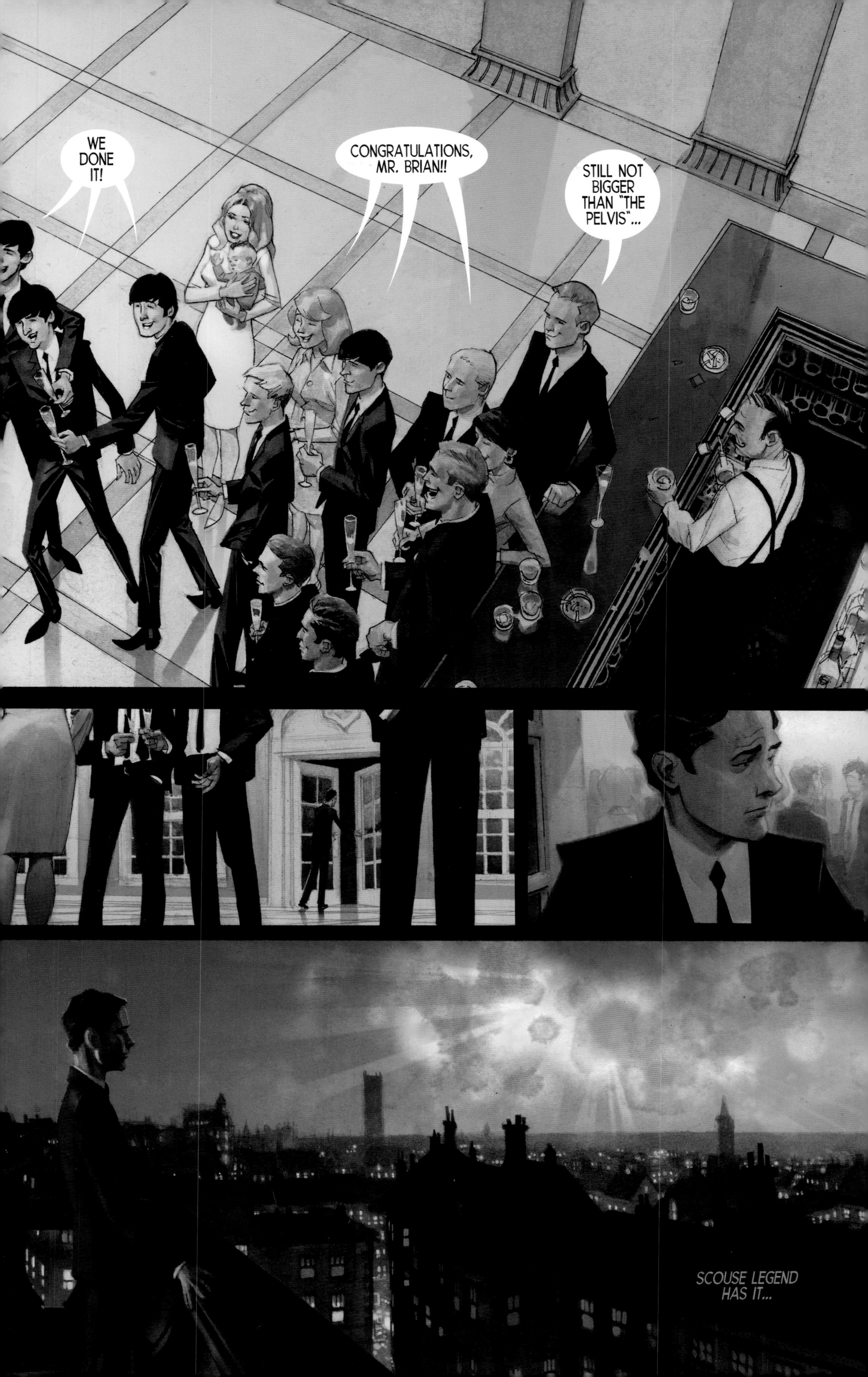
WE DONE IT!
CONGRATULATIONS, MR. BRIAN!!
STILL NOT BIGGER THAN "THE PELVIS"...
SCOUSE LEGEND HAS IT...

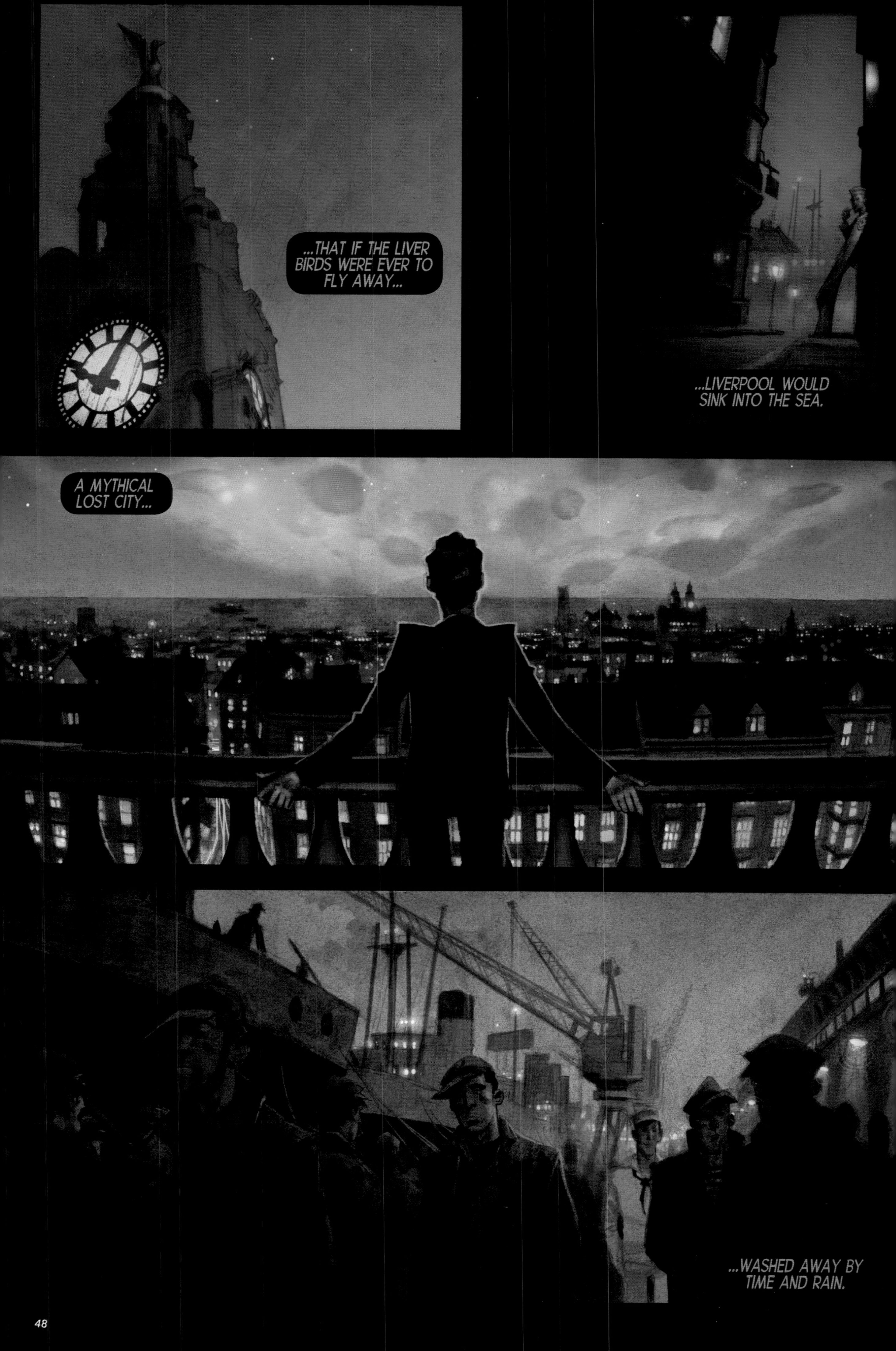
...THAT IF THE LIVER BIRDS WERE EVER TO FLY AWAY...
...LIVERPOOL WOULD SINK INTO THE SEA.
A MYTHICAL LOST CITY...
...WASHED AWAY BY TIME AND RAIN.

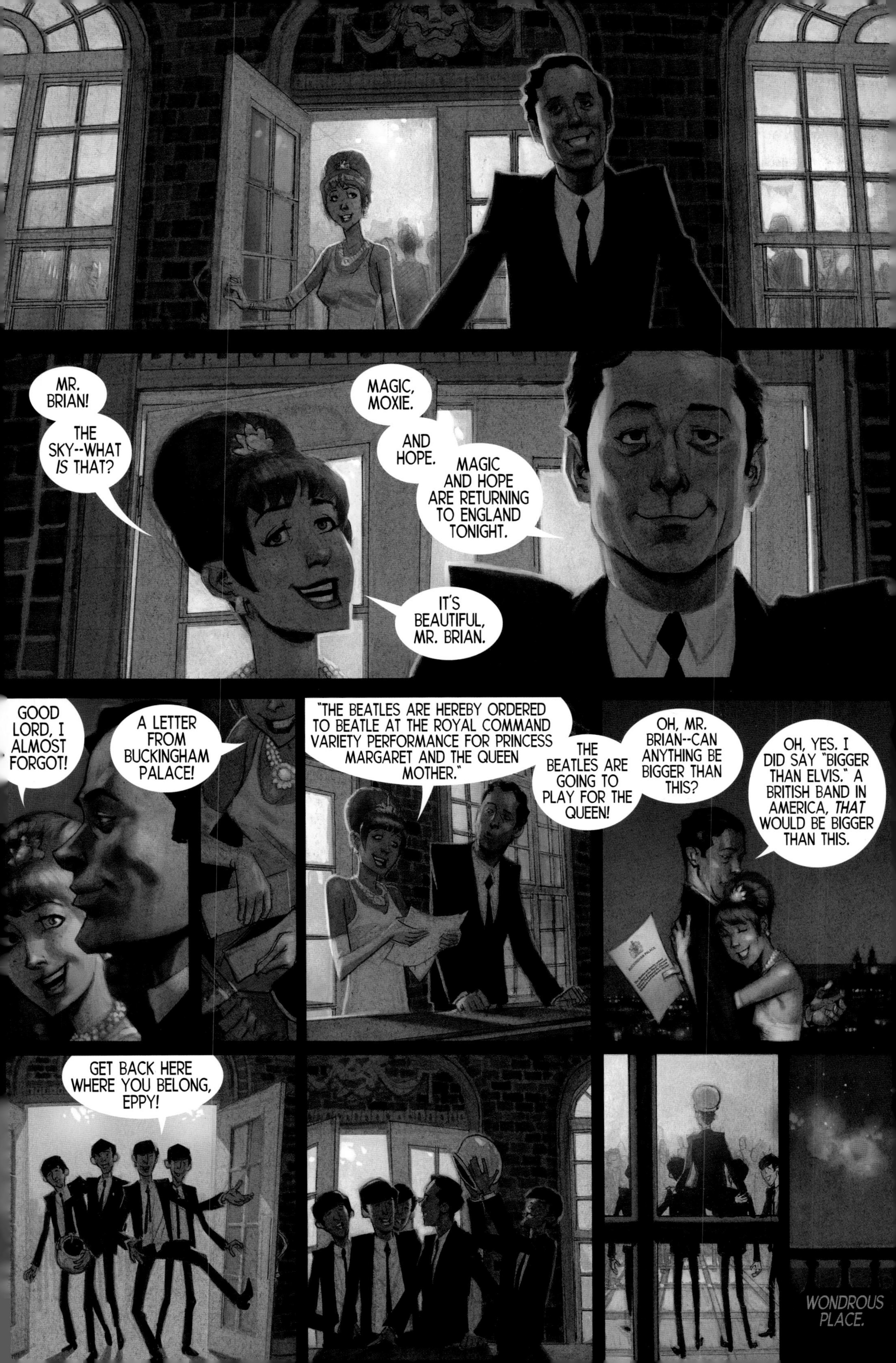
MR. BRIAN!
THE SKY--WHAT *IS* THAT?
MAGIC, MOXIE.
AND HOPE.
MAGIC AND HOPE ARE RETURNING TO ENGLAND TONIGHT.
IT'S BEAUTIFUL, MR. BRIAN.
GOOD LORD, I ALMOST FORGOT!
A LETTER FROM BUCKINGHAM PALACE!
"THE BEATLES ARE HEREBY ORDERED TO BEATLE AT THE ROYAL COMMAND VARIETY PERFORMANCE FOR PRINCESS MARGARET AND THE QUEEN MOTHER."
THE BEATLES ARE GOING TO PLAY FOR THE QUEEN!
OH, MR. BRIAN--CAN ANYTHING BE BIGGER THAN THIS?
OH, YES. I DID SAY "BIGGER THAN ELVIS." A BRITISH BAND IN AMERICA, *THAT* WOULD BE BIGGER THAN THIS.
GET BACK HERE WHERE YOU BELONG, EPPY!
WONDROUS PLACE.

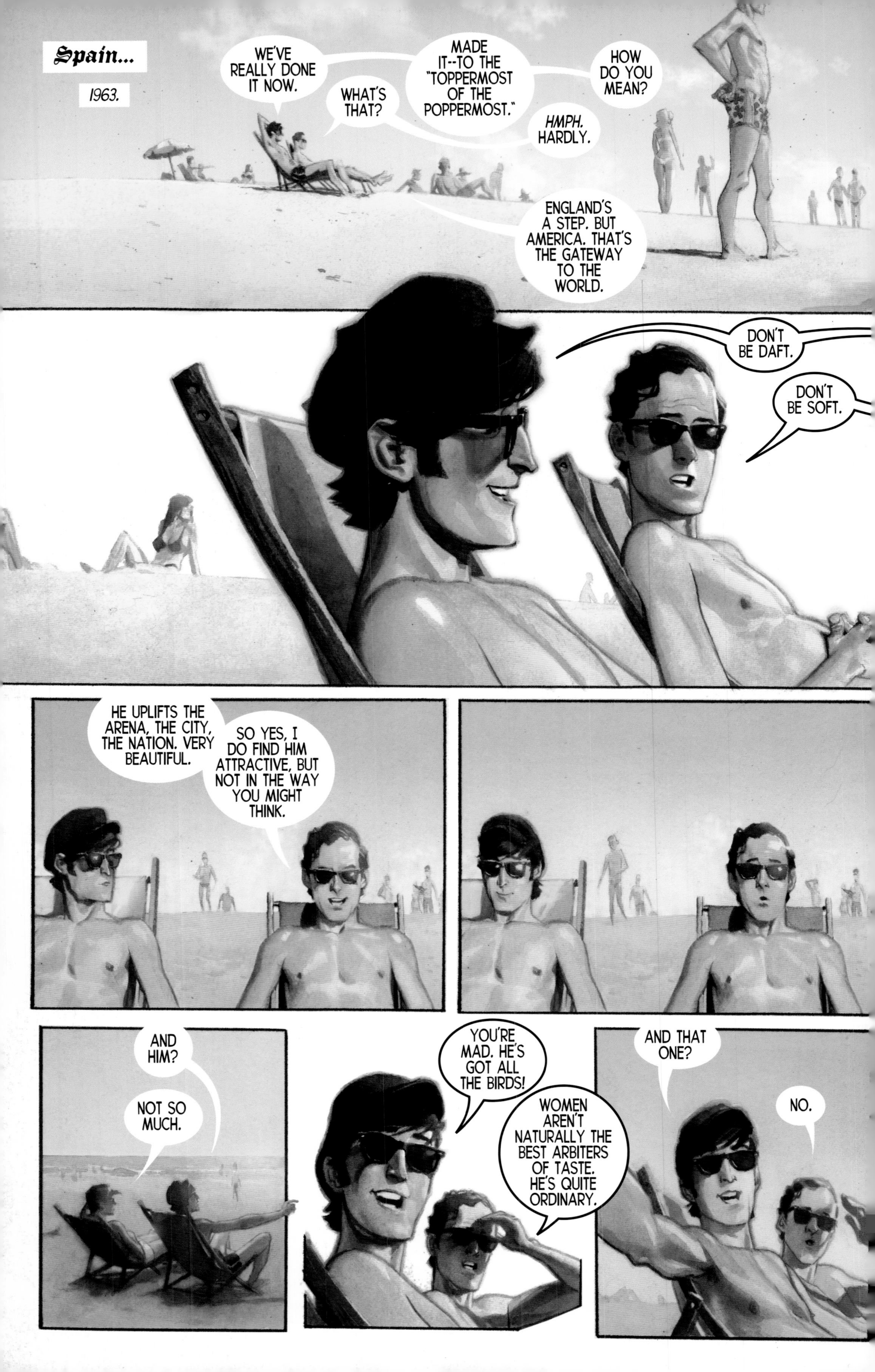
Spain...
1963.
WE'VE REALLY DONE IT NOW.
WHAT'S THAT?
MADE IT--TO THE "TOPPERMOST OF THE POPPERMOST."
HOW DO YOU MEAN?
HMPH. HARDLY.
ENGLAND'S A STEP. BUT AMERICA. THAT'S THE GATEWAY TO THE WORLD.
DON'T BE DAFT.
DON'T BE SOFT.
HE UPLIFTS THE ARENA, THE CITY, THE NATION. VERY BEAUTIFUL.
SO YES, I DO FIND HIM ATTRACTIVE, BUT NOT IN THE WAY YOU MIGHT THINK.
AND HIM?
NOT SO MUCH.
YOU'RE MAD. HE'S GOT ALL THE BIRDS!
WOMEN AREN'T NATURALLY THE BEST ARBITERS OF TASTE. HE'S QUITE ORDINARY.
AND THAT ONE?
NO.

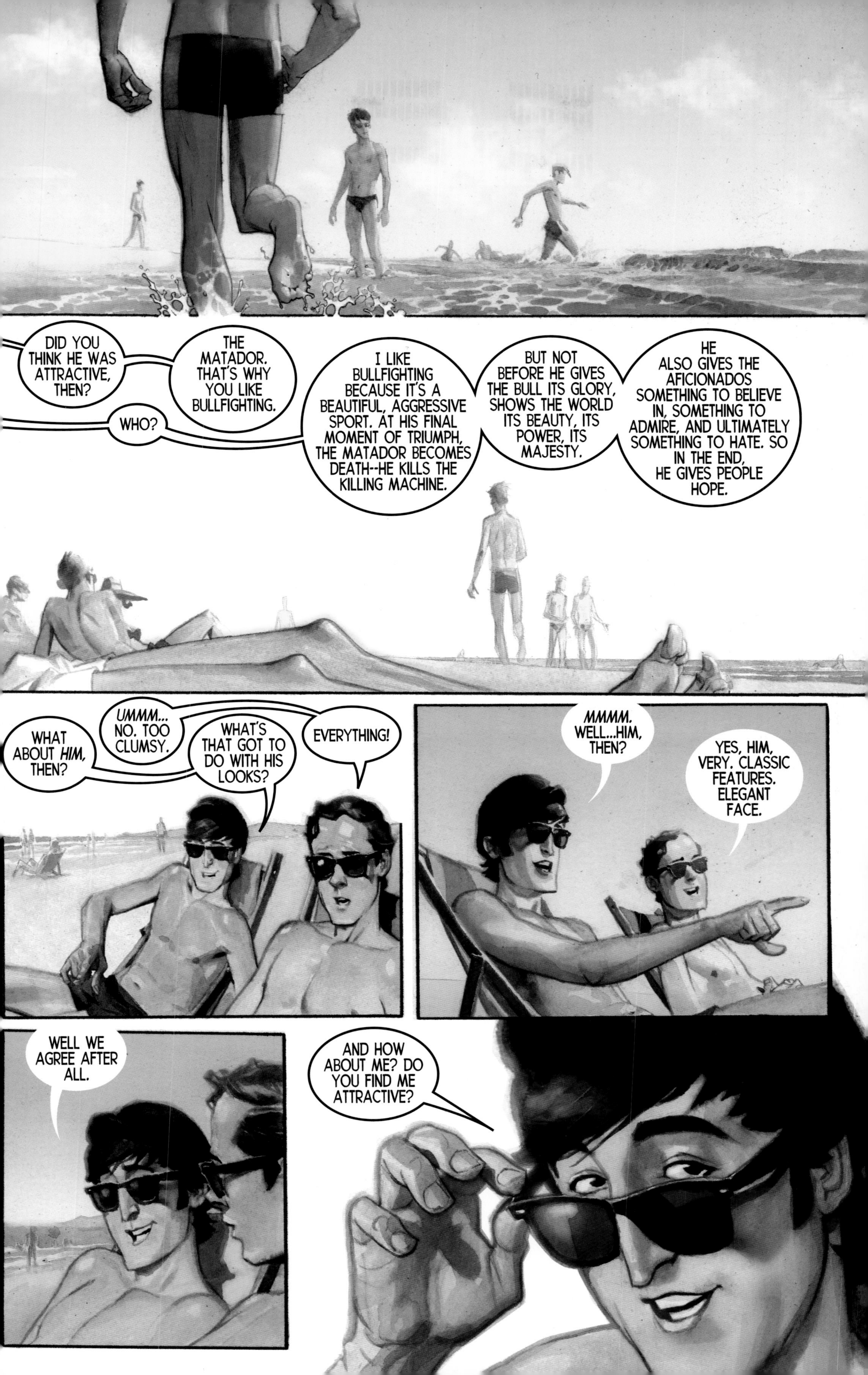
DID YOU THINK HE WAS ATTRACTIVE, THEN?
WHO?
THE MATADOR. THAT'S WHY YOU LIKE BULLFIGHTING.
I LIKE BULLFIGHTING BECAUSE IT'S A BEAUTIFUL, AGGRESSIVE SPORT. AT HIS FINAL MOMENT OF TRIUMPH, THE MATADOR BECOMES DEATH--HE KILLS THE KILLING MACHINE.
BUT NOT BEFORE HE GIVES THE BULL ITS GLORY, SHOWS THE WORLD ITS BEAUTY, ITS POWER, ITS MAJESTY.
HE ALSO GIVES THE AFICIONADOS SOMETHING TO BELIEVE IN, SOMETHING TO ADMIRE, AND ULTIMATELY SOMETHING TO HATE. SO IN THE END, HE GIVES PEOPLE HOPE.
WHAT ABOUT *HIM*, THEN?
UMMM... NO. TOO CLUMSY.
WHAT'S THAT GOT TO DO WITH HIS LOOKS?
EVERYTHING!
MMMM. WELL...HIM, THEN?
YES, HIM, VERY. CLASSIC FEATURES. ELEGANT FACE.
WELL WE AGREE AFTER ALL.
AND HOW ABOUT ME? DO YOU FIND ME ATTRACTIVE?

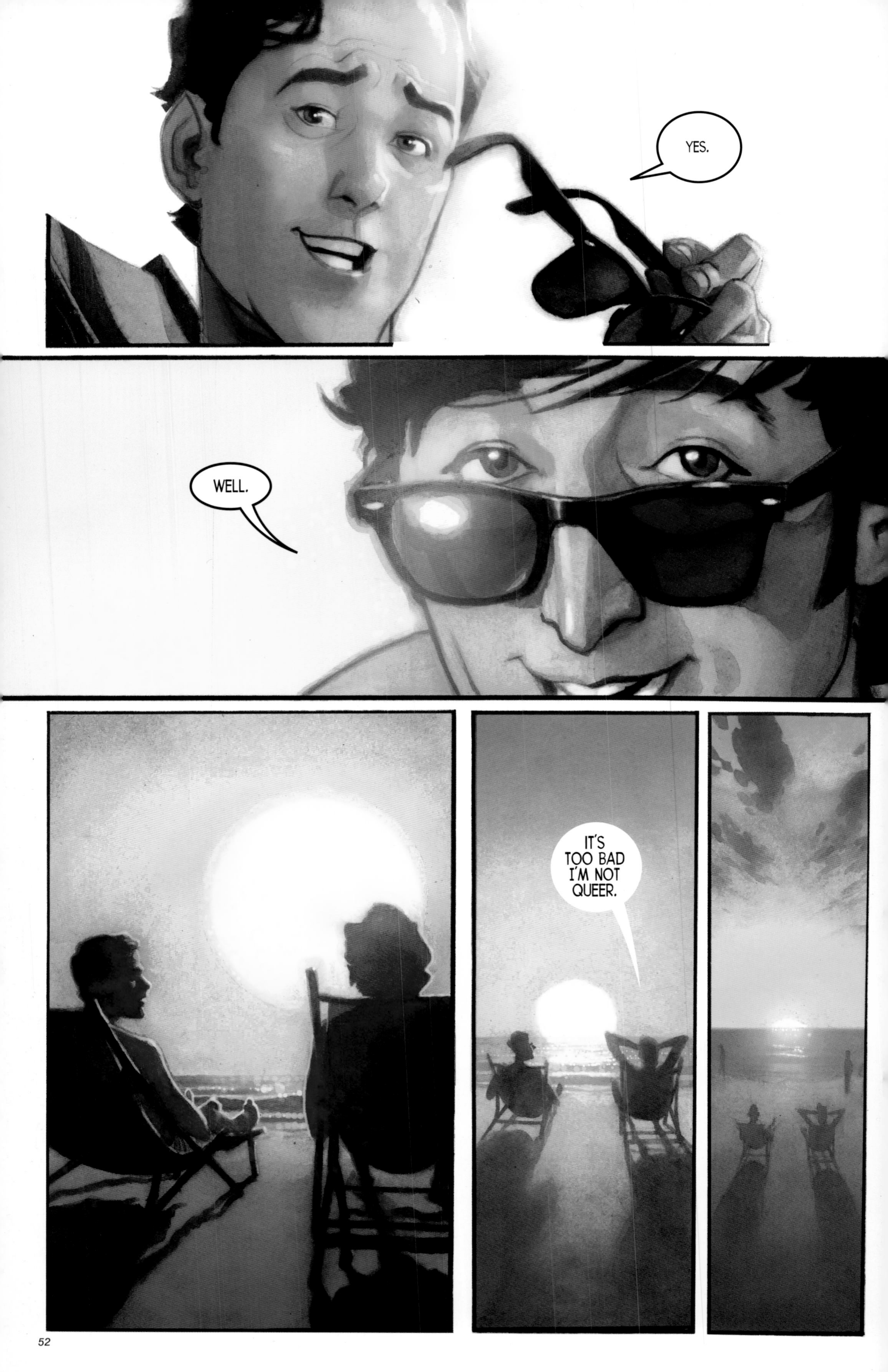
YES.
WELL.
IT'S TOO BAD I'M NOT QUEER.

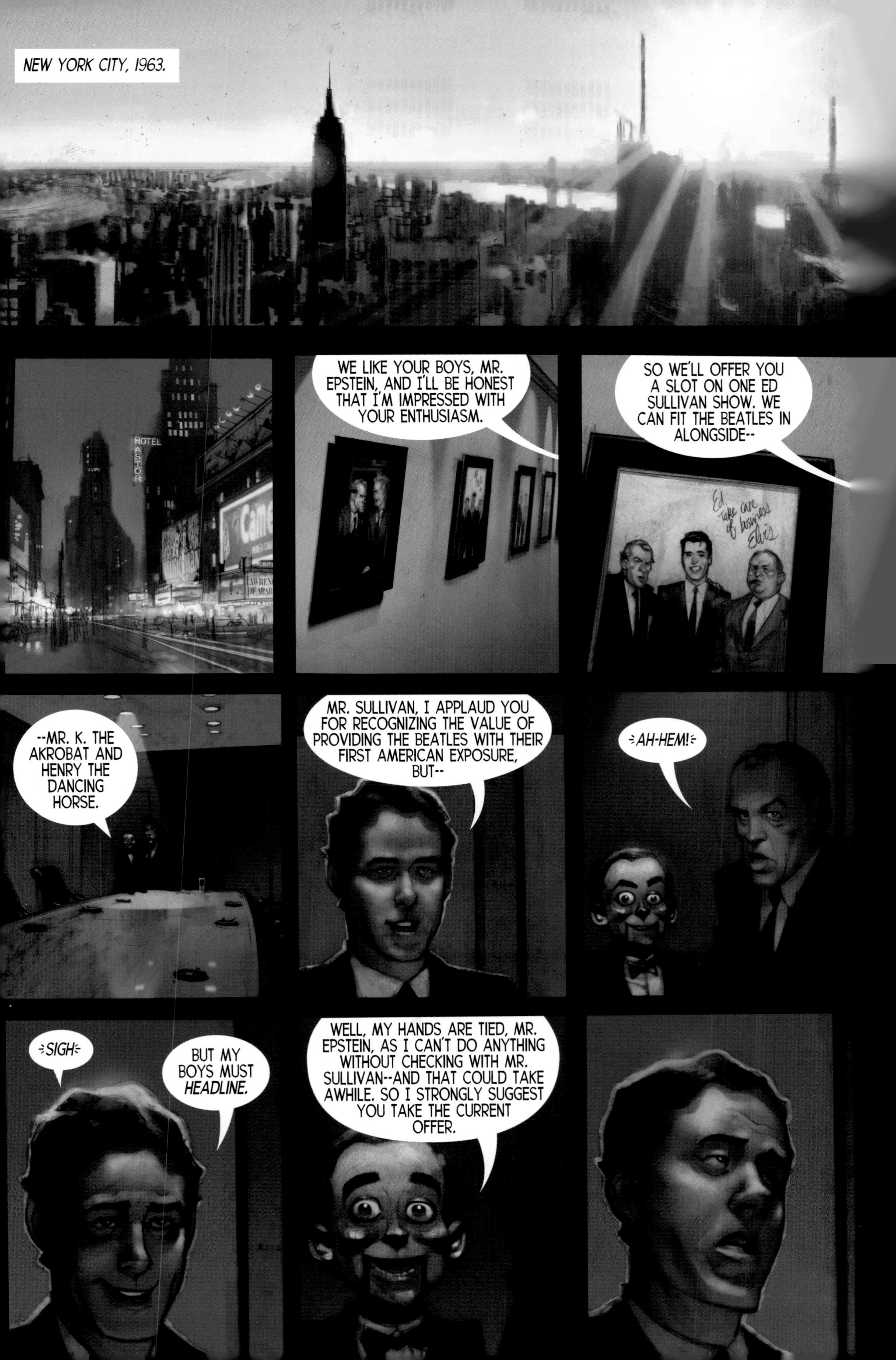
NEW YORK CITY, 1963.
HOTEL ASTOR
WE LIKE YOUR BOYS, MR. EPSTEIN, AND I'LL BE HONEST THAT I'M IMPRESSED WITH YOUR ENTHUSIASM.
SO WE'LL OFFER YOU A SLOT ON ONE ED SULLIVAN SHOW. WE CAN FIT THE BEATLES IN ALONGSIDE--
Ed, take care of business Elvis
--MR. K. THE AKROBAT AND HENRY THE DANCING HORSE.
MR. SULLIVAN, I APPLAUD YOU FOR RECOGNIZING THE VALUE OF PROVIDING THE BEATLES WITH THEIR FIRST AMERICAN EXPOSURE, BUT--
AH-HEM!
SIGH
BUT MY BOYS MUST *HEADLINE.*
WELL, MY HANDS ARE TIED, MR. EPSTEIN, AS I CAN'T DO ANYTHING WITHOUT CHECKING WITH MR. SULLIVAN--AND THAT COULD TAKE AWHILE. SO I STRONGLY SUGGEST YOU TAKE THE CURRENT OFFER.

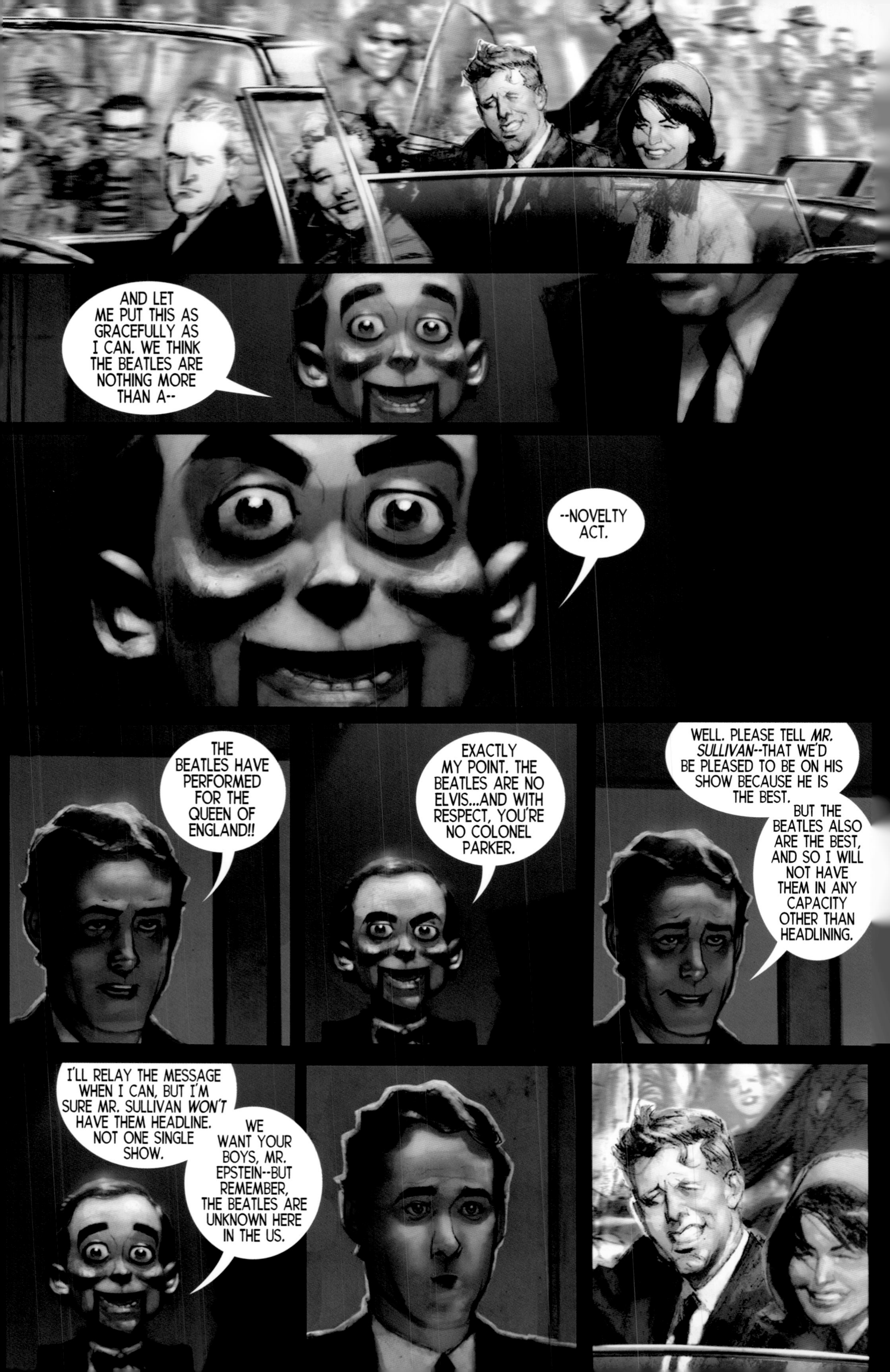

AND LET ME PUT THIS AS GRACEFULLY AS I CAN. WE THINK THE BEATLES ARE NOTHING MORE THAN A--
--NOVELTY ACT.
THE BEATLES HAVE PERFORMED FOR THE QUEEN OF ENGLAND!!
EXACTLY MY POINT. THE BEATLES ARE NO ELVIS...AND WITH RESPECT, YOU'RE NO COLONEL PARKER.
WELL. PLEASE TELL *MR. SULLIVAN*--THAT WE'D BE PLEASED TO BE ON HIS SHOW BECAUSE HE IS THE BEST.
BUT THE BEATLES ALSO ARE THE BEST, AND SO I WILL NOT HAVE THEM IN ANY CAPACITY OTHER THAN HEADLINING.
I'LL RELAY THE MESSAGE WHEN I CAN, BUT I'M SURE MR. SULLIVAN *WON'T* HAVE THEM HEADLINE. NOT ONE SINGLE SHOW.
WE WANT YOUR BOYS, MR. EPSTEIN--BUT REMEMBER, THE BEATLES ARE UNKNOWN HERE IN THE US.

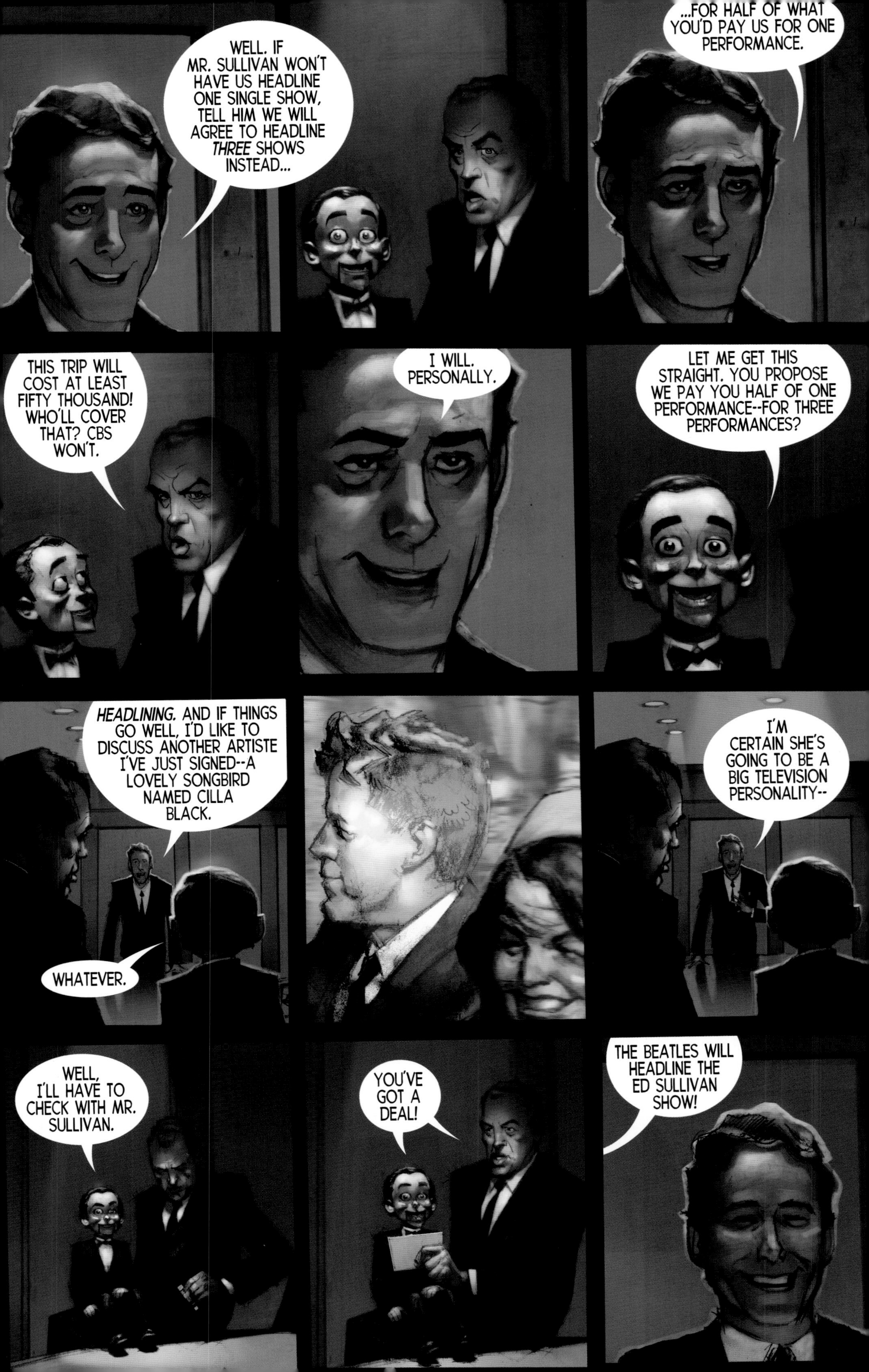
WELL. IF MR. SULLIVAN WON'T HAVE US HEADLINE ONE SINGLE SHOW, TELL HIM WE WILL AGREE TO HEADLINE *THREE* SHOWS INSTEAD...
...FOR HALF OF WHAT YOU'D PAY US FOR ONE PERFORMANCE.
THIS TRIP WILL COST AT LEAST FIFTY THOUSAND! WHO'LL COVER THAT? CBS WON'T.
I WILL. PERSONALLY.
LET ME GET THIS STRAIGHT. YOU PROPOSE WE PAY YOU HALF OF ONE PERFORMANCE--FOR THREE PERFORMANCES?
HEADLINING. AND IF THINGS GO WELL, I'D LIKE TO DISCUSS ANOTHER ARTISTE I'VE JUST SIGNED--A LOVELY SONGBIRD NAMED CILLA BLACK.
WHATEVER.
I'M CERTAIN SHE'S GOING TO BE A BIG TELEVISION PERSONALITY--
WELL, I'LL HAVE TO CHECK WITH MR. SULLIVAN.
YOU'VE GOT A DEAL!
THE BEATLES WILL HEADLINE THE ED SULLIVAN SHOW!

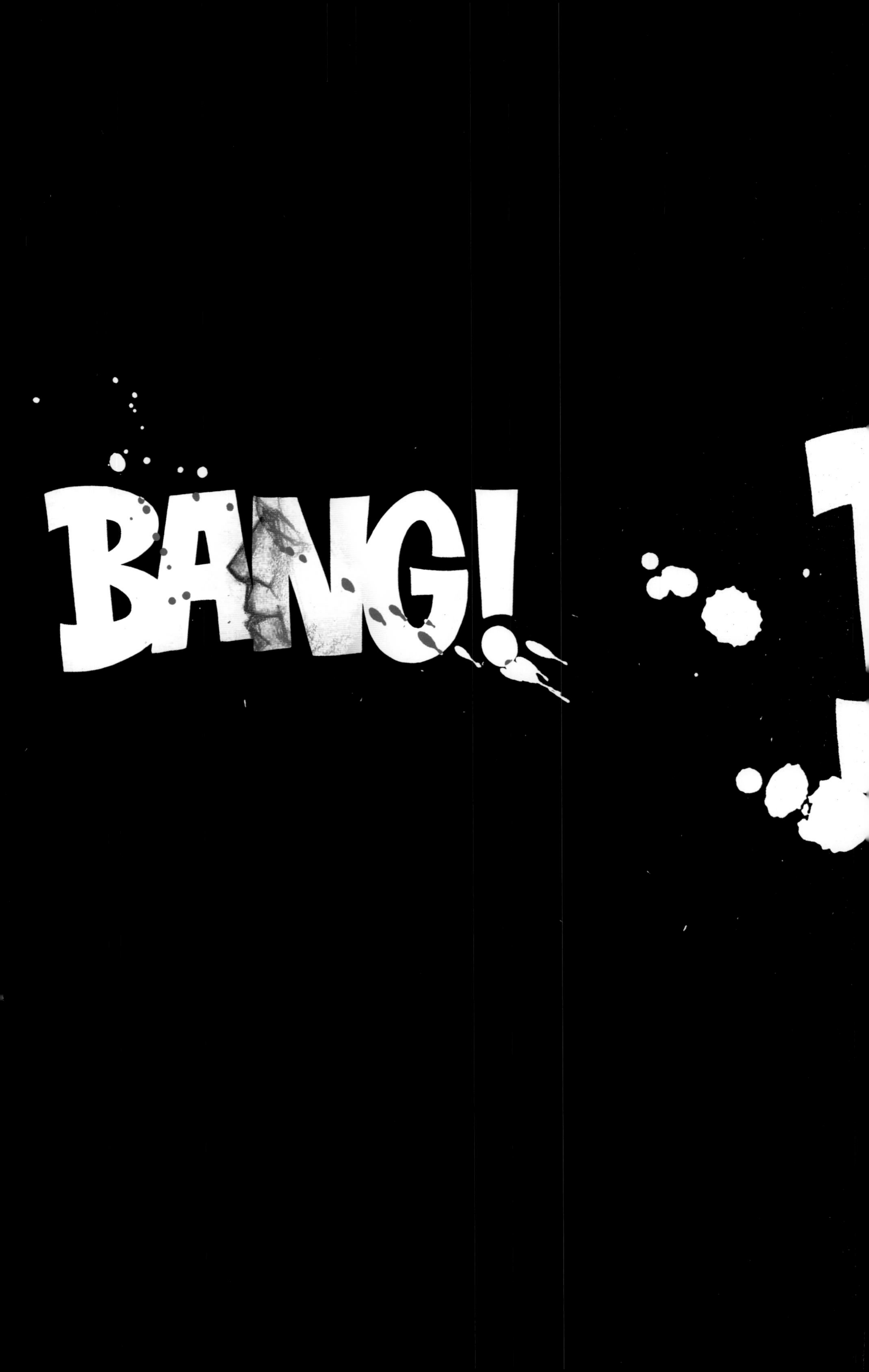
BANG!

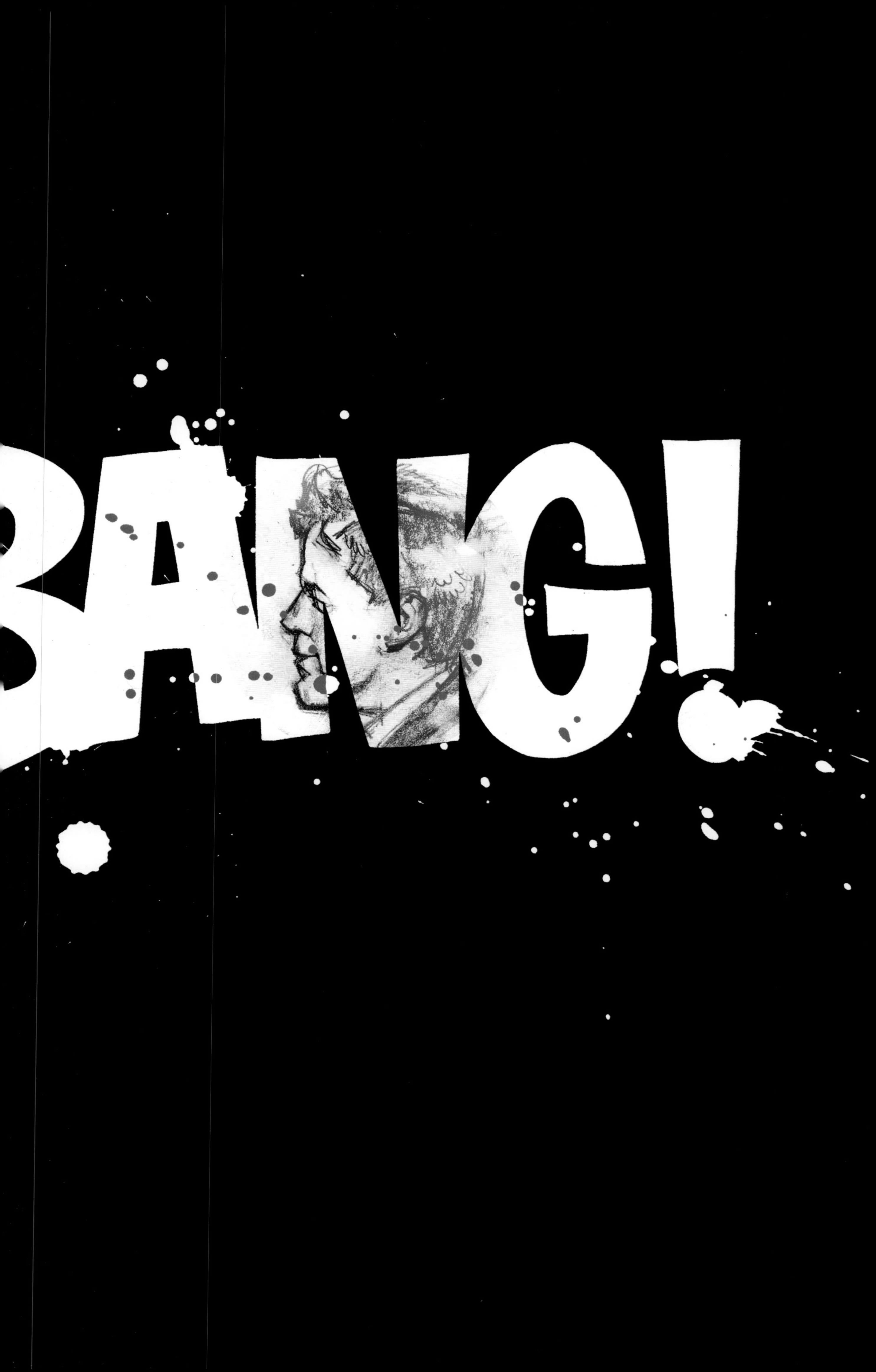
BANG!

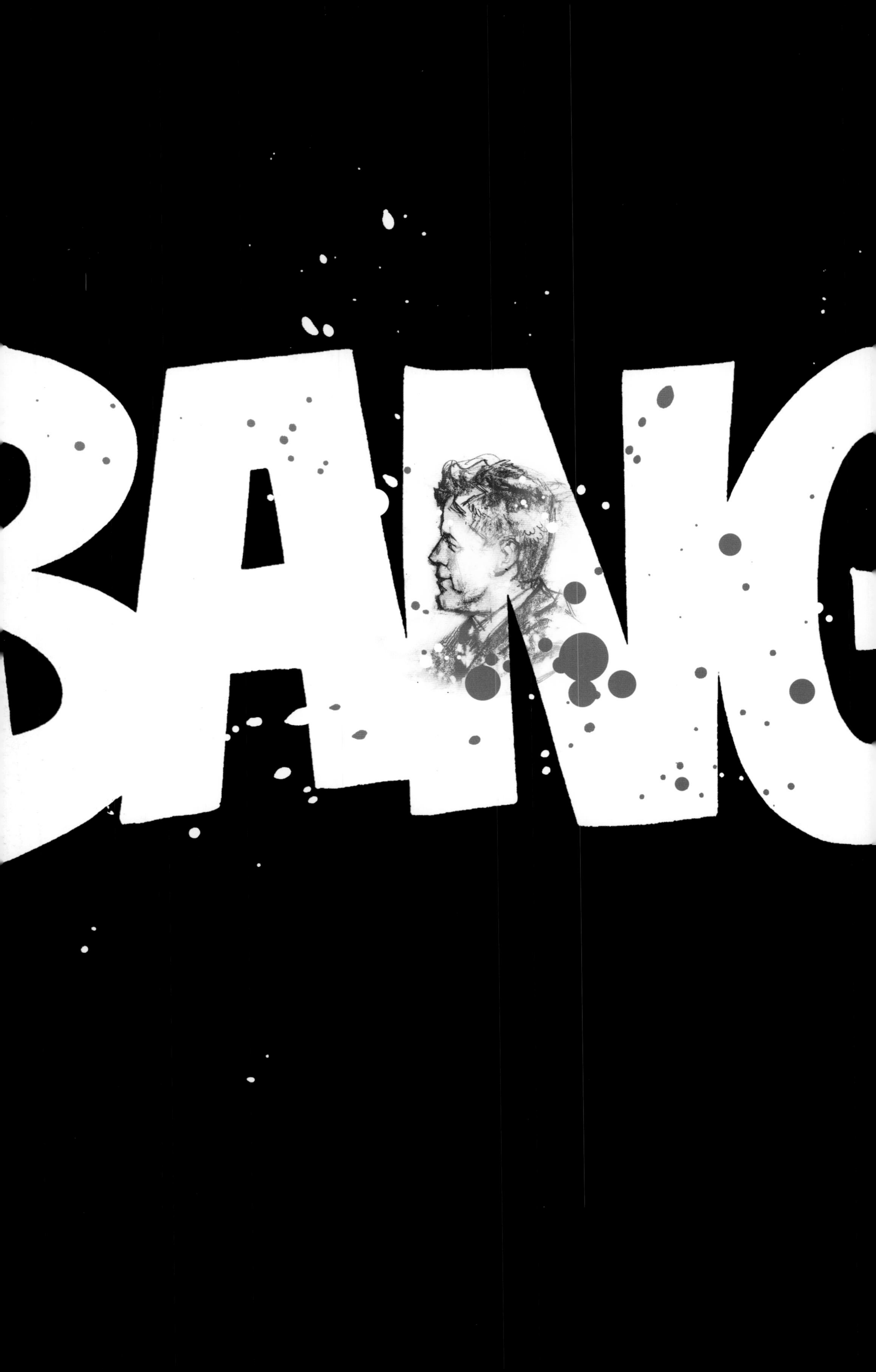
BANG

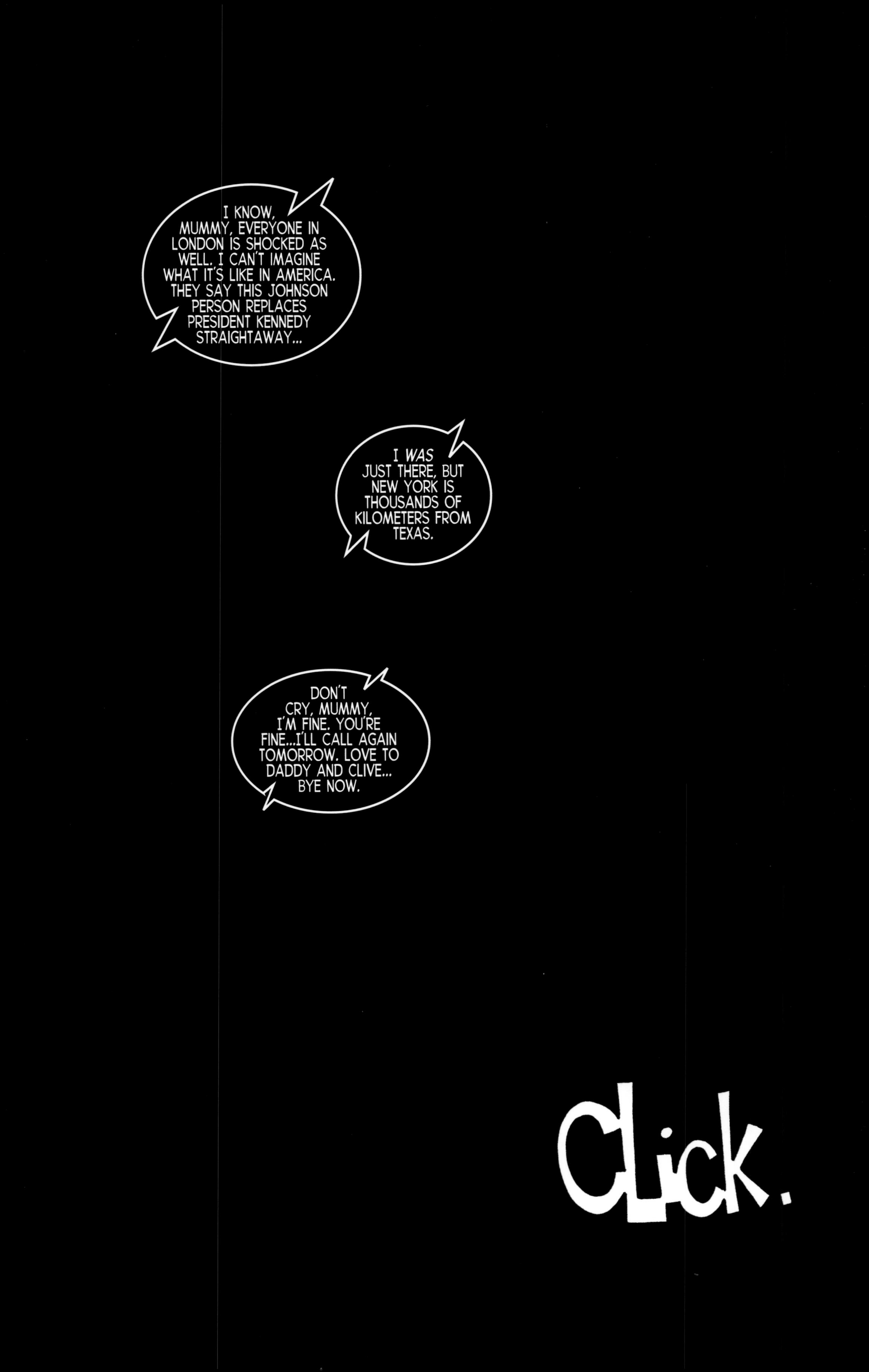
I KNOW, MUMMY, EVERYONE IN LONDON IS SHOCKED AS WELL. I CAN'T IMAGINE WHAT IT'S LIKE IN AMERICA. THEY SAY THIS JOHNSON PERSON REPLACES PRESIDENT KENNEDY STRAIGHTAWAY...
I WAS JUST THERE, BUT NEW YORK IS THOUSANDS OF KILOMETERS FROM TEXAS.
DON'T CRY, MUMMY, I'M FINE. YOU'RE FINE...I'LL CALL AGAIN TOMORROW. LOVE TO DADDY AND CLIVE... BYE NOW.
Click.

"As a bullfighter you're completely alone, even if thousands of people are watching your fight. It is an unimaginable loneliness. The only thing you can sense at that moment is the bull."

—The great matador Juan Belmonte

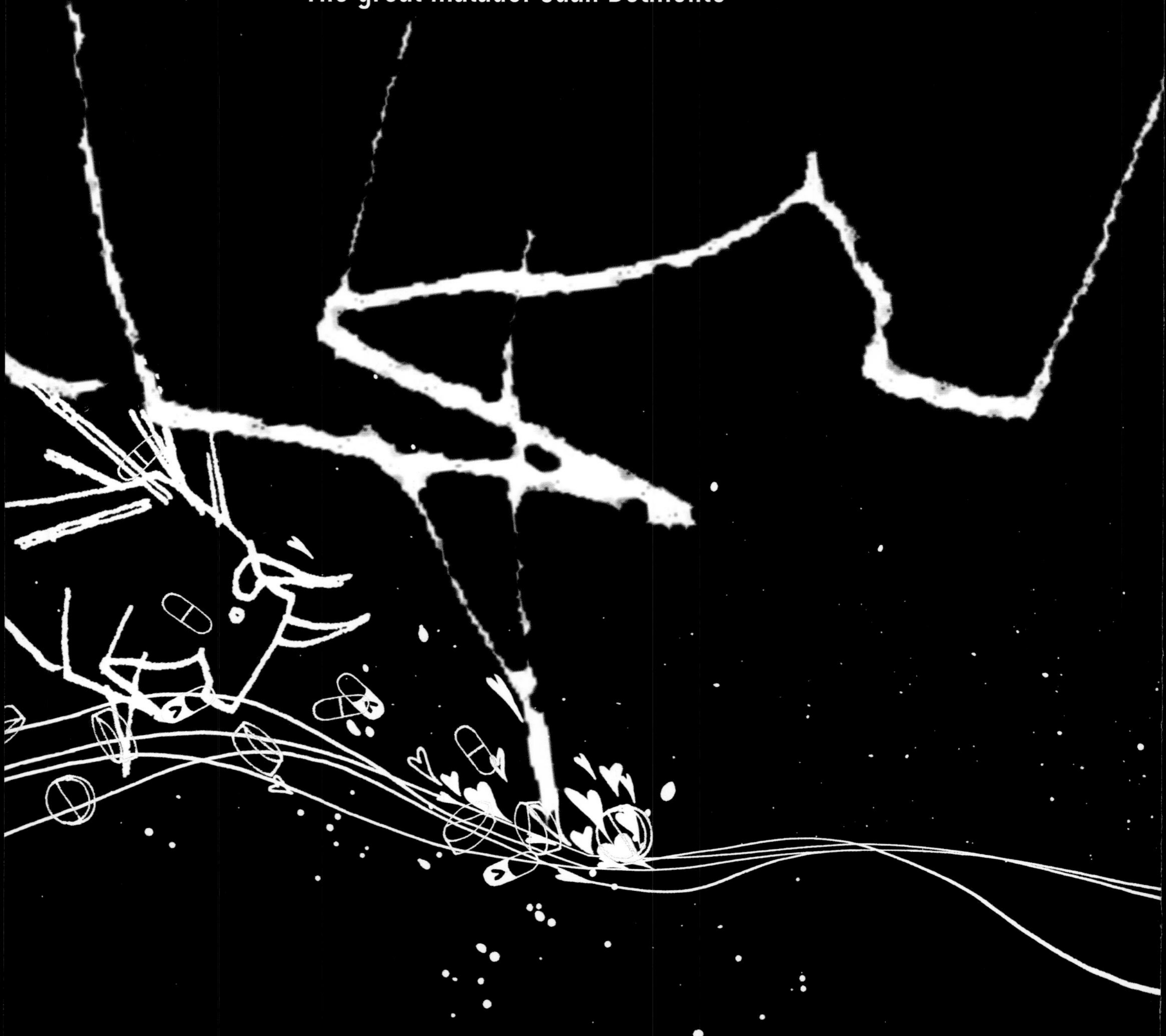

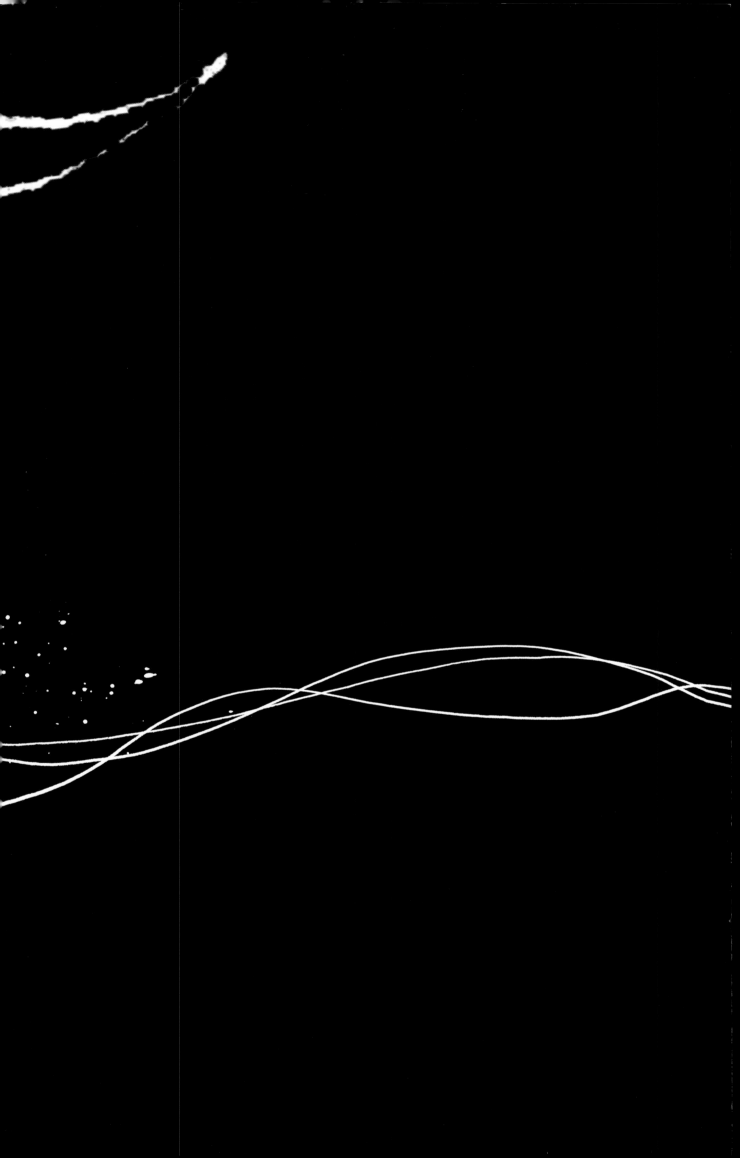

Part II: The Great Cause

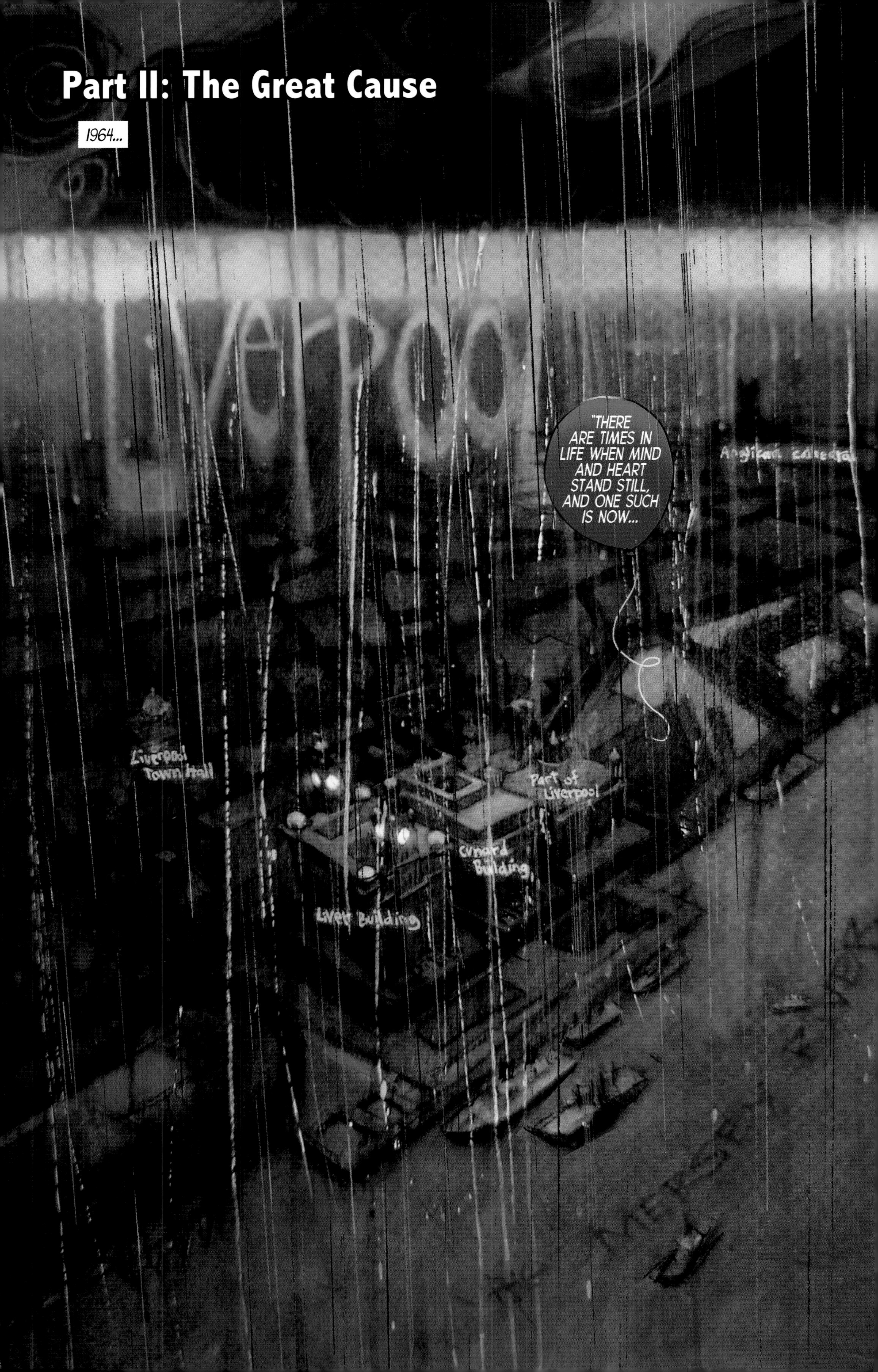
1964...
"THERE ARE TIMES IN LIFE WHEN MIND AND HEART STAND STILL, AND ONE SUCH IS NOW...
Liverpool Town Hall
Port of Liverpool
Cunard Building
Liver Building

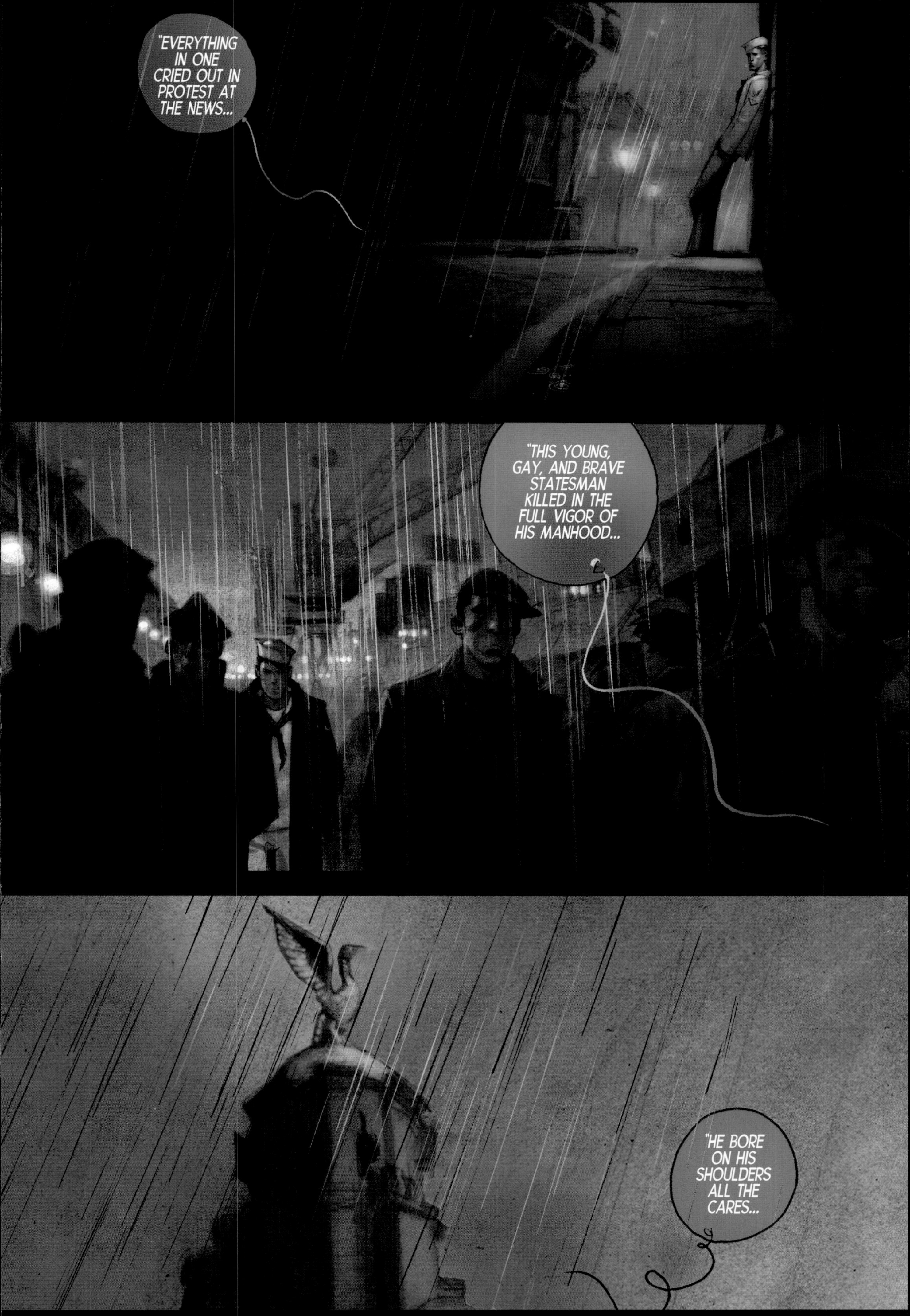
"EVERYTHING IN ONE CRIED OUT IN PROTEST AT THE NEWS...
"THIS YOUNG, GAY, AND BRAVE STATESMAN KILLED IN THE FULL VIGOR OF HIS MANHOOD...
"HE BORE ON HIS SHOULDERS ALL THE CARES...

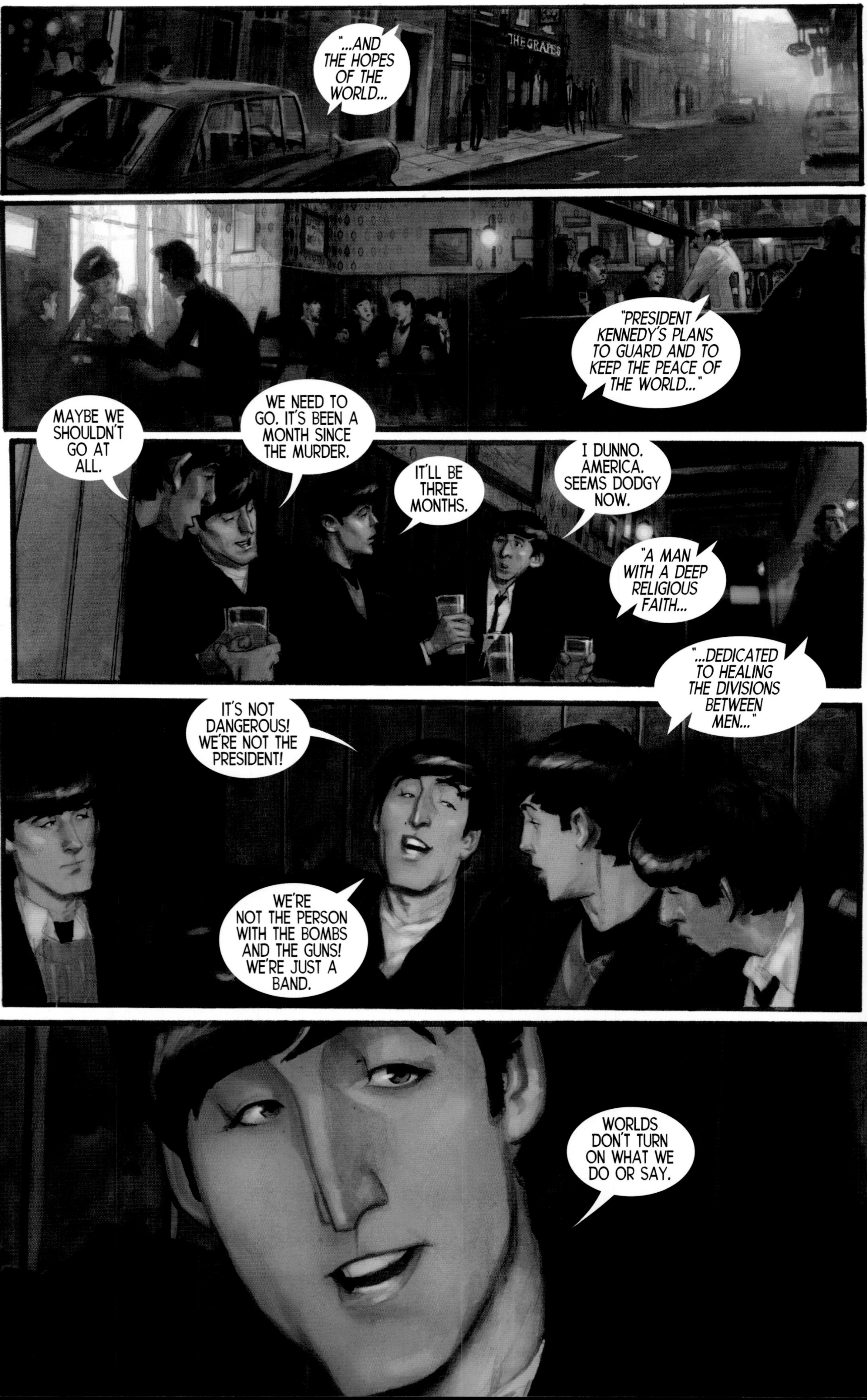
"...AND THE HOPES OF THE WORLD...
THE GRAPES
"PRESIDENT KENNEDY'S PLANS TO GUARD AND TO KEEP THE PEACE OF THE WORLD..."
MAYBE WE SHOULDN'T GO AT ALL.
WE NEED TO GO. IT'S BEEN A MONTH SINCE THE MURDER.
IT'LL BE THREE MONTHS.
I DUNNO. AMERICA. SEEMS DODGY NOW.
"A MAN WITH A DEEP RELIGIOUS FAITH...
"...DEDICATED TO HEALING THE DIVISIONS BETWEEN MEN..."
IT'S NOT DANGEROUS! WE'RE NOT THE PRESIDENT!
WE'RE NOT THE PERSON WITH THE BOMBS AND THE GUNS! WE'RE JUST A BAND.
WORLDS DON'T TURN ON WHAT WE DO OR SAY.

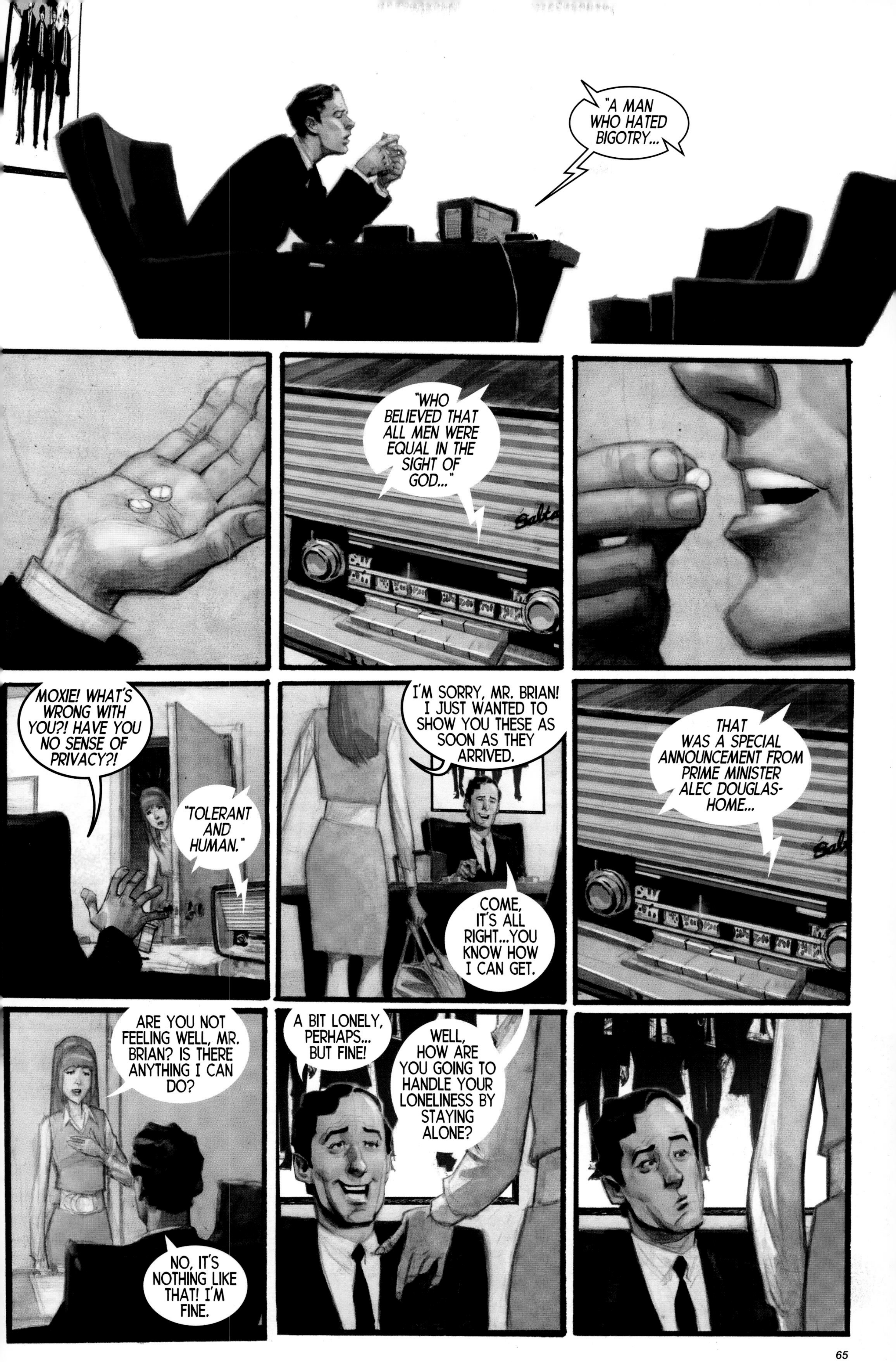
"A MAN WHO HATED BIGOTRY...
"WHO BELIEVED THAT ALL MEN WERE EQUAL IN THE SIGHT OF GOD..."
MOXIE! WHAT'S WRONG WITH YOU?! HAVE YOU NO SENSE OF PRIVACY?!
"TOLERANT AND HUMAN."
I'M SORRY, MR. BRIAN! I JUST WANTED TO SHOW YOU THESE AS SOON AS THEY ARRIVED.
COME, IT'S ALL RIGHT...YOU KNOW HOW I CAN GET.
THAT WAS A SPECIAL ANNOUNCEMENT FROM PRIME MINISTER ALEC DOUGLAS-HOME...
ARE YOU NOT FEELING WELL, MR. BRIAN? IS THERE ANYTHING I CAN DO?
NO, IT'S NOTHING LIKE THAT! I'M FINE.
A BIT LONELY, PERHAPS... BUT FINE!
WELL, HOW ARE YOU GOING TO HANDLE YOUR LONELINESS BY STAYING ALONE?

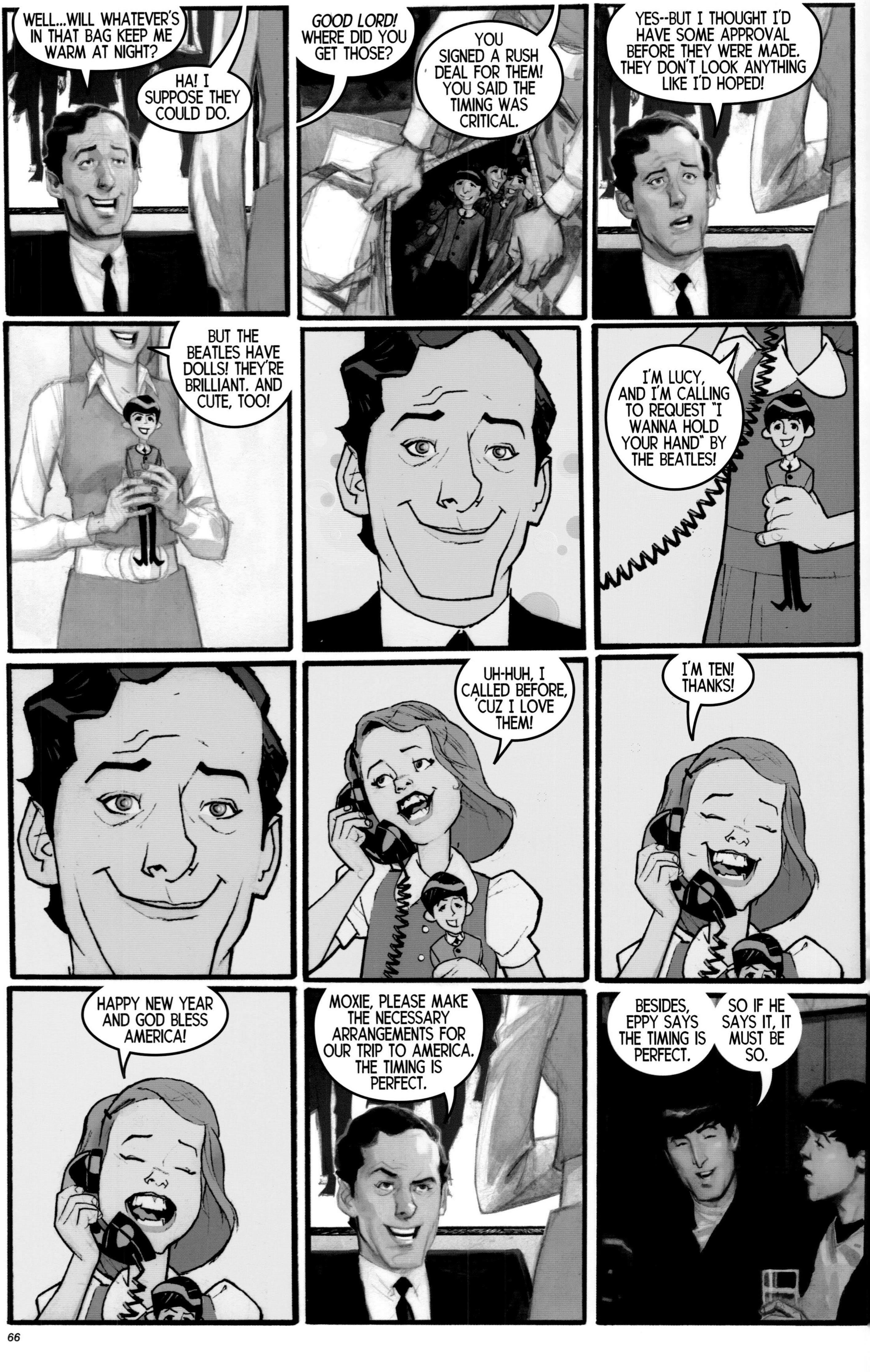
WELL...WILL WHATEVER'S IN THAT BAG KEEP ME WARM AT NIGHT?
HA! I SUPPOSE THEY COULD DO.
GOOD LORD! WHERE DID YOU GET THOSE?
YOU SIGNED A RUSH DEAL FOR THEM! YOU SAID THE TIMING WAS CRITICAL.
YES--BUT I THOUGHT I'D HAVE SOME APPROVAL BEFORE THEY WERE MADE. THEY DON'T LOOK ANYTHING LIKE I'D HOPED!
BUT THE BEATLES HAVE DOLLS! THEY'RE BRILLIANT. AND CUTE, TOO!
I'M LUCY, AND I'M CALLING TO REQUEST "I WANNA HOLD YOUR HAND" BY THE BEATLES!
UH-HUH, I CALLED BEFORE, 'CUZ I LOVE THEM!
I'M TEN! THANKS!
HAPPY NEW YEAR AND GOD BLESS AMERICA!
MOXIE, PLEASE MAKE THE NECESSARY ARRANGEMENTS FOR OUR TRIP TO AMERICA. THE TIMING IS PERFECT.
BESIDES, EPPY SAYS THE TIMING IS PERFECT.
SO IF HE SAYS IT, IT MUST BE SO.

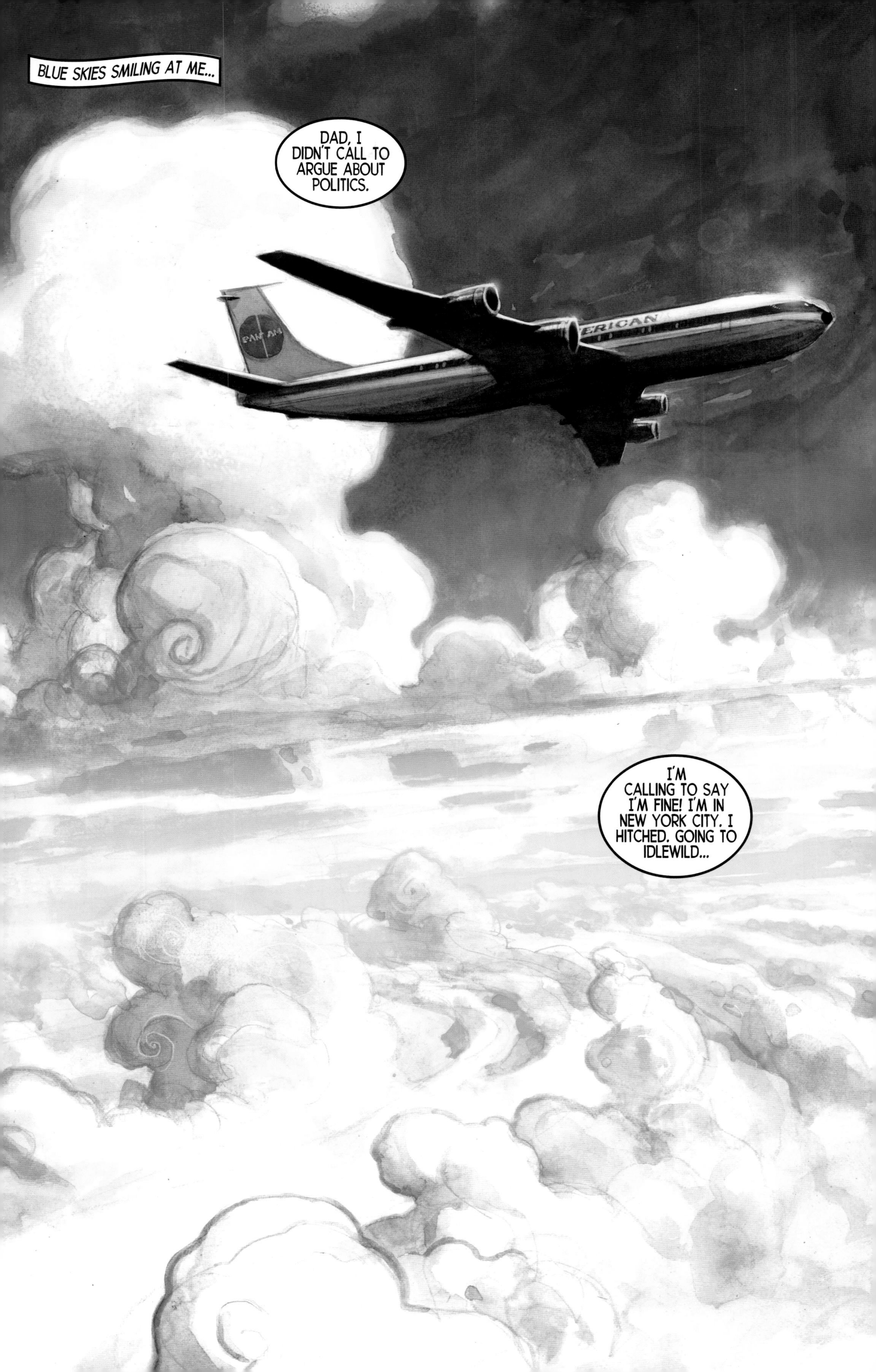
BLUE SKIES SMILING AT ME...
DAD, I DIDN'T CALL TO ARGUE ABOUT POLITICS.
PAN AM
AMERICAN
I'M CALLING TO SAY I'M FINE! I'M IN NEW YORK CITY. I HITCHED. GOING TO IDLEWILD...

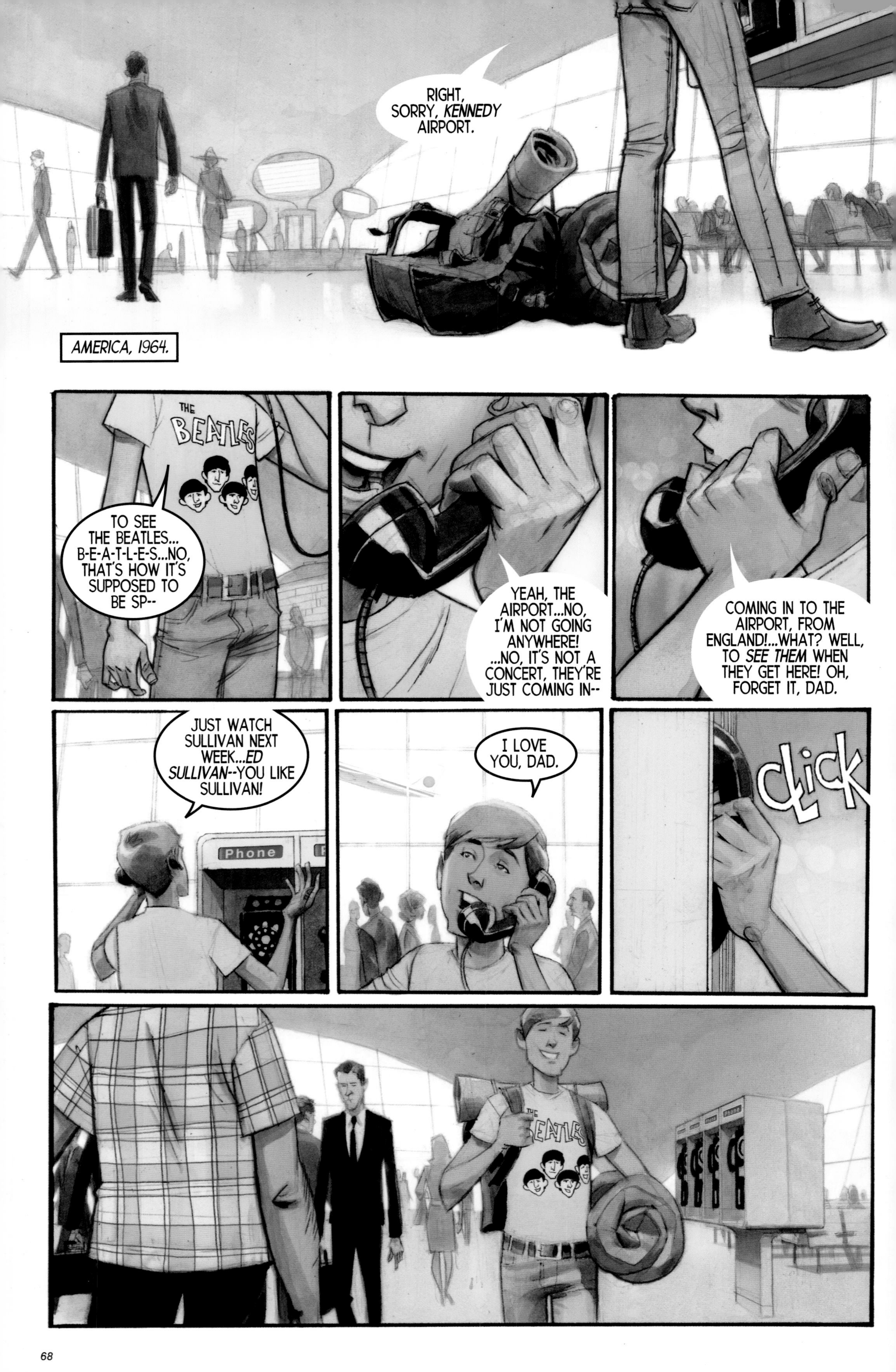
RIGHT, SORRY, *KENNEDY* AIRPORT.
AMERICA, 1964.
THE BEATLES
TO SEE THE BEATLES... B-E-A-T-L-E-S...NO, THAT'S HOW IT'S SUPPOSED TO BE SP--
YEAH, THE AIRPORT...NO, I'M NOT GOING ANYWHERE! ...NO, IT'S NOT A CONCERT, THEY'RE JUST COMING IN--
COMING IN TO THE AIRPORT, FROM ENGLAND!...WHAT? WELL, TO *SEE THEM* WHEN THEY GET HERE! OH, FORGET IT, DAD.
JUST WATCH SULLIVAN NEXT WEEK...*ED SULLIVAN*--YOU LIKE SULLIVAN!
Phone
I LOVE YOU, DAD.
CLICK
THE BEATLES
Phone

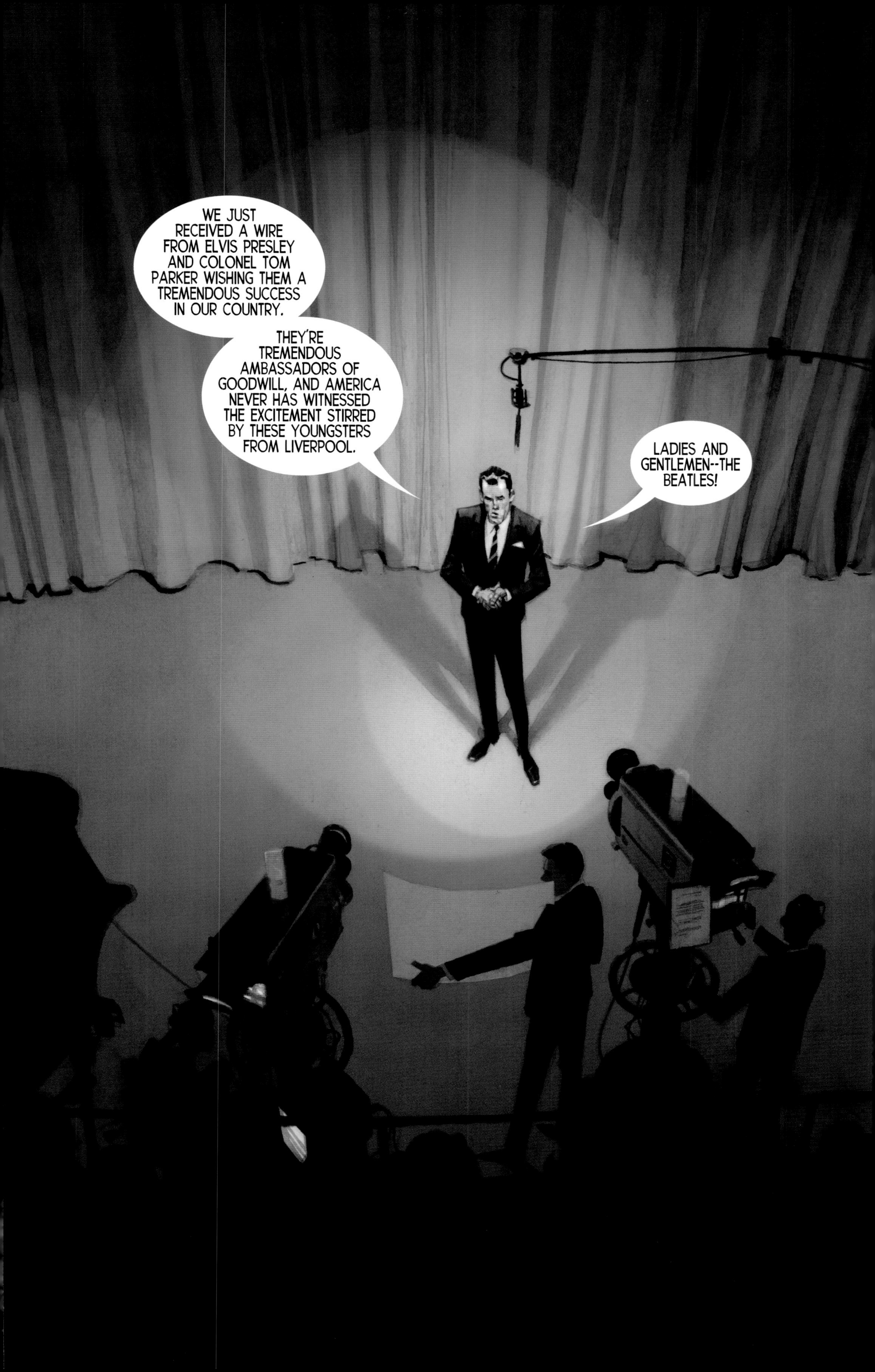
WE JUST RECEIVED A WIRE FROM ELVIS PRESLEY AND COLONEL TOM PARKER WISHING THEM A TREMENDOUS SUCCESS IN OUR COUNTRY.
THEY'RE TREMENDOUS AMBASSADORS OF GOODWILL, AND AMERICA NEVER HAS WITNESSED THE EXCITEMENT STIRRED BY THESE YOUNGSTERS FROM LIVERPOOL.
LADIES AND GENTLEMEN--THE BEATLES!

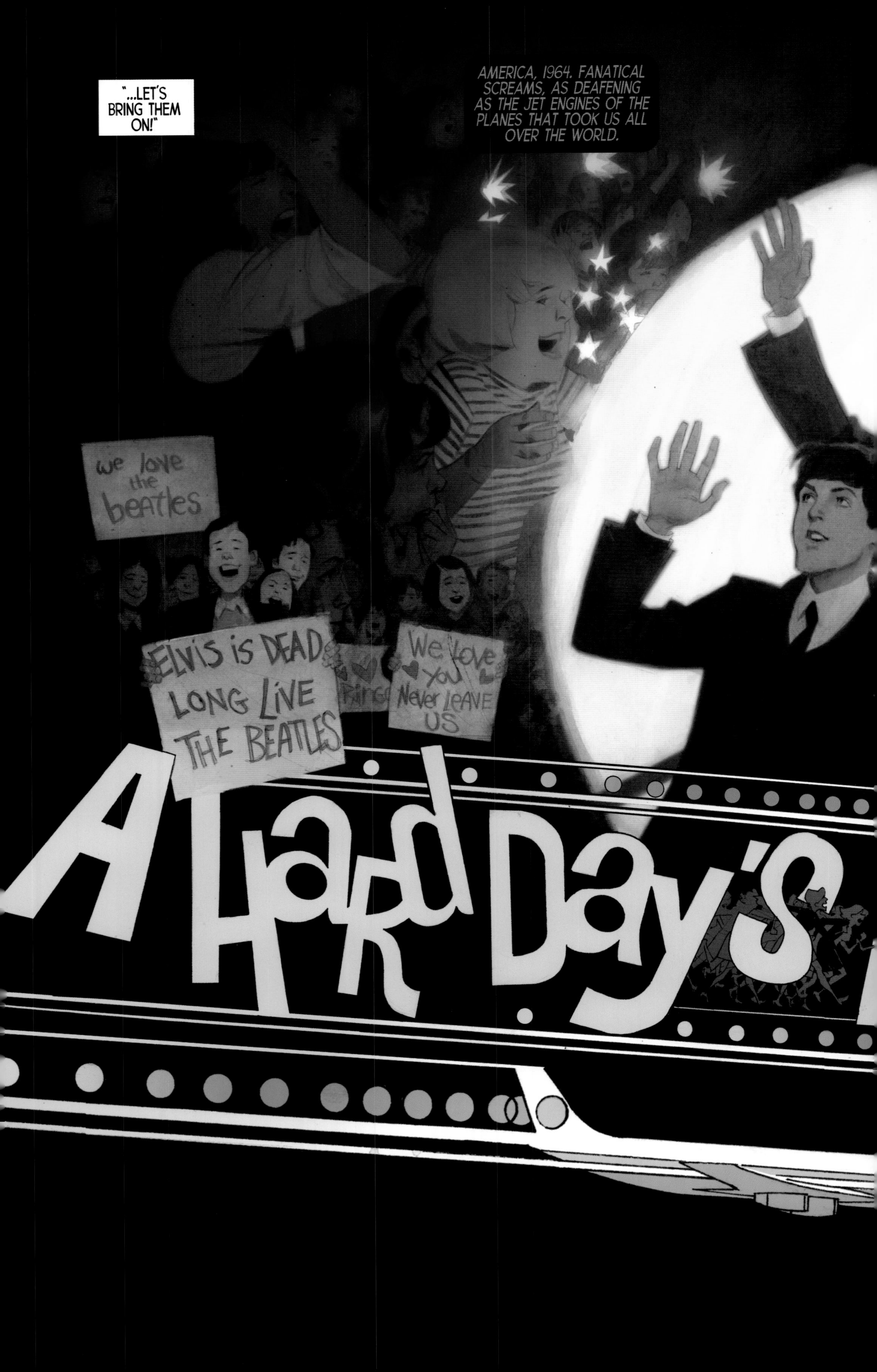
"...LET'S BRING THEM ON!"
AMERICA, 1964. FANATICAL SCREAMS, AS DEAFENING AS THE JET ENGINES OF THE PLANES THAT TOOK US ALL OVER THE WORLD.
we love the beatles
ELVIS IS DEAD LONG LIVE THE BEATLES
We Love You Never LEAVE US
A HARD DAY'S

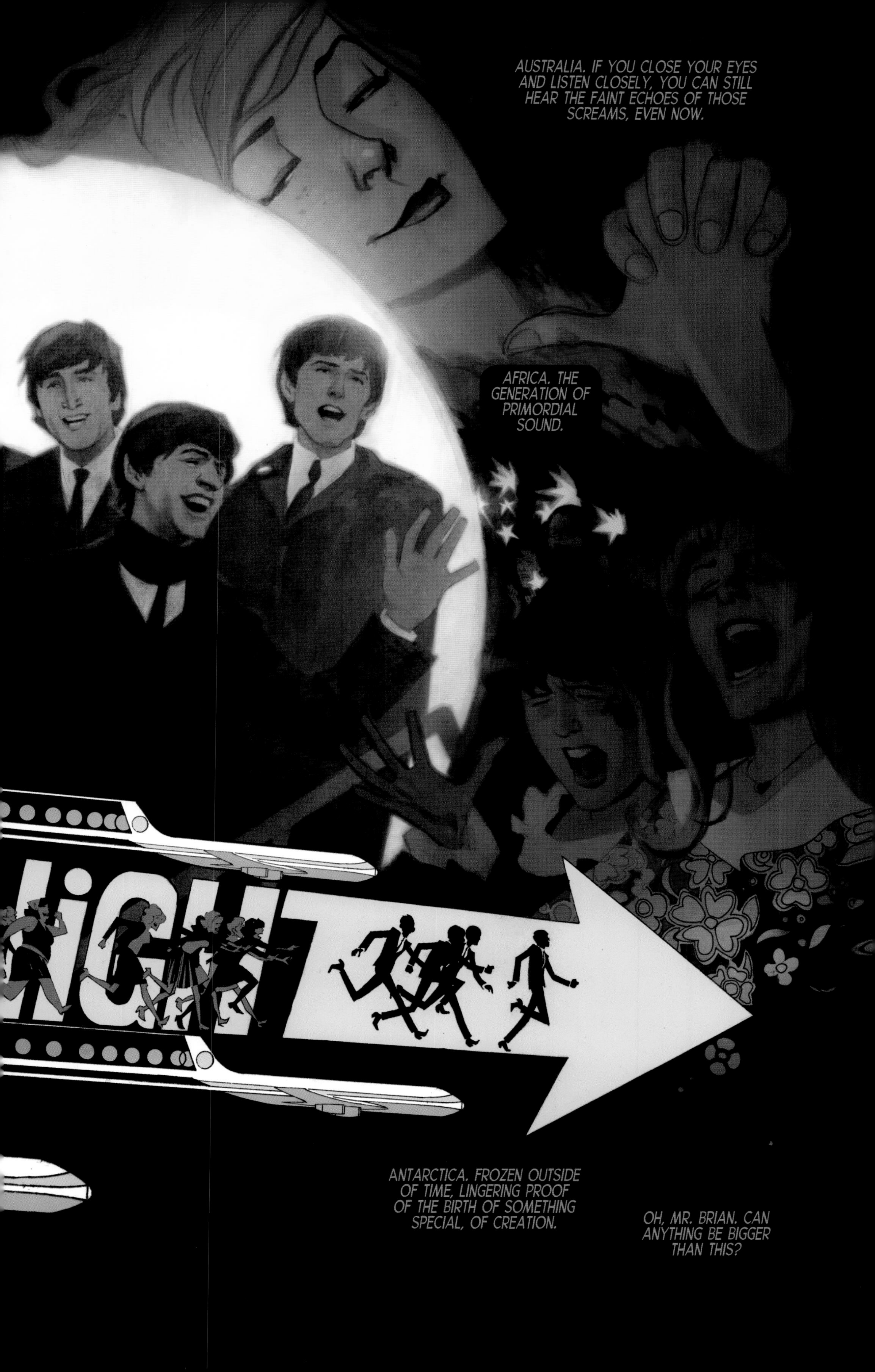
AUSTRALIA. IF YOU CLOSE YOUR EYES AND LISTEN CLOSELY, YOU CAN STILL HEAR THE FAINT ECHOES OF THOSE SCREAMS, EVEN NOW.
AFRICA. THE GENERATION OF PRIMORDIAL SOUND.
ANTARCTICA. FROZEN OUTSIDE OF TIME, LINGERING PROOF OF THE BIRTH OF SOMETHING SPECIAL, OF CREATION.
OH, MR. BRIAN. CAN ANYTHING BE BIGGER THAN THIS?

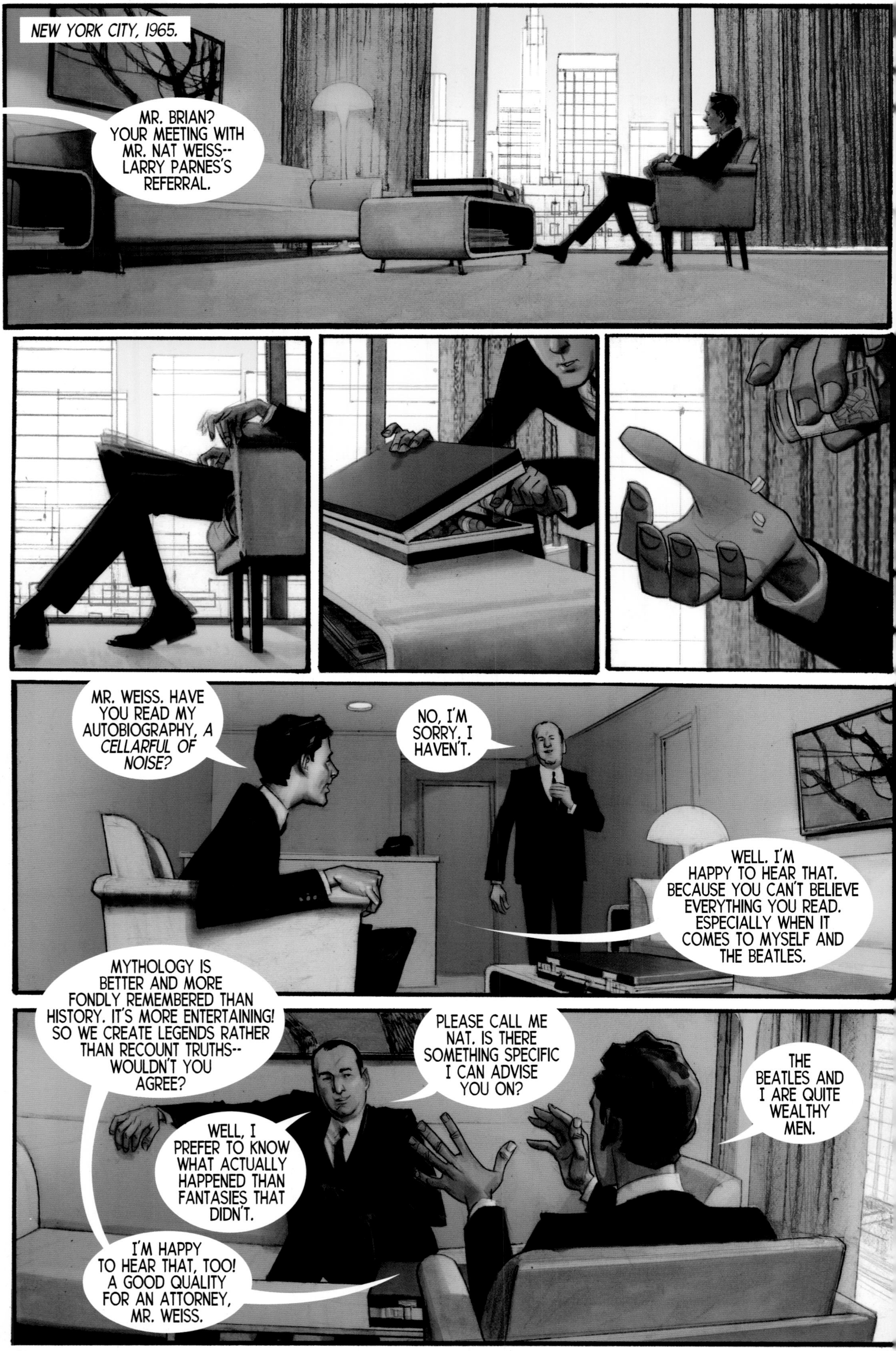
NEW YORK CITY, 1965.
MR. BRIAN? YOUR MEETING WITH MR. NAT WEISS-- LARRY PARNES'S REFERRAL.
MR. WEISS. HAVE YOU READ MY AUTOBIOGRAPHY, A *CELLARFUL OF NOISE?*
NO, I'M SORRY, I HAVEN'T.
WELL. I'M HAPPY TO HEAR THAT. BECAUSE YOU CAN'T BELIEVE EVERYTHING YOU READ. ESPECIALLY WHEN IT COMES TO MYSELF AND THE BEATLES.
MYTHOLOGY IS BETTER AND MORE FONDLY REMEMBERED THAN HISTORY. IT'S MORE ENTERTAINING! SO WE CREATE LEGENDS RATHER THAN RECOUNT TRUTHS-- WOULDN'T YOU AGREE?
WELL, I PREFER TO KNOW WHAT ACTUALLY HAPPENED THAN FANTASIES THAT DIDN'T.
I'M HAPPY TO HEAR THAT, TOO! A GOOD QUALITY FOR AN ATTORNEY, MR. WEISS.
PLEASE CALL ME NAT. IS THERE SOMETHING SPECIFIC I CAN ADVISE YOU ON?
THE BEATLES AND I ARE QUITE WEALTHY MEN.

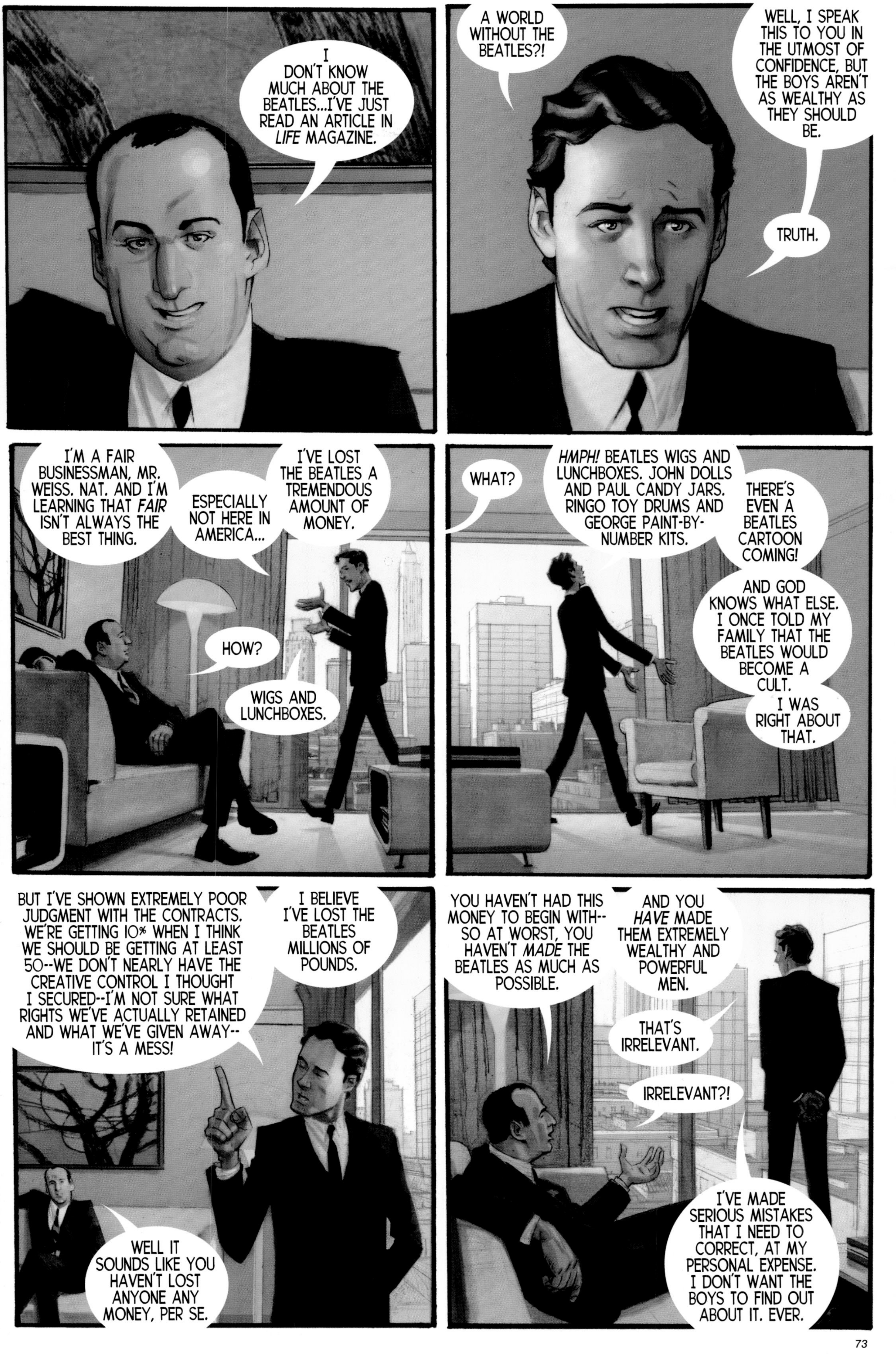
I DON'T KNOW MUCH ABOUT THE BEATLES...I'VE JUST READ AN ARTICLE IN *LIFE* MAGAZINE.
A WORLD WITHOUT THE BEATLES?!
WELL, I SPEAK THIS TO YOU IN THE UTMOST OF CONFIDENCE, BUT THE BOYS AREN'T AS WEALTHY AS THEY SHOULD BE.
TRUTH.
I'M A FAIR BUSINESSMAN, MR. WEISS. NAT. AND I'M LEARNING THAT *FAIR* ISN'T ALWAYS THE BEST THING.
ESPECIALLY NOT HERE IN AMERICA...
I'VE LOST THE BEATLES A TREMENDOUS AMOUNT OF MONEY.
HOW?
WIGS AND LUNCHBOXES.
WHAT?
HMPH! BEATLES WIGS AND LUNCHBOXES. JOHN DOLLS AND PAUL CANDY JARS. RINGO TOY DRUMS AND GEORGE PAINT-BY-NUMBER KITS.
THERE'S EVEN A BEATLES CARTOON COMING!
AND GOD KNOWS WHAT ELSE. I ONCE TOLD MY FAMILY THAT THE BEATLES WOULD BECOME A CULT.
I WAS RIGHT ABOUT THAT.
BUT I'VE SHOWN EXTREMELY POOR JUDGMENT WITH THE CONTRACTS. WE'RE GETTING 10% WHEN I THINK WE SHOULD BE GETTING AT LEAST 50--WE DON'T NEARLY HAVE THE CREATIVE CONTROL I THOUGHT I SECURED--I'M NOT SURE WHAT RIGHTS WE'VE ACTUALLY RETAINED AND WHAT WE'VE GIVEN AWAY--IT'S A MESS!
I BELIEVE I'VE LOST THE BEATLES MILLIONS OF POUNDS.
WELL IT SOUNDS LIKE YOU HAVEN'T LOST ANYONE ANY MONEY, PER SE.
YOU HAVEN'T HAD THIS MONEY TO BEGIN WITH--SO AT WORST, YOU HAVEN'T *MADE* THE BEATLES AS MUCH AS POSSIBLE.
AND YOU *HAVE* MADE THEM EXTREMELY WEALTHY AND POWERFUL MEN.
THAT'S IRRELEVANT.
IRRELEVANT?!
I'VE MADE SERIOUS MISTAKES THAT I NEED TO CORRECT, AT MY PERSONAL EXPENSE. I DON'T WANT THE BOYS TO FIND OUT ABOUT IT. EVER.

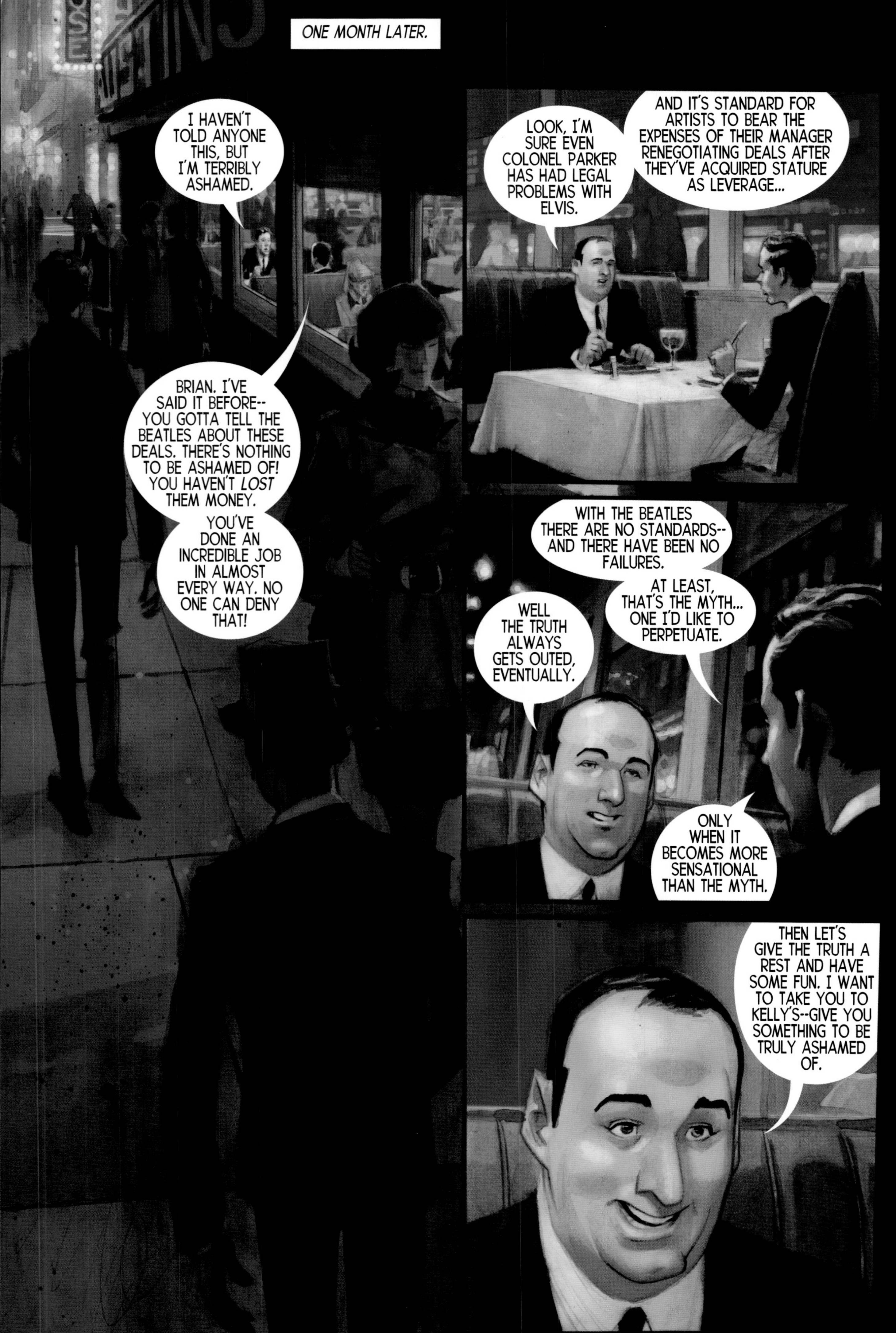
ONE MONTH LATER.
I HAVEN'T TOLD ANYONE THIS, BUT I'M TERRIBLY ASHAMED.
BRIAN. I'VE SAID IT BEFORE--YOU GOTTA TELL THE BEATLES ABOUT THESE DEALS. THERE'S NOTHING TO BE ASHAMED OF! YOU HAVEN'T *LOST* THEM MONEY.
YOU'VE DONE AN INCREDIBLE JOB IN ALMOST EVERY WAY. NO ONE CAN DENY THAT!
LOOK, I'M SURE EVEN COLONEL PARKER HAS HAD LEGAL PROBLEMS WITH ELVIS.
AND IT'S STANDARD FOR ARTISTS TO BEAR THE EXPENSES OF THEIR MANAGER RENEGOTIATING DEALS AFTER THEY'VE ACQUIRED STATURE AS LEVERAGE...
WITH THE BEATLES THERE ARE NO STANDARDS--AND THERE HAVE BEEN NO FAILURES.
AT LEAST, THAT'S THE MYTH... ONE I'D LIKE TO PERPETUATE.
WELL THE TRUTH ALWAYS GETS OUTED, EVENTUALLY.
ONLY WHEN IT BECOMES MORE SENSATIONAL THAN THE MYTH.
THEN LET'S GIVE THE TRUTH A REST AND HAVE SOME FUN. I WANT TO TAKE YOU TO KELLY'S--GIVE YOU SOMETHING TO BE TRULY ASHAMED OF.

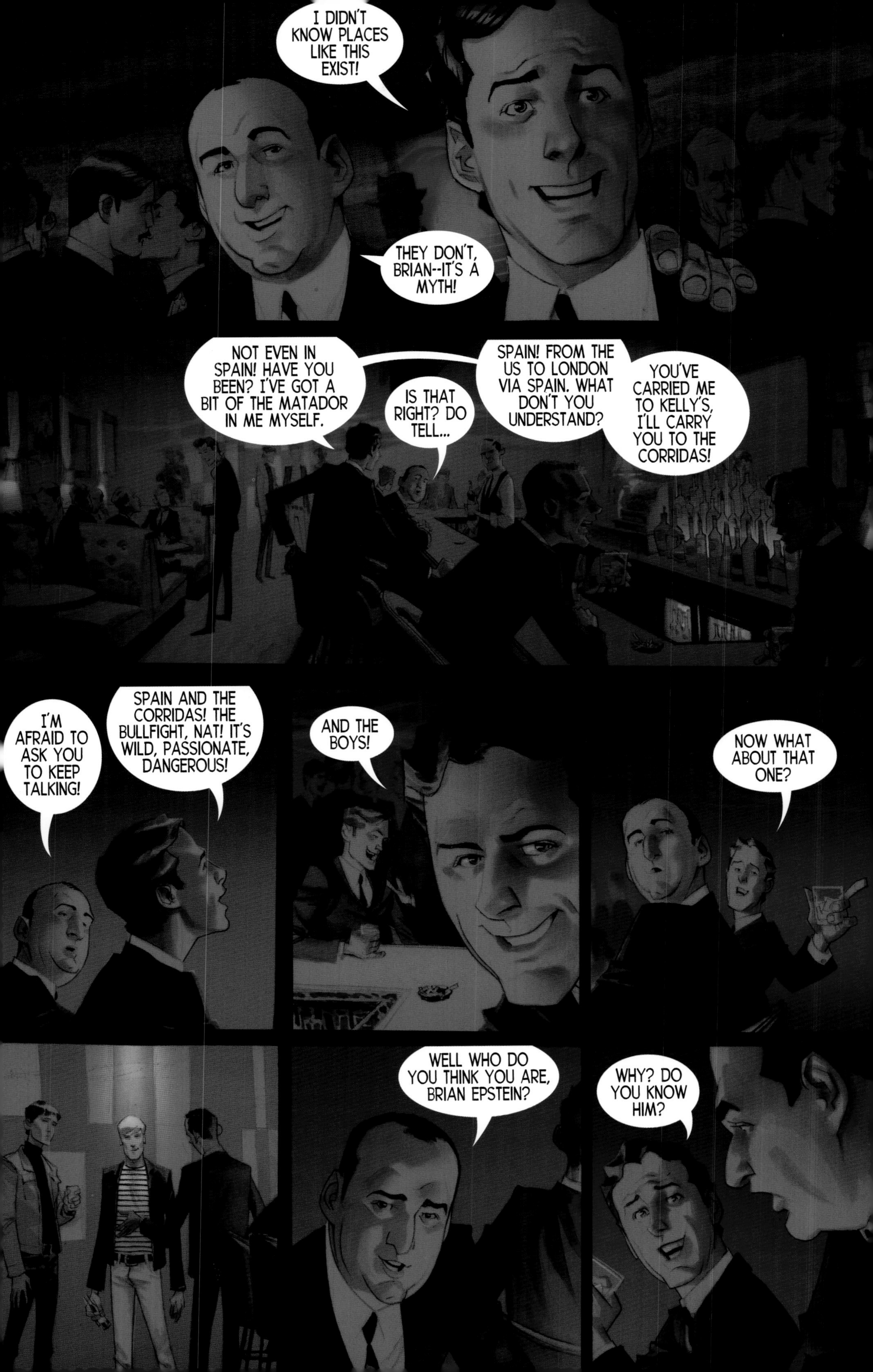
I DIDN'T KNOW PLACES LIKE THIS EXIST!
THEY DON'T, BRIAN--IT'S A MYTH!
NOT EVEN IN SPAIN! HAVE YOU BEEN? I'VE GOT A BIT OF THE MATADOR IN ME MYSELF.
IS THAT RIGHT? DO TELL...
SPAIN! FROM THE US TO LONDON VIA SPAIN. WHAT DON'T YOU UNDERSTAND?
YOU'VE CARRIED ME TO KELLY'S, I'LL CARRY YOU TO THE CORRIDAS!
I'M AFRAID TO ASK YOU TO KEEP TALKING!
SPAIN AND THE CORRIDAS! THE BULLFIGHT, NAT! IT'S WILD, PASSIONATE, DANGEROUS!
AND THE BOYS!
NOW WHAT ABOUT THAT ONE?
WELL WHO DO YOU THINK YOU ARE, BRIAN EPSTEIN?
WHY? DO YOU KNOW HIM?

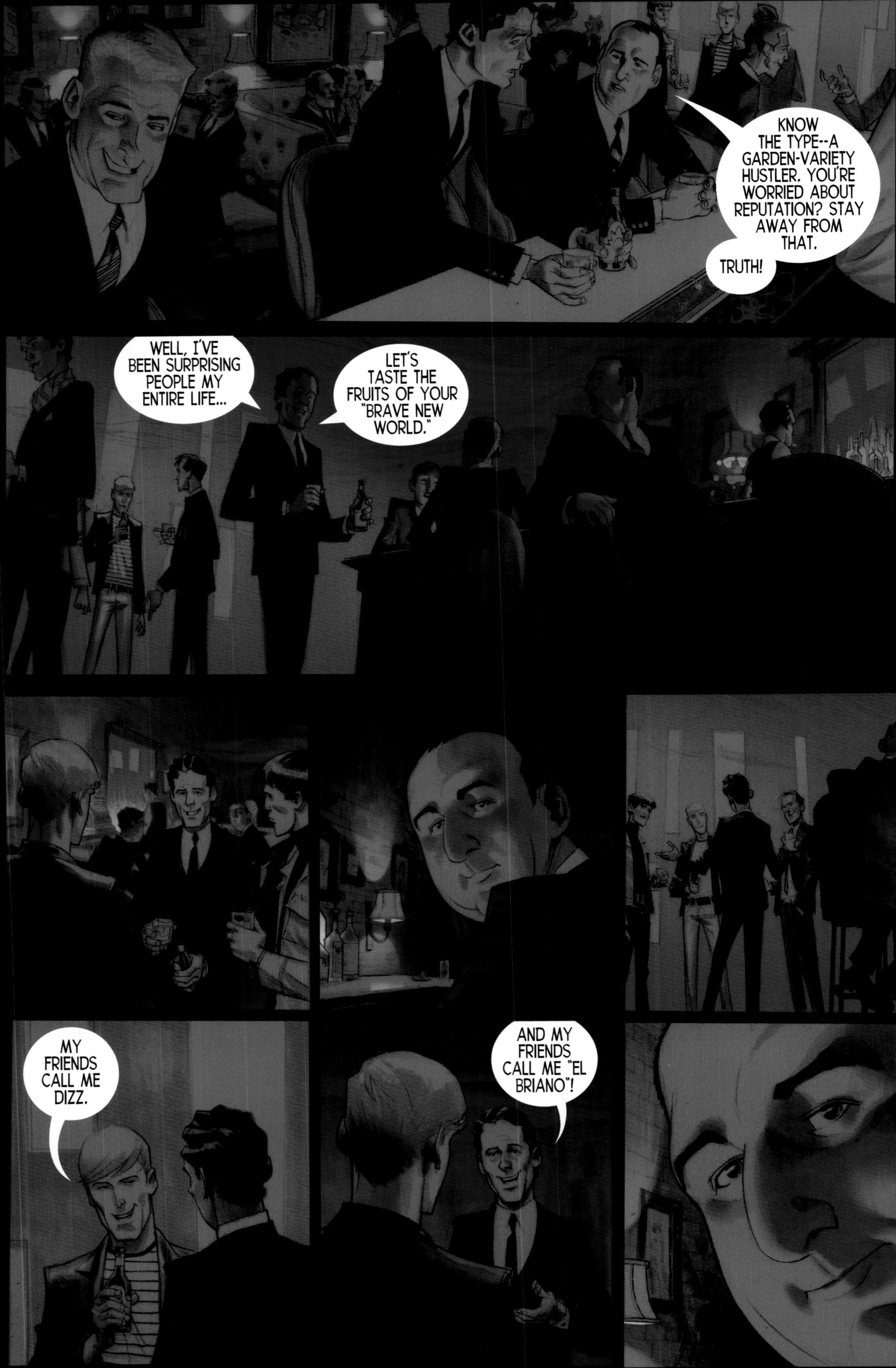
KNOW THE TYPE--A GARDEN-VARIETY HUSTLER. YOU'RE WORRIED ABOUT REPUTATION? STAY AWAY FROM THAT.
TRUTH!
WELL, I'VE BEEN SURPRISING PEOPLE MY ENTIRE LIFE...
LET'S TASTE THE FRUITS OF YOUR "BRAVE NEW WORLD."
MY FRIENDS CALL ME DIZZ.
AND MY FRIENDS CALL ME "EL BRIANO"!

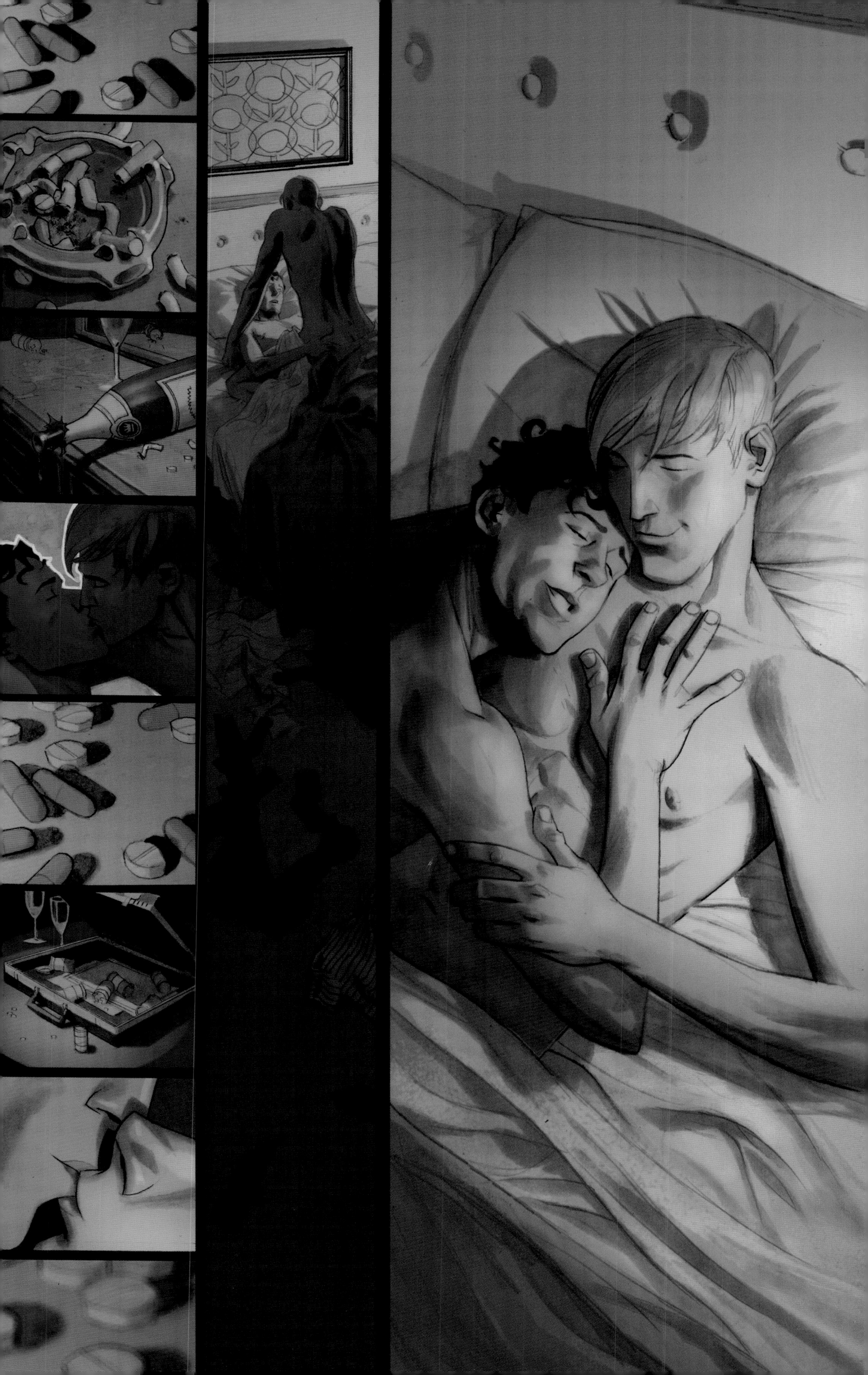

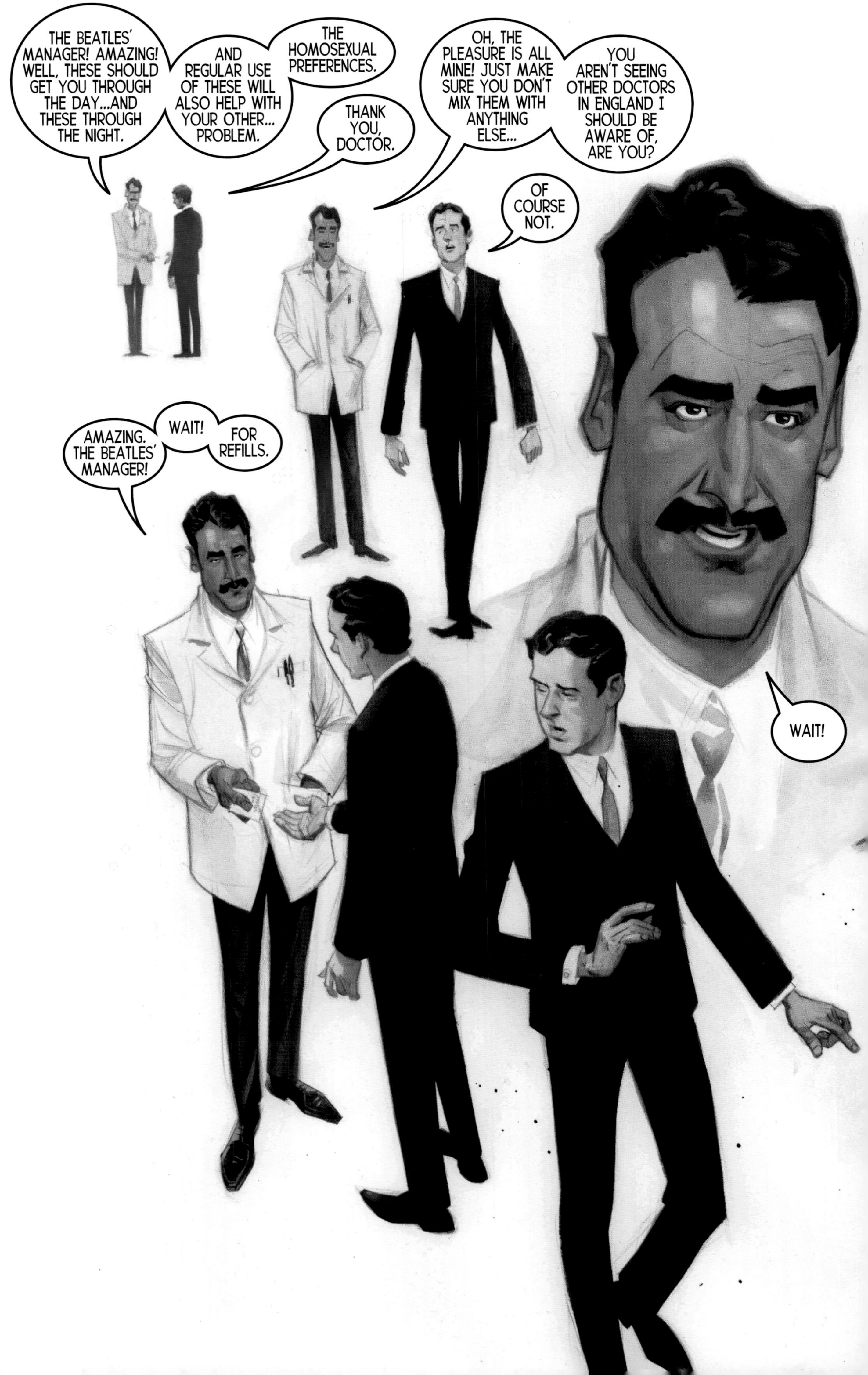
THE BEATLES' MANAGER! AMAZING! WELL, THESE SHOULD GET YOU THROUGH THE DAY...AND THESE THROUGH THE NIGHT.
AND REGULAR USE OF THESE WILL ALSO HELP WITH YOUR OTHER... PROBLEM.
THE HOMOSEXUAL PREFERENCES.
THANK YOU, DOCTOR.
OH, THE PLEASURE IS ALL MINE! JUST MAKE SURE YOU DON'T MIX THEM WITH ANYTHING ELSE...
YOU AREN'T SEEING OTHER DOCTORS IN ENGLAND I SHOULD BE AWARE OF, ARE YOU?
OF COURSE NOT.
AMAZING. THE BEATLES' MANAGER!
WAIT!
FOR REFILLS.
WAIT!

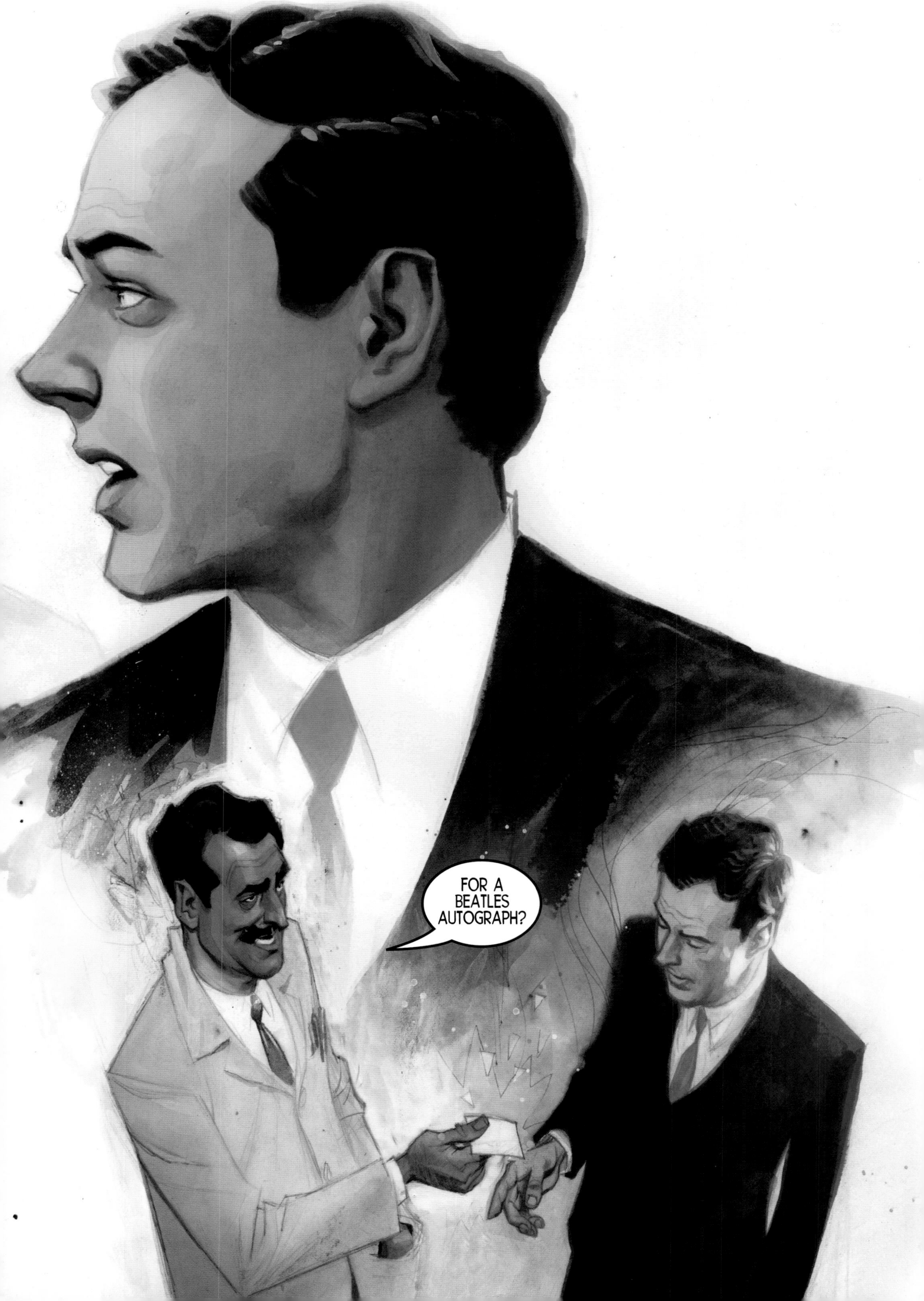
FOR A BEATLES AUTOGRAPH?

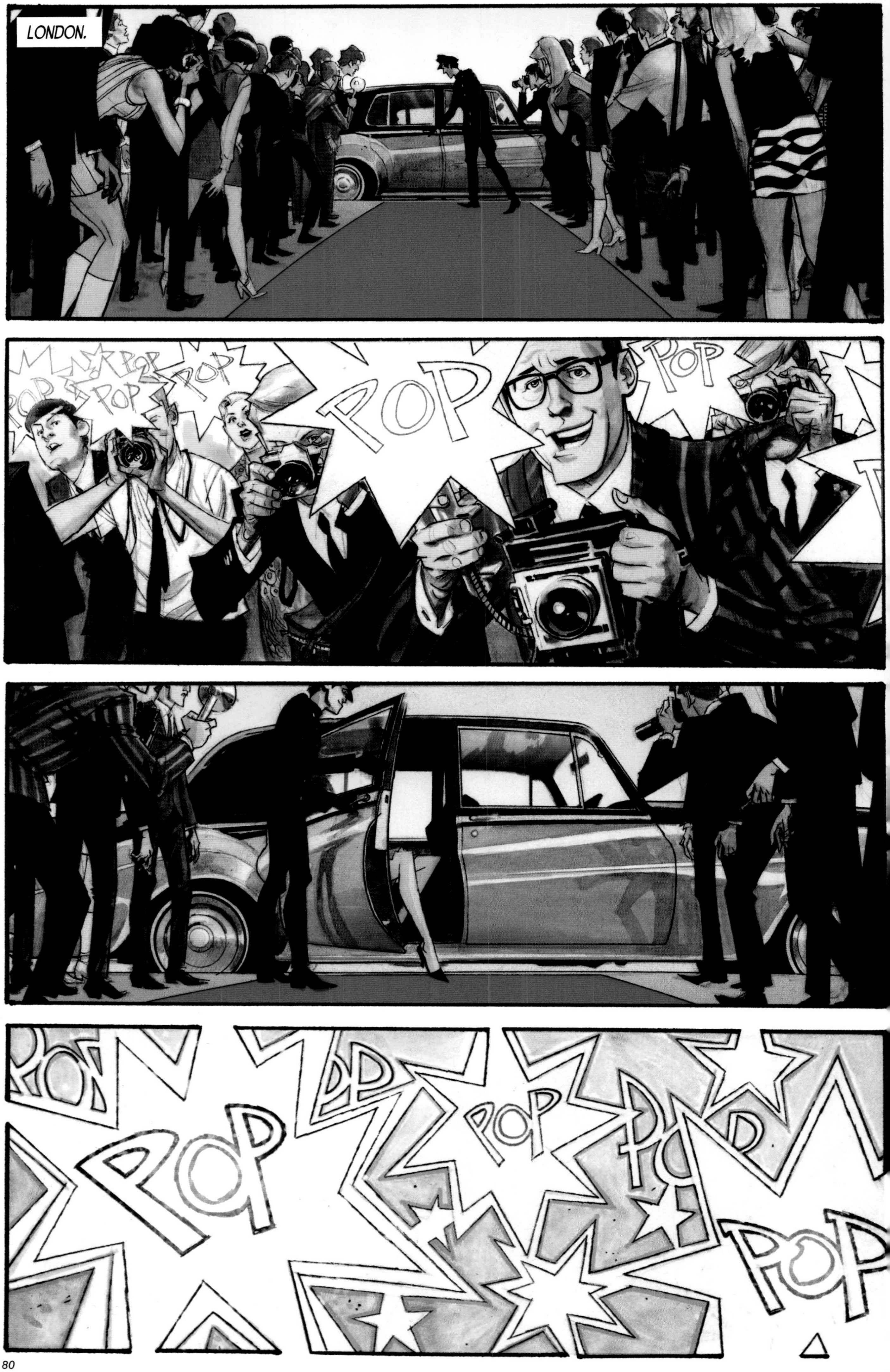
LONDON.
POP POP POP POP
POP
POP
POP
POP
POP
POP
POP

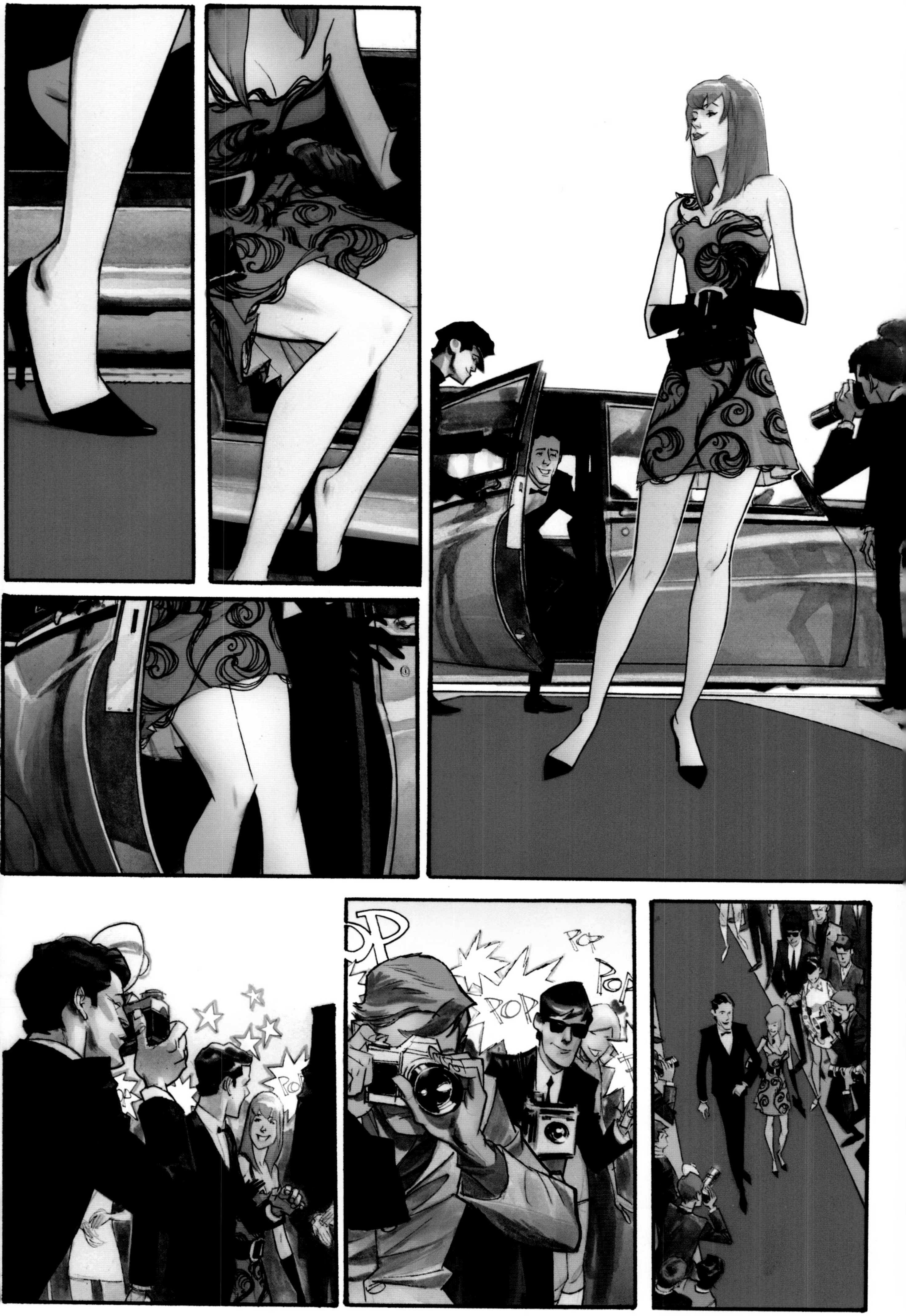
POP
POP
POP

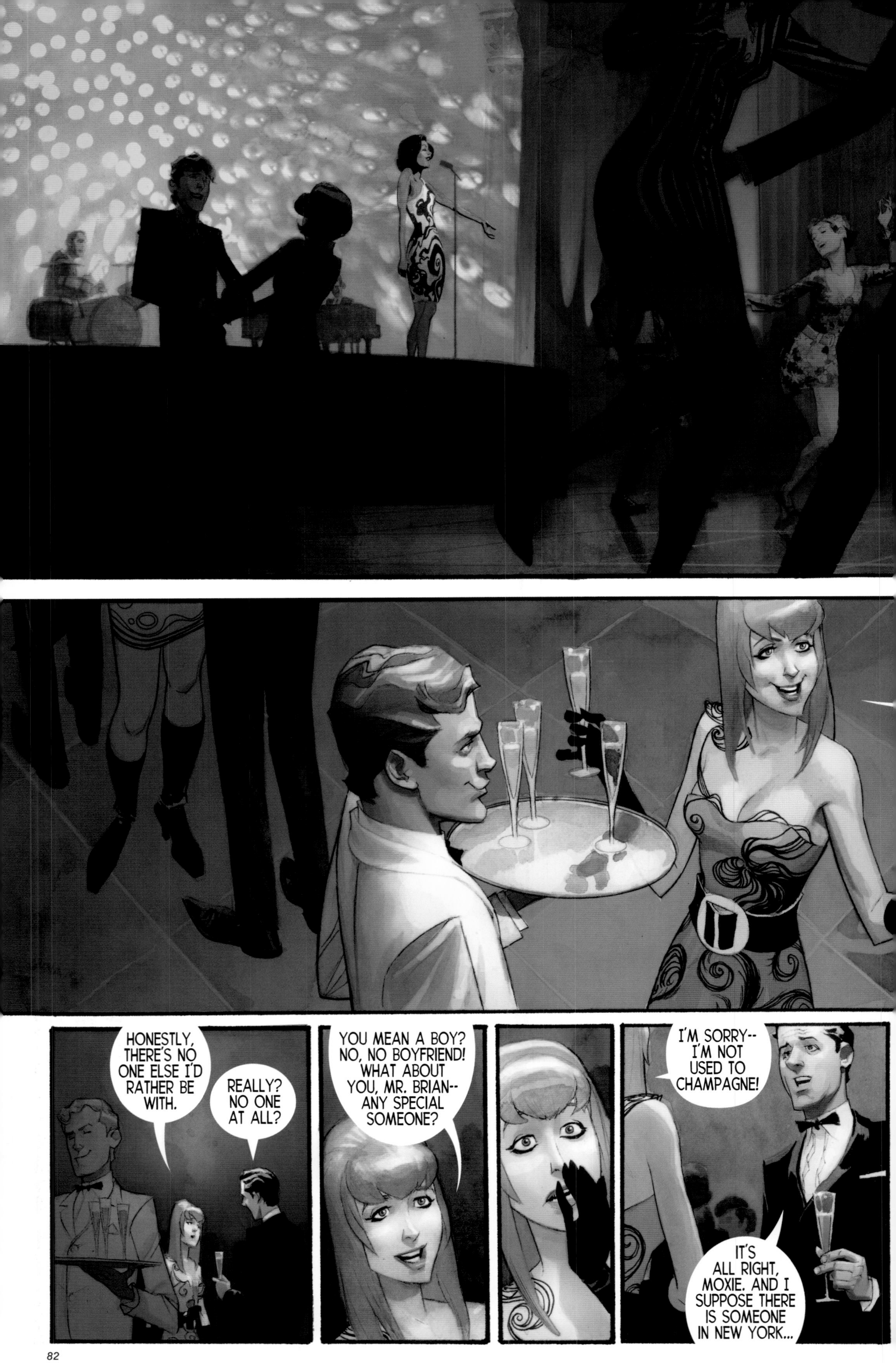
HONESTLY, THERE'S NO ONE ELSE I'D RATHER BE WITH.
REALLY? NO ONE AT ALL?
YOU MEAN A BOY? NO, NO BOYFRIEND! WHAT ABOUT YOU, MR. BRIAN-- ANY SPECIAL SOMEONE?
I'M SORRY-- I'M NOT USED TO CHAMPAGNE!
IT'S ALL RIGHT, MOXIE. AND I SUPPOSE THERE IS SOMEONE IN NEW YORK...

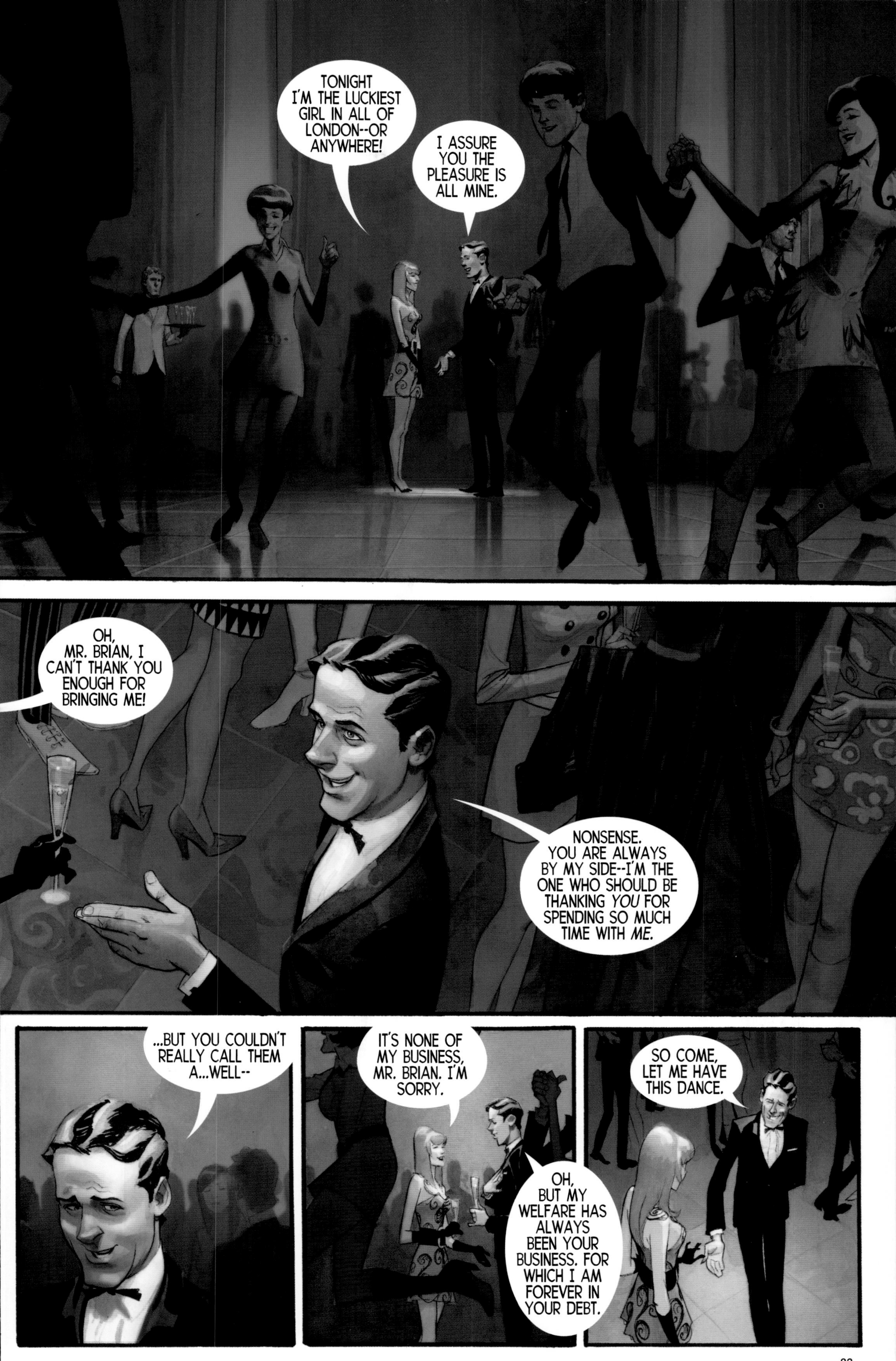
TONIGHT I'M THE LUCKIEST GIRL IN ALL OF LONDON--OR ANYWHERE!
I ASSURE YOU THE PLEASURE IS ALL MINE.
OH, MR. BRIAN, I CAN'T THANK YOU ENOUGH FOR BRINGING ME!
NONSENSE. YOU ARE ALWAYS BY MY SIDE--I'M THE ONE WHO SHOULD BE THANKING *YOU* FOR SPENDING SO MUCH TIME WITH *ME.*
...BUT YOU COULDN'T REALLY CALL THEM A...WELL--
IT'S NONE OF MY BUSINESS, MR. BRIAN. I'M SORRY.
OH, BUT MY WELFARE HAS ALWAYS BEEN YOUR BUSINESS. FOR WHICH I AM FOREVER IN YOUR DEBT.
SO COME, LET ME HAVE THIS DANCE.

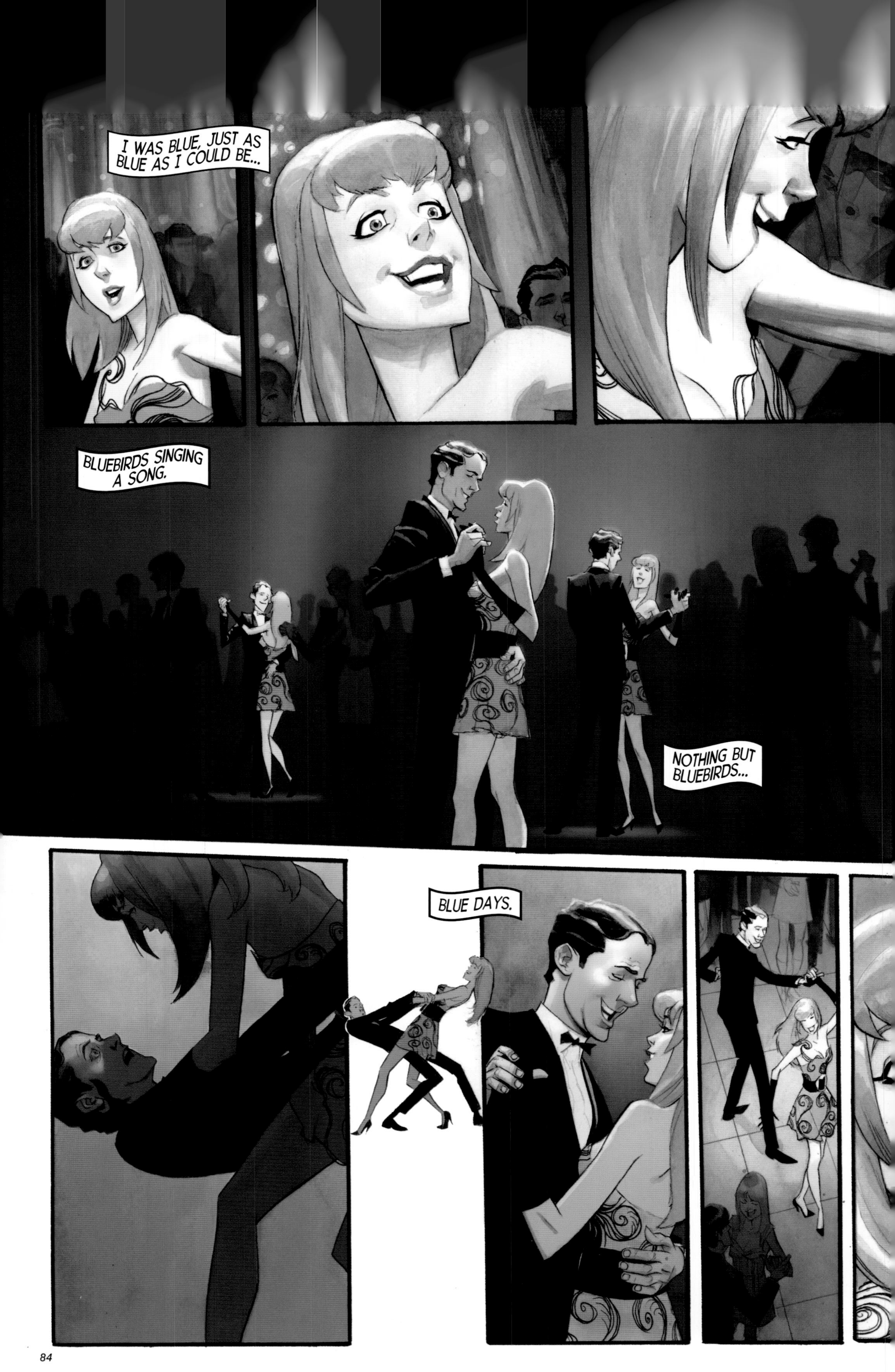
I WAS BLUE, JUST AS BLUE AS I COULD BE...
BLUEBIRDS SINGING A SONG.
NOTHING BUT BLUEBIRDS...
BLUE DAYS.

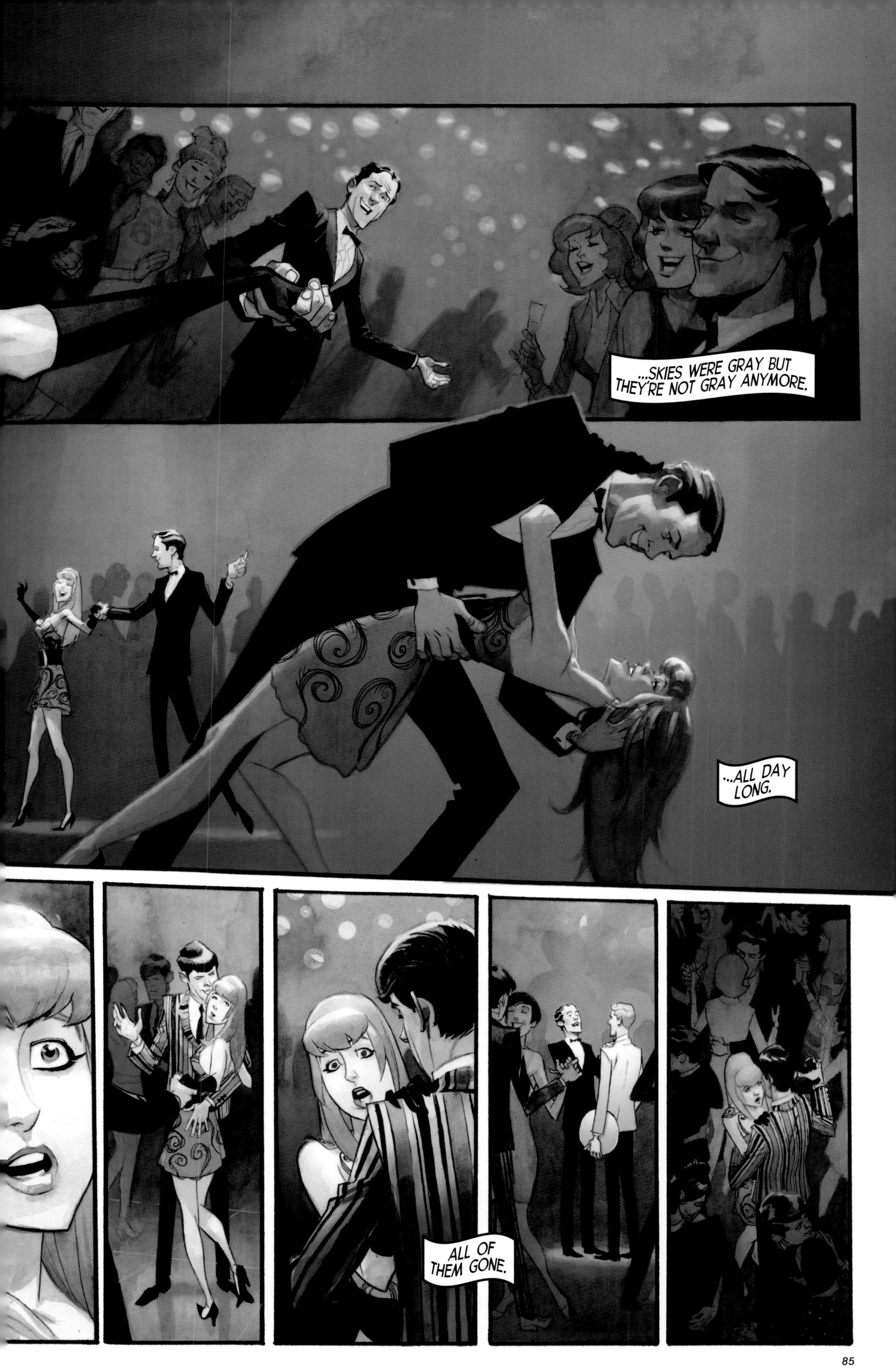
...SKIES WERE GRAY BUT THEY'RE NOT GRAY ANYMORE.
...ALL DAY LONG.
ALL OF THEM GONE.

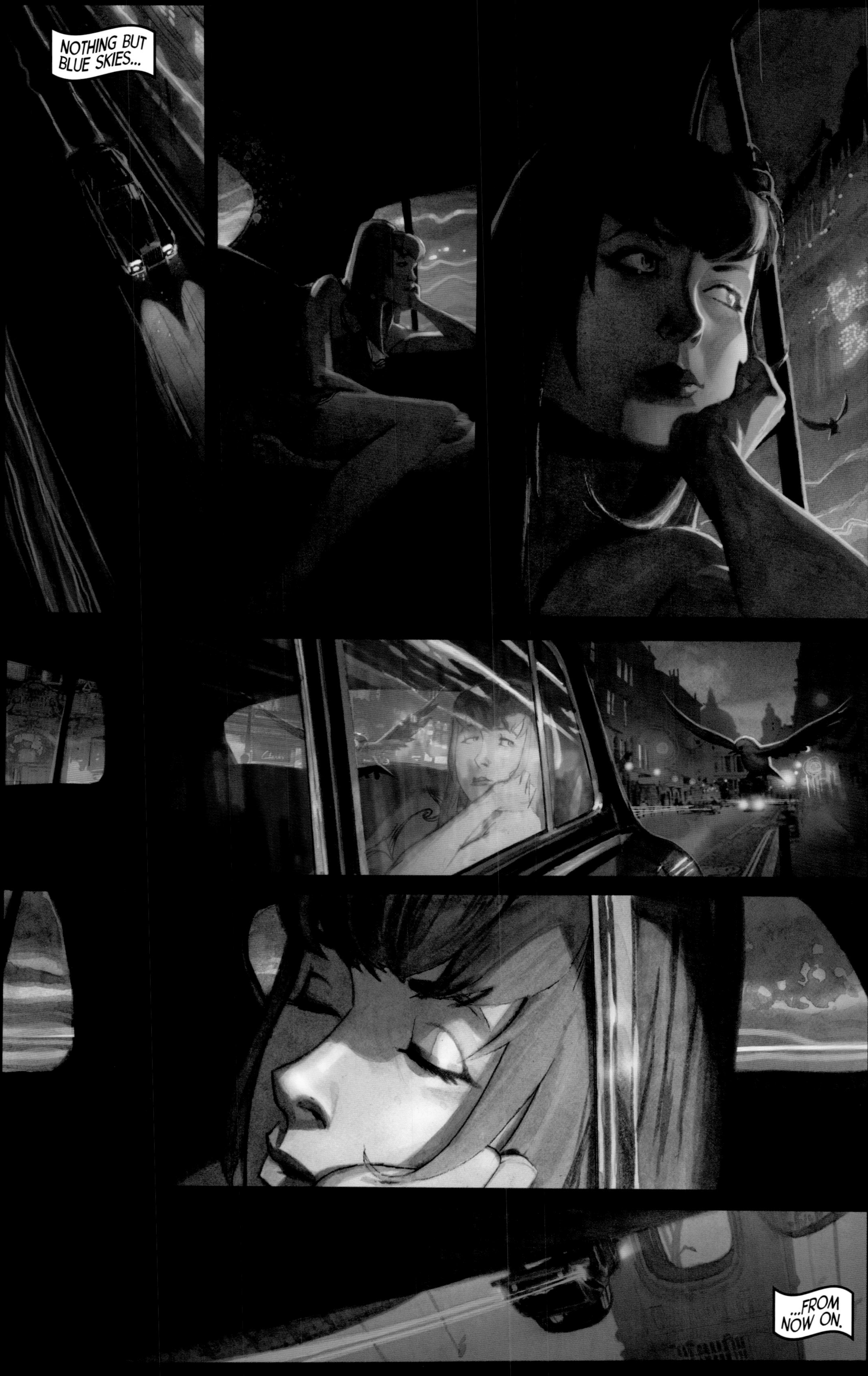
NOTHING BUT BLUE SKIES...
...FROM NOW ON.

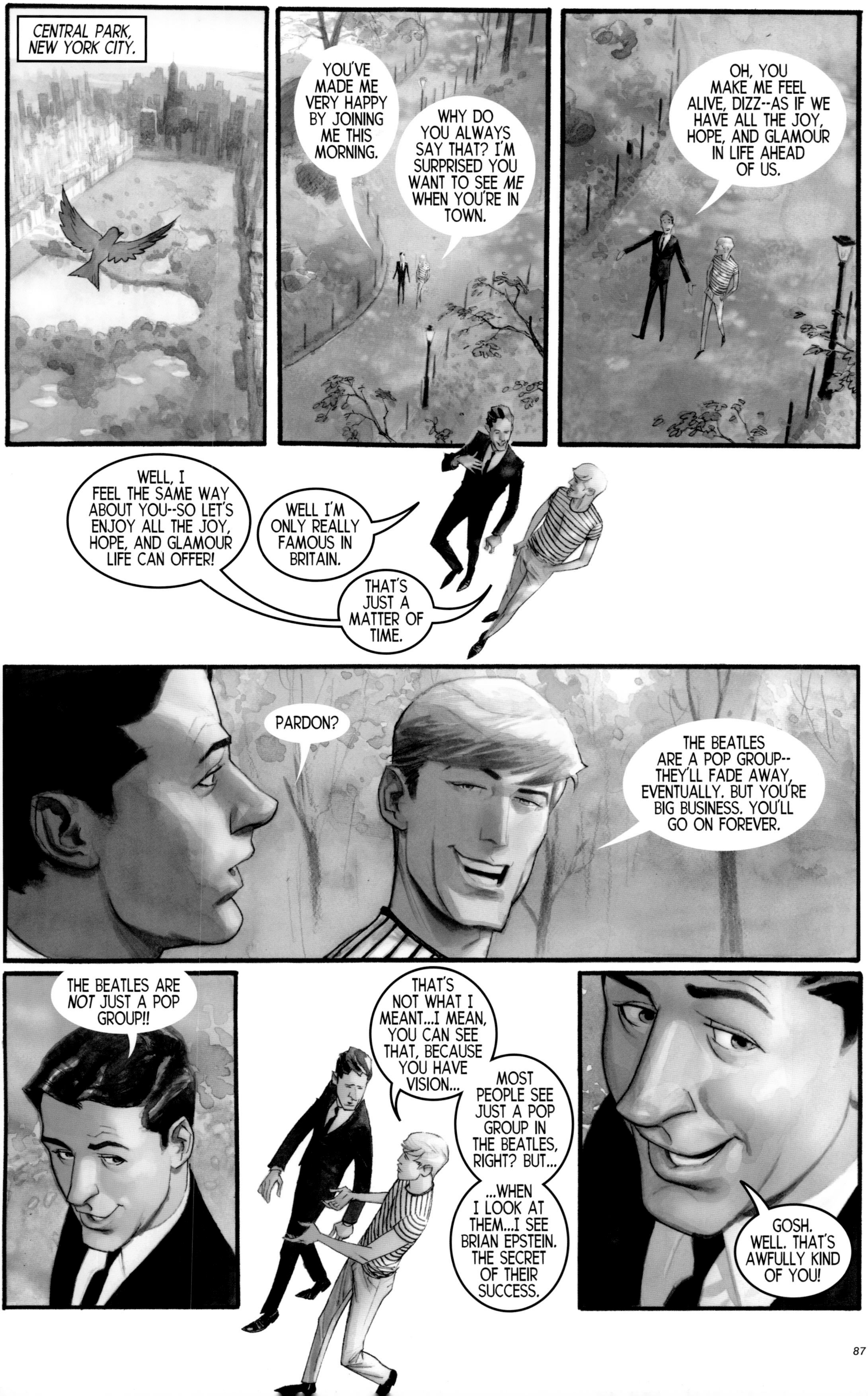
CENTRAL PARK, NEW YORK CITY.
YOU'VE MADE ME VERY HAPPY BY JOINING ME THIS MORNING.
WHY DO YOU ALWAYS SAY THAT? I'M SURPRISED YOU WANT TO SEE *ME* WHEN YOU'RE IN TOWN.
OH, YOU MAKE ME FEEL ALIVE, DIZZ--AS IF WE HAVE ALL THE JOY, HOPE, AND GLAMOUR IN LIFE AHEAD OF US.
WELL, I FEEL THE SAME WAY ABOUT YOU--SO LET'S ENJOY ALL THE JOY, HOPE, AND GLAMOUR LIFE CAN OFFER!
WELL I'M ONLY REALLY FAMOUS IN BRITAIN.
THAT'S JUST A MATTER OF TIME.
PARDON?
THE BEATLES ARE A POP GROUP-- THEY'LL FADE AWAY, EVENTUALLY. BUT YOU'RE BIG BUSINESS. YOU'LL GO ON FOREVER.
THE BEATLES ARE *NOT* JUST A POP GROUP!!
THAT'S NOT WHAT I MEANT...I MEAN, YOU CAN SEE THAT, BECAUSE YOU HAVE VISION...
MOST PEOPLE SEE JUST A POP GROUP IN THE BEATLES, RIGHT? BUT...
...WHEN I LOOK AT THEM...I SEE BRIAN EPSTEIN. THE SECRET OF THEIR SUCCESS.
GOSH. WELL. THAT'S AWFULLY KIND OF YOU!

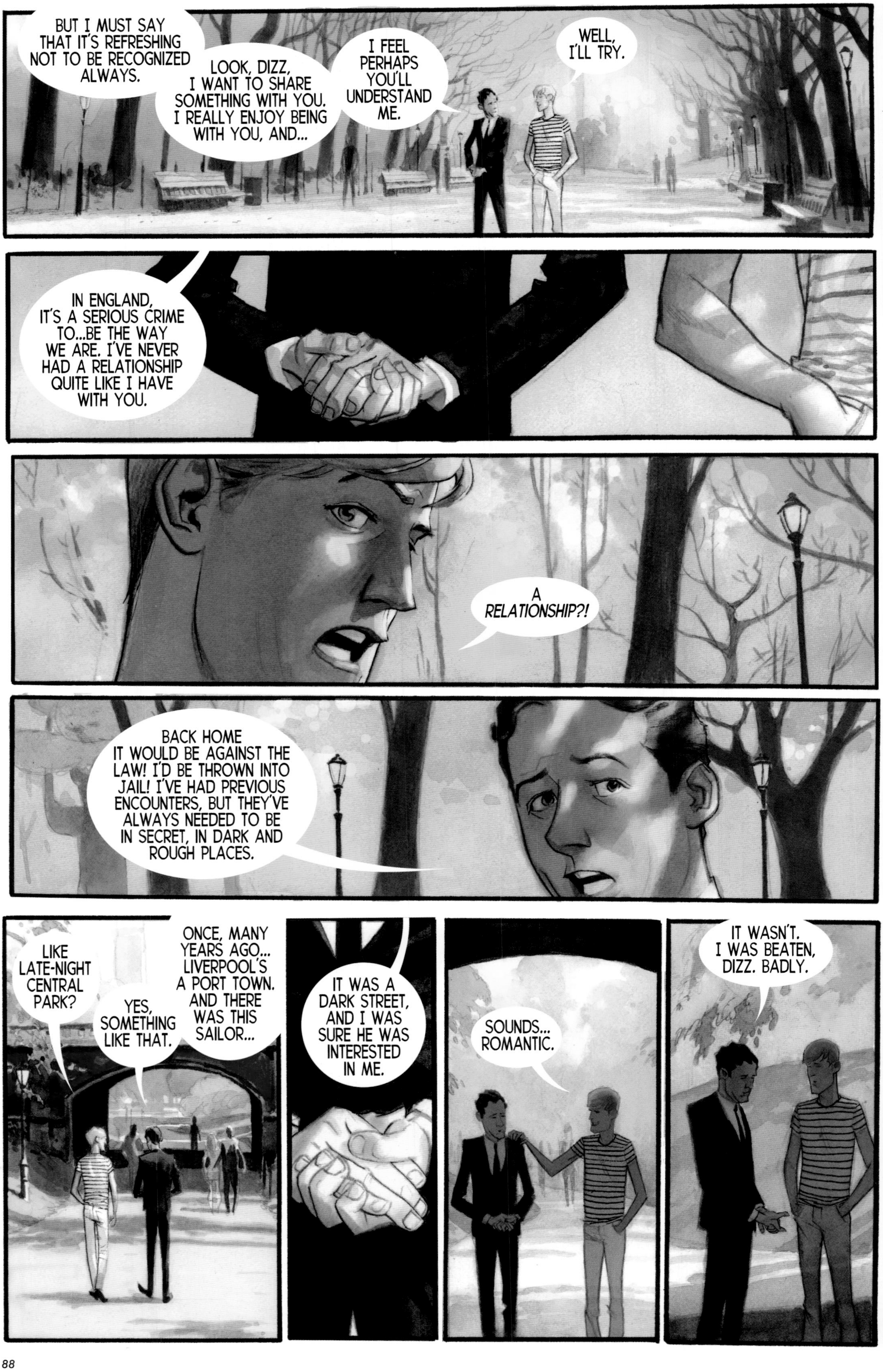
BUT I MUST SAY THAT IT'S REFRESHING NOT TO BE RECOGNIZED ALWAYS.
LOOK, DIZZ, I WANT TO SHARE SOMETHING WITH YOU. I REALLY ENJOY BEING WITH YOU, AND...
I FEEL PERHAPS YOU'LL UNDERSTAND ME.
WELL, I'LL TRY.
IN ENGLAND, IT'S A SERIOUS CRIME TO...BE THE WAY WE ARE. I'VE NEVER HAD A RELATIONSHIP QUITE LIKE I HAVE WITH YOU.
A *RELATIONSHIP*?!
BACK HOME IT WOULD BE AGAINST THE LAW! I'D BE THROWN INTO JAIL! I'VE HAD PREVIOUS ENCOUNTERS, BUT THEY'VE ALWAYS NEEDED TO BE IN SECRET, IN DARK AND ROUGH PLACES.
LIKE LATE-NIGHT CENTRAL PARK?
YES, SOMETHING LIKE THAT.
ONCE, MANY YEARS AGO... LIVERPOOL'S A PORT TOWN. AND THERE WAS THIS SAILOR...
IT WAS A DARK STREET, AND I WAS SURE HE WAS INTERESTED IN ME.
SOUNDS... ROMANTIC.
IT WASN'T. I WAS BEATEN, DIZZ. BADLY.

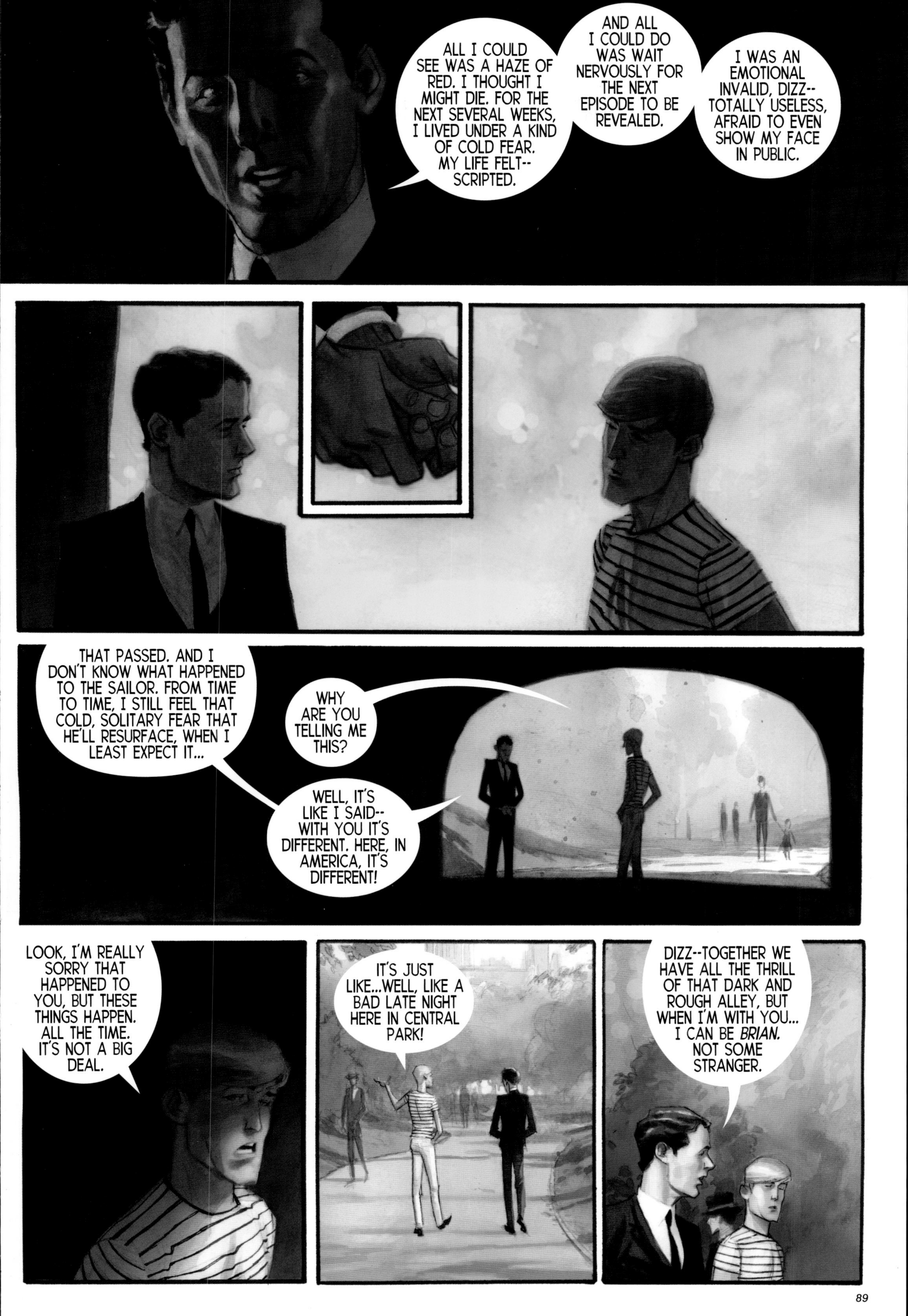
ALL I COULD SEE WAS A HAZE OF RED. I THOUGHT I MIGHT DIE. FOR THE NEXT SEVERAL WEEKS, I LIVED UNDER A KIND OF COLD FEAR. MY LIFE FELT--SCRIPTED.
AND ALL I COULD DO WAS WAIT NERVOUSLY FOR THE NEXT EPISODE TO BE REVEALED.
I WAS AN EMOTIONAL INVALID, DIZZ--TOTALLY USELESS, AFRAID TO EVEN SHOW MY FACE IN PUBLIC.
THAT PASSED. AND I DON'T KNOW WHAT HAPPENED TO THE SAILOR. FROM TIME TO TIME, I STILL FEEL THAT COLD, SOLITARY FEAR THAT HE'LL RESURFACE, WHEN I LEAST EXPECT IT...
WHY ARE YOU TELLING ME THIS?
WELL, IT'S LIKE I SAID--WITH YOU IT'S DIFFERENT. HERE, IN AMERICA, IT'S DIFFERENT!
LOOK, I'M REALLY SORRY THAT HAPPENED TO YOU, BUT THESE THINGS HAPPEN. ALL THE TIME. IT'S NOT A BIG DEAL.
IT'S JUST LIKE...WELL, LIKE A BAD LATE NIGHT HERE IN CENTRAL PARK!
DIZZ--TOGETHER WE HAVE ALL THE THRILL OF THAT DARK AND ROUGH ALLEY, BUT WHEN I'M WITH YOU... I CAN BE *BRIAN.* NOT SOME STRANGER.

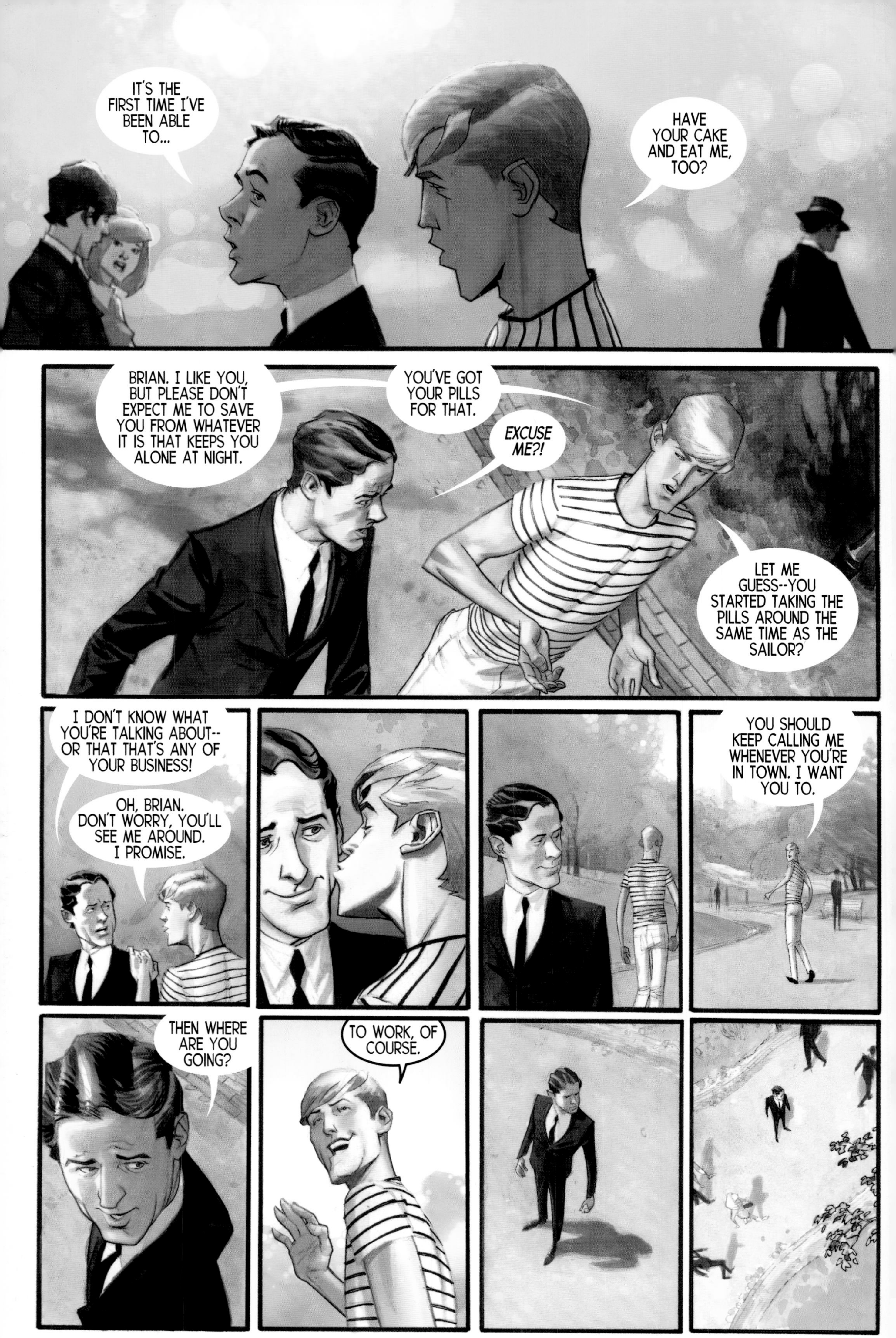
IT'S THE FIRST TIME I'VE BEEN ABLE TO...
HAVE YOUR CAKE AND EAT ME, TOO?
BRIAN. I LIKE YOU, BUT PLEASE DON'T EXPECT ME TO SAVE YOU FROM WHATEVER IT IS THAT KEEPS YOU ALONE AT NIGHT.
YOU'VE GOT YOUR PILLS FOR THAT.
EXCUSE ME?!
LET ME GUESS--YOU STARTED TAKING THE PILLS AROUND THE SAME TIME AS THE SAILOR?
I DON'T KNOW WHAT YOU'RE TALKING ABOUT-- OR THAT THAT'S ANY OF YOUR BUSINESS!
OH, BRIAN. DON'T WORRY, YOU'LL SEE ME AROUND. I PROMISE.
YOU SHOULD KEEP CALLING ME WHENEVER YOU'RE IN TOWN. I WANT YOU TO.
THEN WHERE ARE YOU GOING?
TO WORK, OF COURSE.

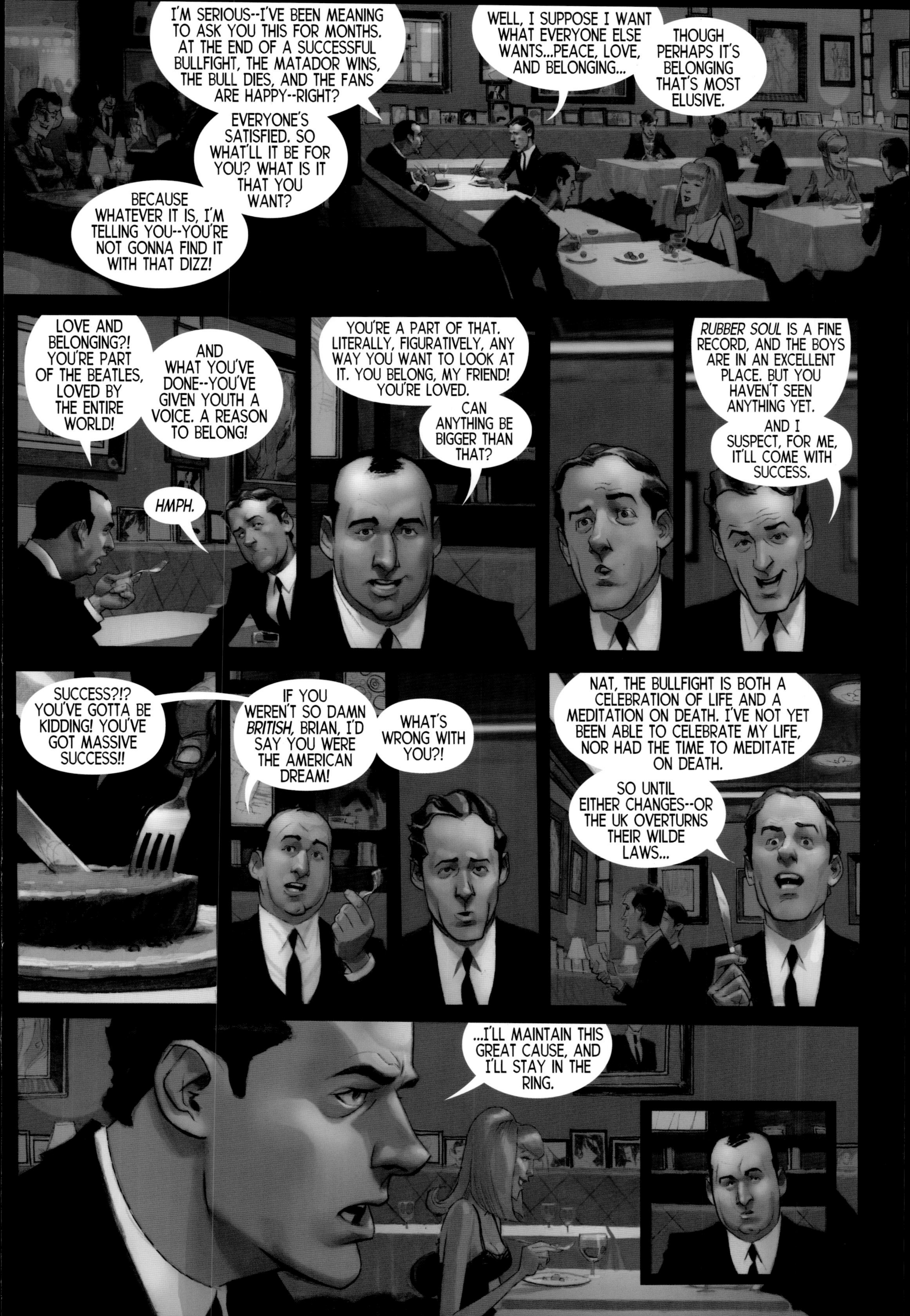
I'M SERIOUS--I'VE BEEN MEANING TO ASK YOU THIS FOR MONTHS. AT THE END OF A SUCCESSFUL BULLFIGHT, THE MATADOR WINS, THE BULL DIES, AND THE FANS ARE HAPPY--RIGHT?
EVERYONE'S SATISFIED. SO WHAT'LL IT BE FOR YOU? WHAT IS IT THAT YOU WANT?
BECAUSE WHATEVER IT IS, I'M TELLING YOU--YOU'RE NOT GONNA FIND IT WITH THAT DIZZ!
WELL, I SUPPOSE I WANT WHAT EVERYONE ELSE WANTS...PEACE, LOVE, AND BELONGING...
THOUGH PERHAPS IT'S BELONGING THAT'S MOST ELUSIVE.
LOVE AND BELONGING?! YOU'RE PART OF THE BEATLES, LOVED BY THE ENTIRE WORLD!
AND WHAT YOU'VE DONE--YOU'VE GIVEN YOUTH A VOICE. A REASON TO BELONG!
HMPH.
YOU'RE A PART OF THAT. LITERALLY, FIGURATIVELY, ANY WAY YOU WANT TO LOOK AT IT. YOU BELONG, MY FRIEND! YOU'RE LOVED.
CAN ANYTHING BE BIGGER THAN THAT?
RUBBER SOUL IS A FINE RECORD, AND THE BOYS ARE IN AN EXCELLENT PLACE. BUT YOU HAVEN'T SEEN ANYTHING YET.
AND I SUSPECT, FOR ME, IT'LL COME WITH SUCCESS.
SUCCESS?!? YOU'VE GOTTA BE KIDDING! YOU'VE GOT MASSIVE SUCCESS!!
IF YOU WEREN'T SO DAMN BRITISH, BRIAN, I'D SAY YOU WERE THE AMERICAN DREAM!
WHAT'S WRONG WITH YOU?!
NAT, THE BULLFIGHT IS BOTH A CELEBRATION OF LIFE AND A MEDITATION ON DEATH. I'VE NOT YET BEEN ABLE TO CELEBRATE MY LIFE, NOR HAD THE TIME TO MEDITATE ON DEATH.
SO UNTIL EITHER CHANGES--OR THE UK OVERTURNS THEIR WILDE LAWS...
...I'LL MAINTAIN THIS GREAT CAUSE, AND I'LL STAY IN THE RING.

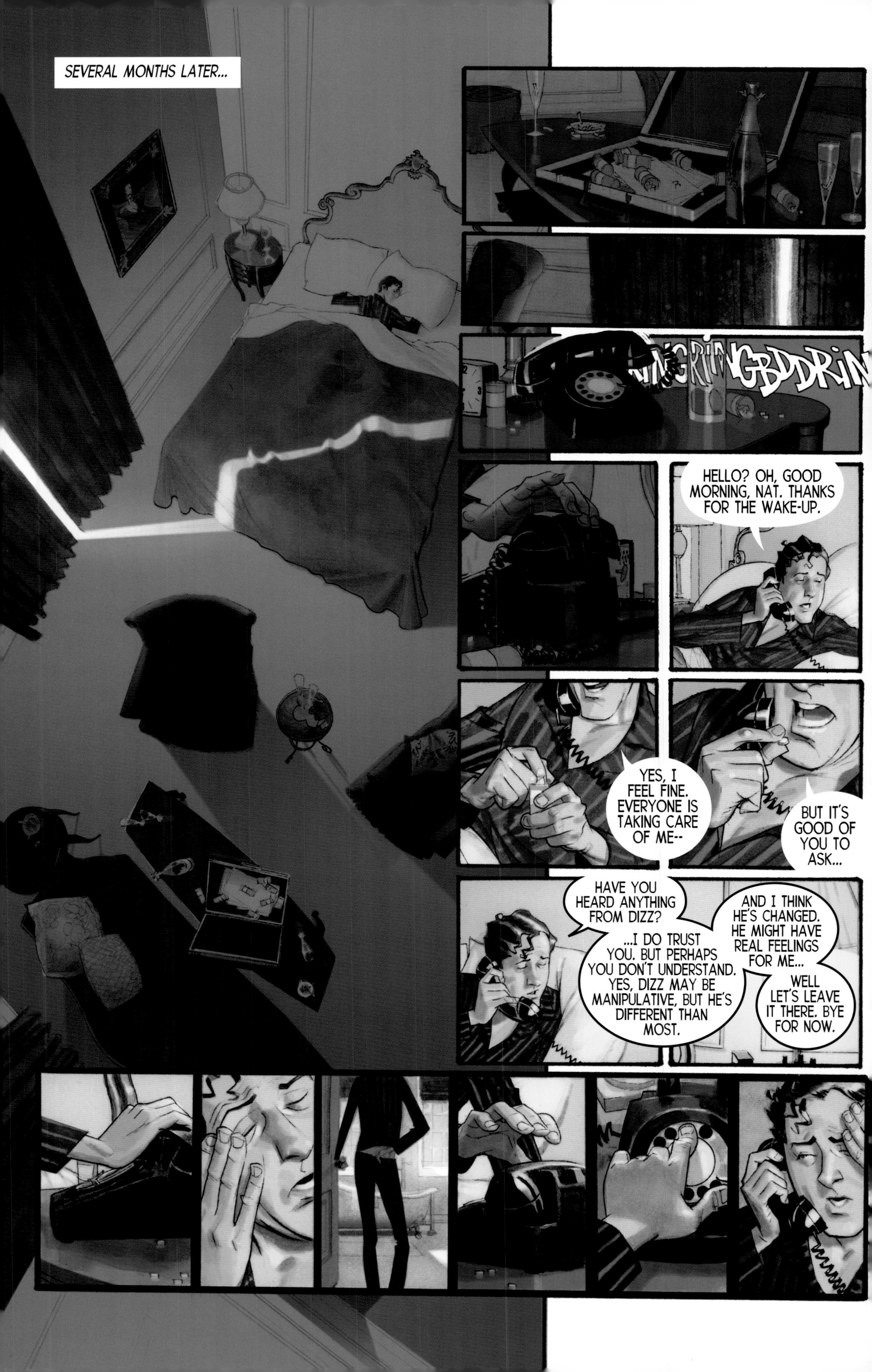
SEVERAL MONTHS LATER...
RINGRINGBDDRIN
HELLO? OH, GOOD MORNING, NAT. THANKS FOR THE WAKE-UP.
YES, I FEEL FINE. EVERYONE IS TAKING CARE OF ME--
BUT IT'S GOOD OF YOU TO ASK...
HAVE YOU HEARD ANYTHING FROM DIZZ?
...I DO TRUST YOU. BUT PERHAPS YOU DON'T UNDERSTAND. YES, DIZZ MAY BE MANIPULATIVE, BUT HE'S DIFFERENT THAN MOST.
AND I THINK HE'S CHANGED. HE MIGHT HAVE REAL FEELINGS FOR ME...
WELL LET'S LEAVE IT THERE. BYE FOR NOW.

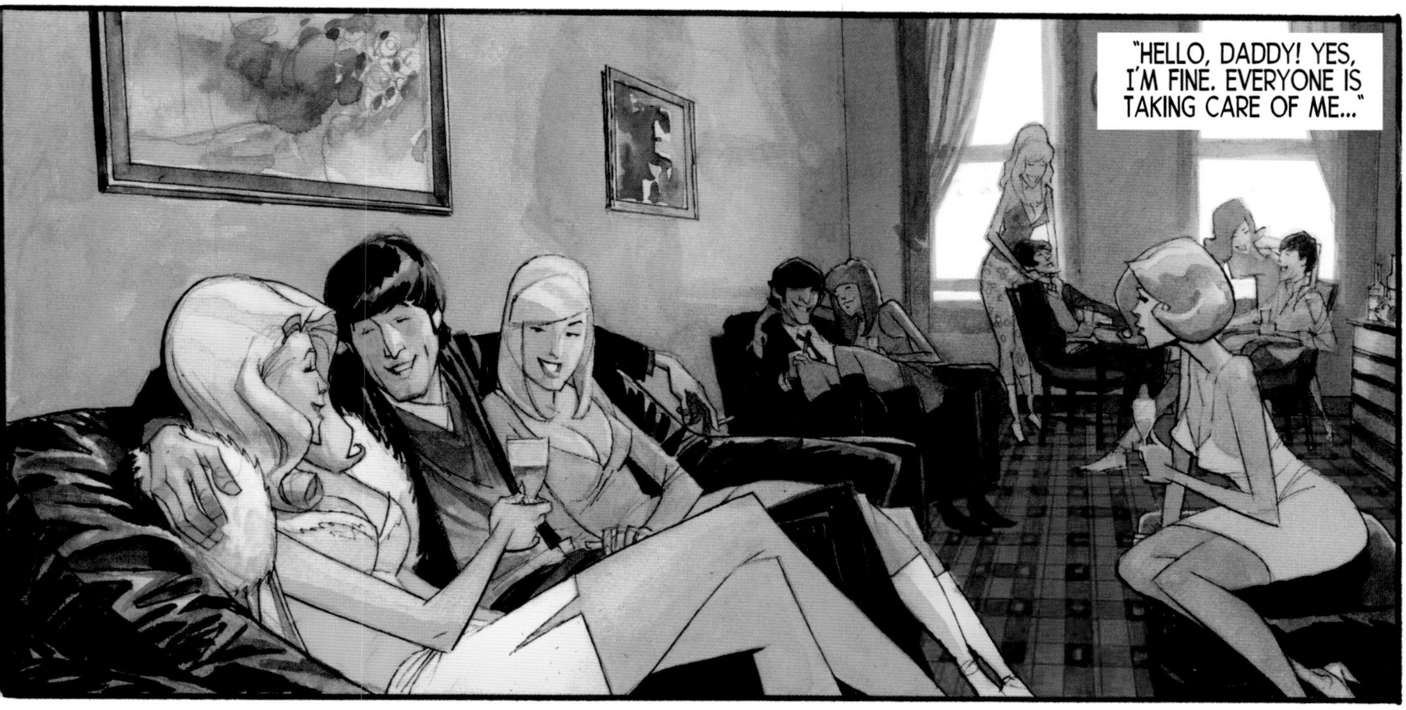
"HELLO, DADDY! YES, I'M FINE. EVERYONE IS TAKING CARE OF ME..."

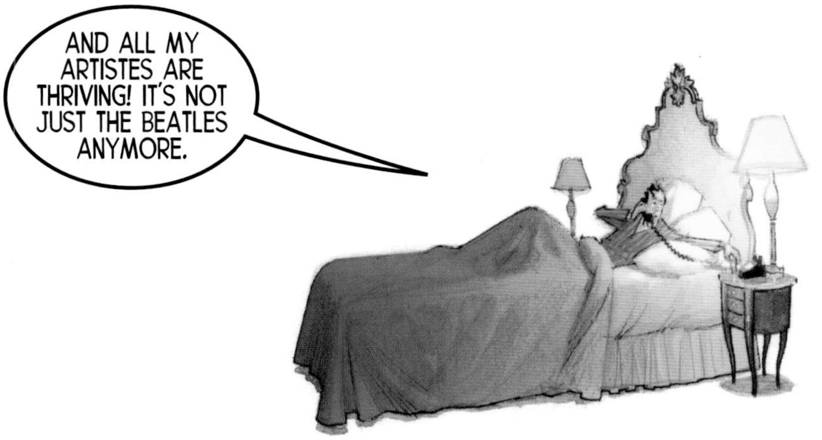
AND ALL MY ARTISTES ARE THRIVING! IT'S NOT JUST THE BEATLES ANYMORE.

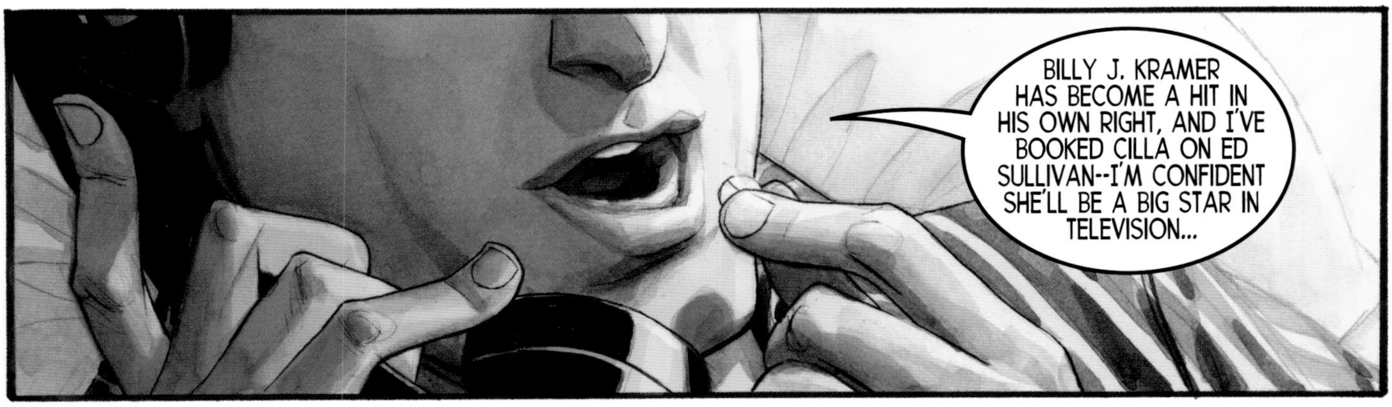
BILLY J. KRAMER HAS BECOME A HIT IN HIS OWN RIGHT, AND I'VE BOOKED CILLA ON ED SULLIVAN--I'M CONFIDENT SHE'LL BE A BIG STAR IN TELEVISION...

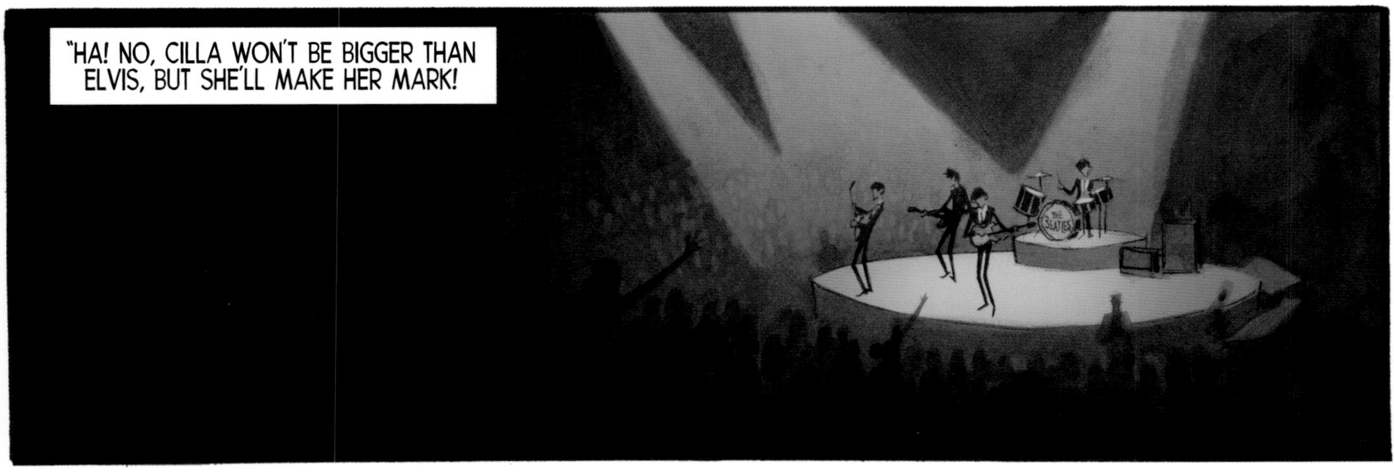
"HA! NO, CILLA WON'T BE BIGGER THAN ELVIS, BUT SHE'LL MAKE HER MARK!

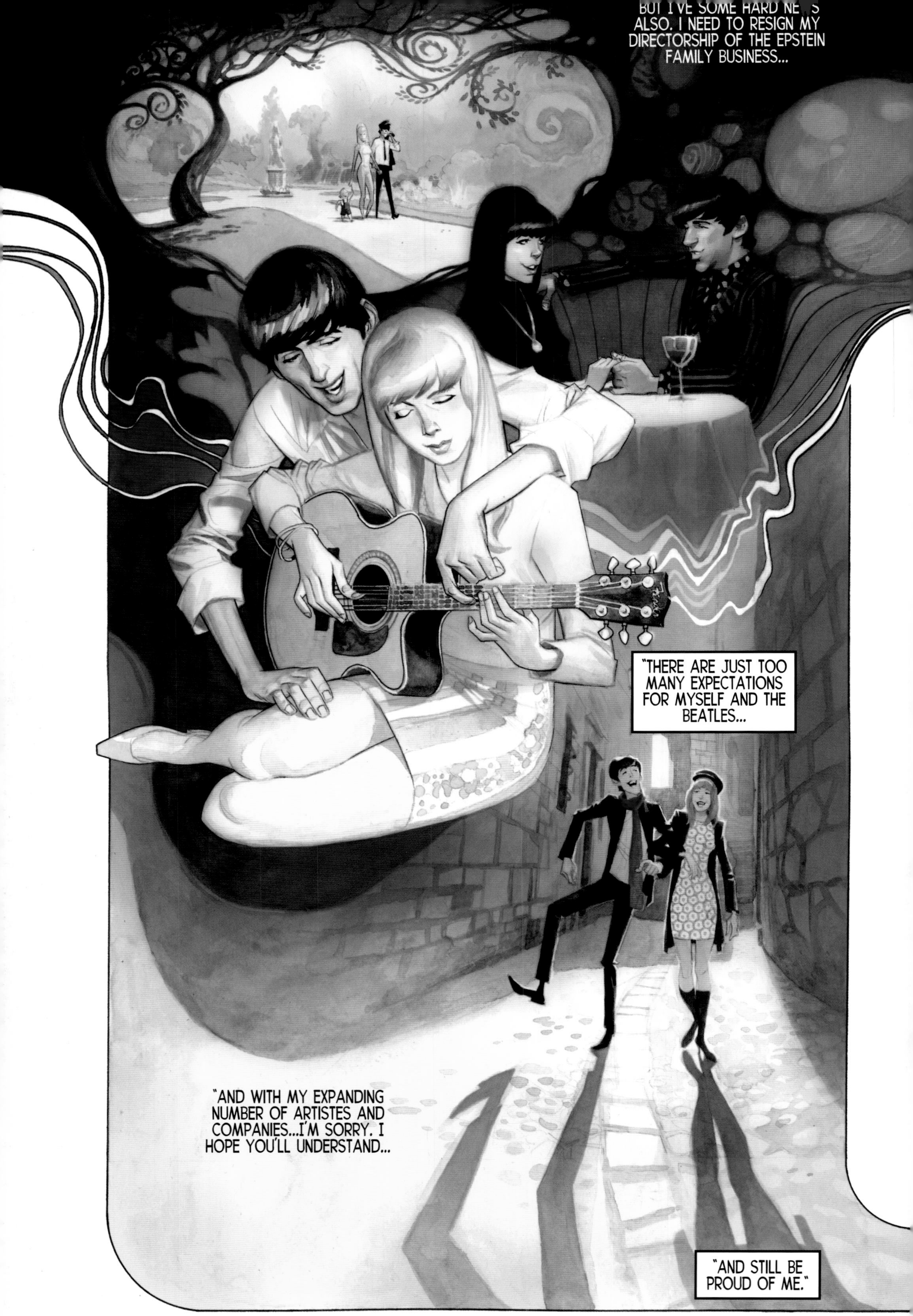
BUT I'VE SOME HARD NE S ALSO. I NEED TO RESIGN MY DIRECTORSHIP OF THE EPSTEIN FAMILY BUSINESS...
"THERE ARE JUST TOO MANY EXPECTATIONS FOR MYSELF AND THE BEATLES...
"AND WITH MY EXPANDING NUMBER OF ARTISTES AND COMPANIES...I'M SORRY. I HOPE YOU'LL UNDERSTAND...
"AND STILL BE PROUD OF ME."

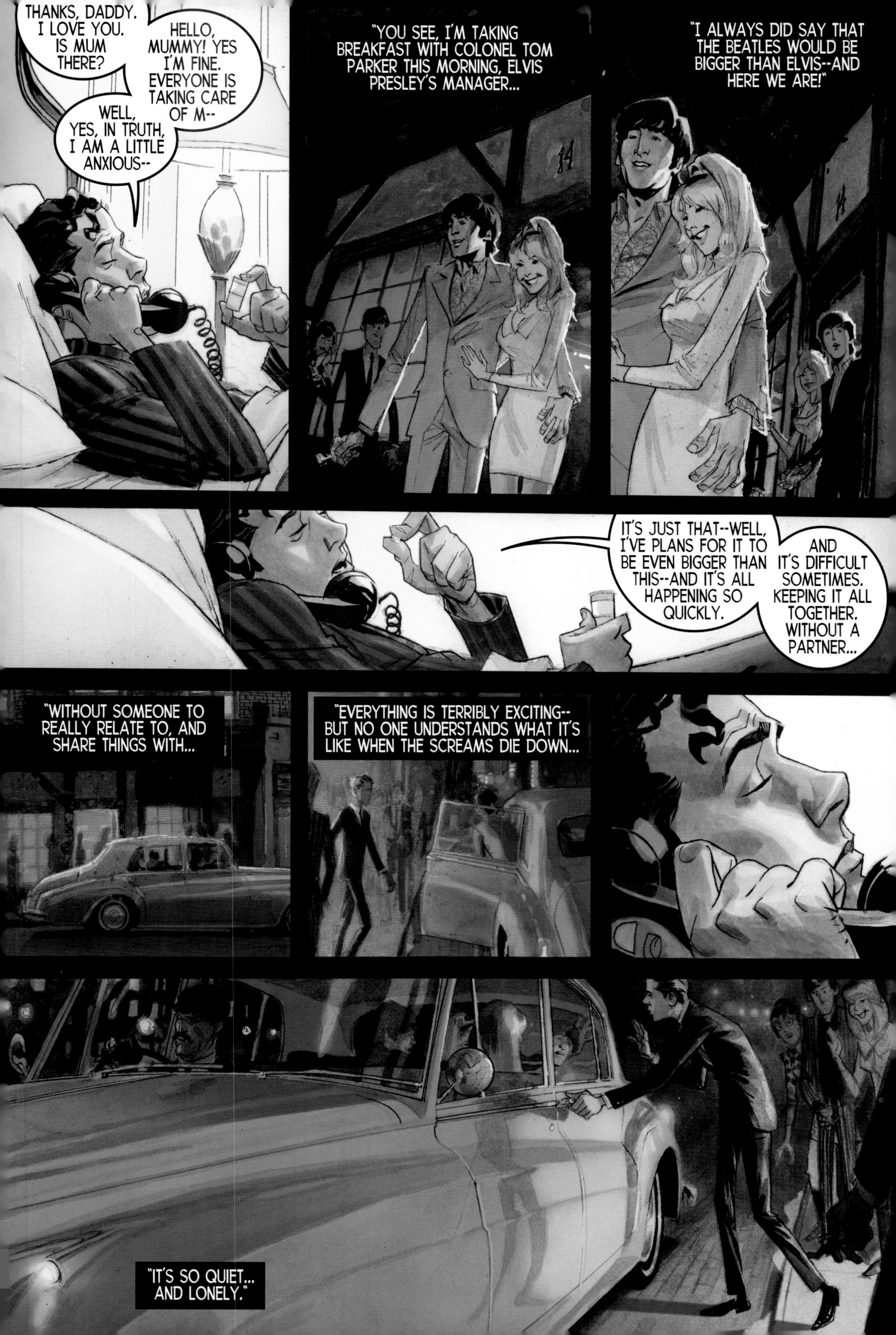
THANKS, DADDY. I LOVE YOU. IS MUM THERE?
HELLO, MUMMY! YES I'M FINE. EVERYONE IS TAKING CARE OF M--
WELL, YES, IN TRUTH, I AM A LITTLE ANXIOUS--
"YOU SEE, I'M TAKING BREAKFAST WITH COLONEL TOM PARKER THIS MORNING, ELVIS PRESLEY'S MANAGER...
"I ALWAYS DID SAY THAT THE BEATLES WOULD BE BIGGER THAN ELVIS--AND HERE WE ARE!"
IT'S JUST THAT--WELL, I'VE PLANS FOR IT TO BE EVEN BIGGER THAN THIS--AND IT'S ALL HAPPENING SO QUICKLY.
AND IT'S DIFFICULT SOMETIMES. KEEPING IT ALL TOGETHER. WITHOUT A PARTNER...
"WITHOUT SOMEONE TO REALLY RELATE TO, AND SHARE THINGS WITH...
"EVERYTHING IS TERRIBLY EXCITING--BUT NO ONE UNDERSTANDS WHAT IT'S LIKE WHEN THE SCREAMS DIE DOWN...
"IT'S SO QUIET... AND LONELY."

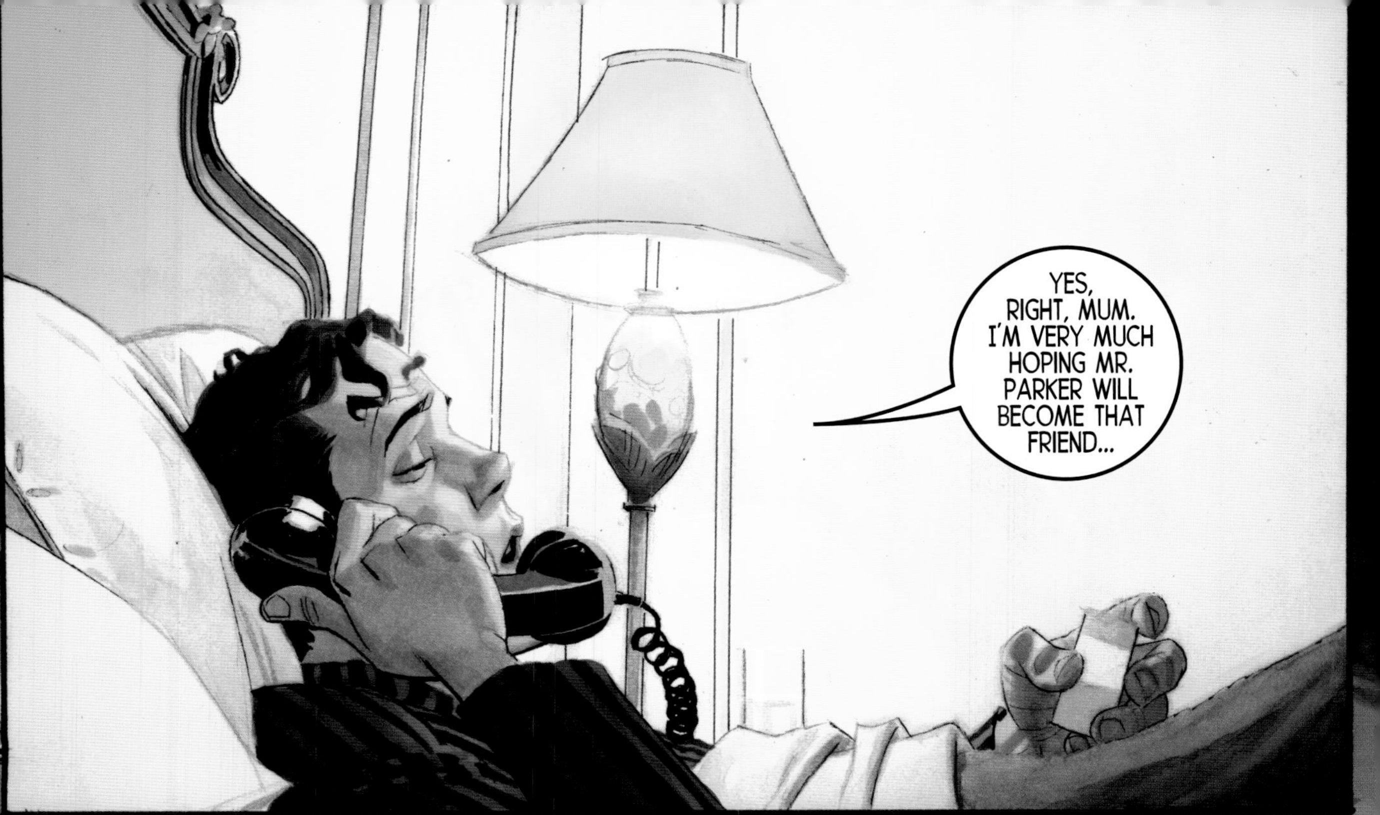
YES, RIGHT, MUM. I'M VERY MUCH HOPING MR. PARKER WILL BECOME THAT FRIEND...

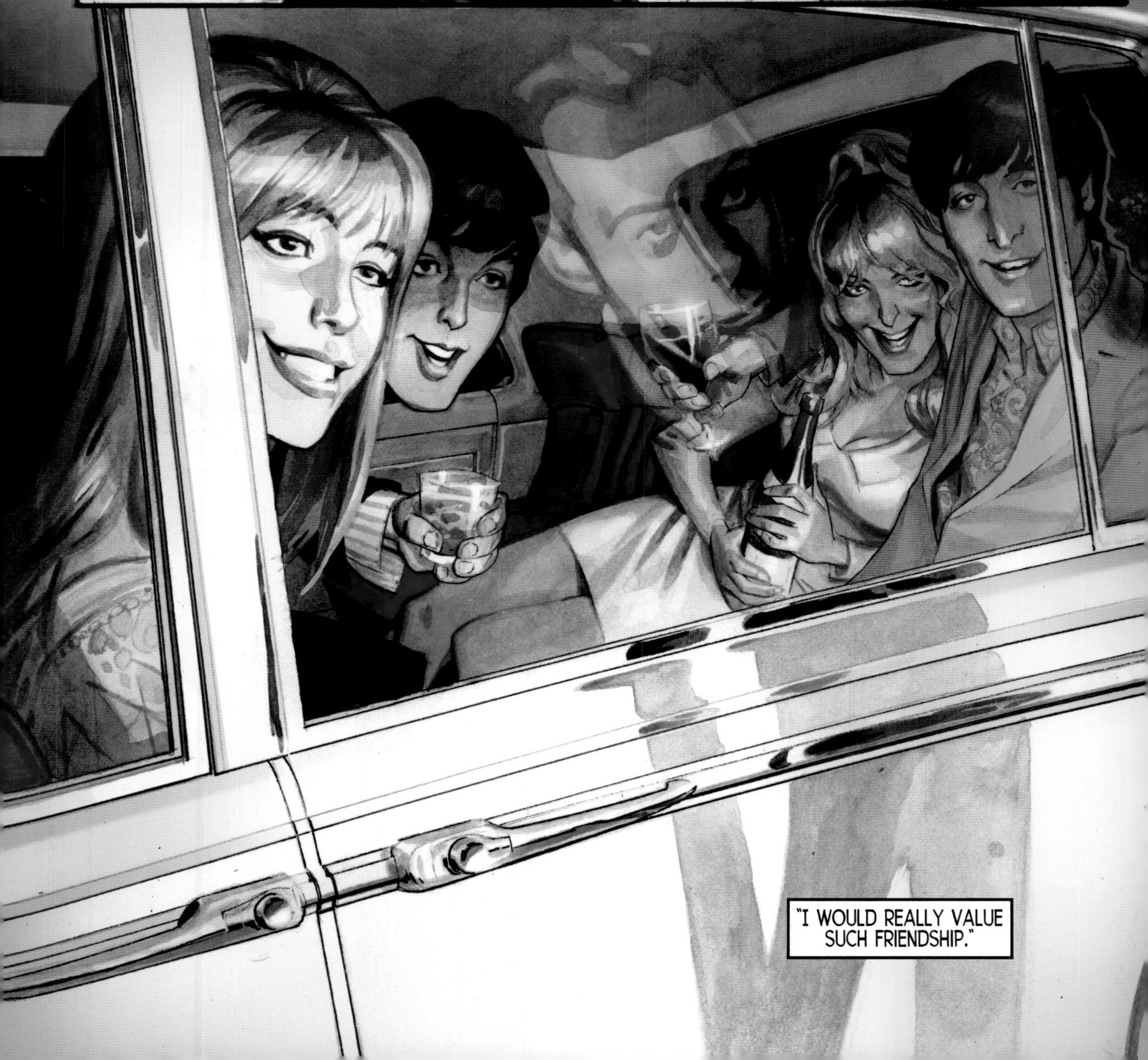
"I WOULD REALLY VALUE SUCH FRIENDSHIP."

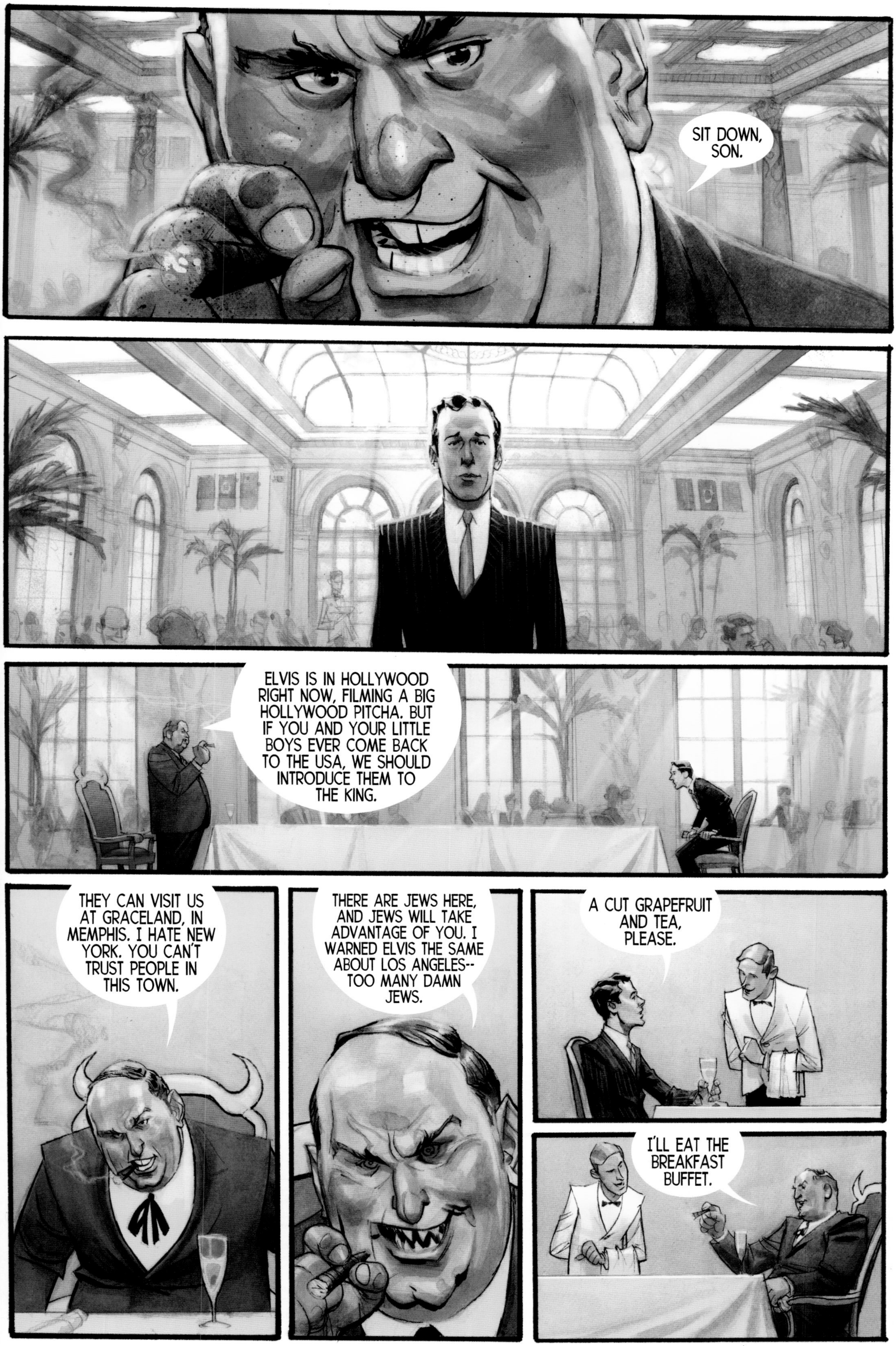
SIT DOWN, SON.
ELVIS IS IN HOLLYWOOD RIGHT NOW, FILMING A BIG HOLLYWOOD PITCHA. BUT IF YOU AND YOUR LITTLE BOYS EVER COME BACK TO THE USA, WE SHOULD INTRODUCE THEM TO THE KING.
THEY CAN VISIT US AT GRACELAND, IN MEMPHIS. I HATE NEW YORK. YOU CAN'T TRUST PEOPLE IN THIS TOWN.
THERE ARE JEWS HERE, AND JEWS WILL TAKE ADVANTAGE OF YOU. I WARNED ELVIS THE SAME ABOUT LOS ANGELES-- TOO MANY DAMN JEWS.
A CUT GRAPEFRUIT AND TEA, PLEASE.
I'LL EAT THE BREAKFAST BUFFET.

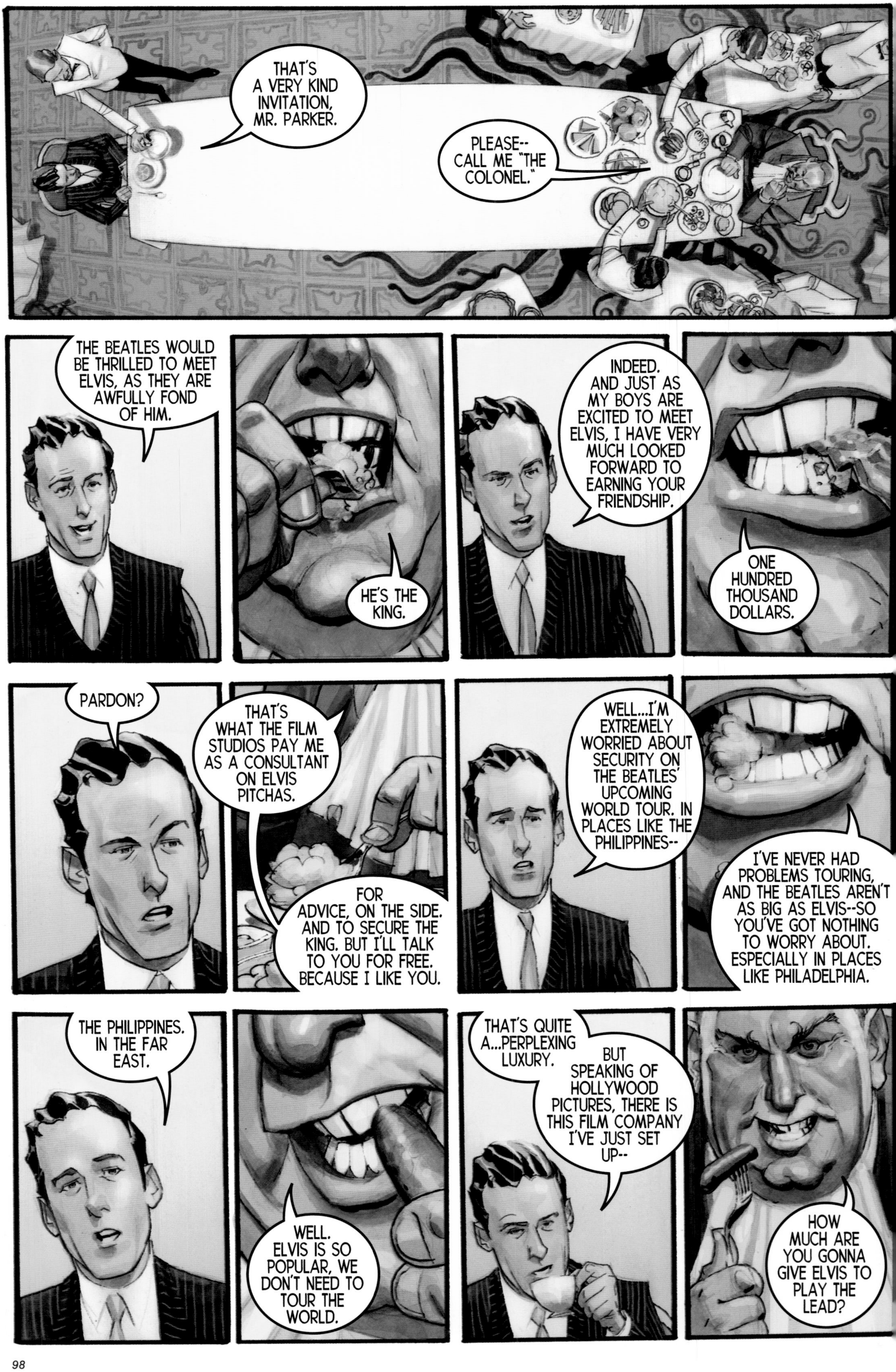
THAT'S A VERY KIND INVITATION, MR. PARKER.
PLEASE-- CALL ME "THE COLONEL."
THE BEATLES WOULD BE THRILLED TO MEET ELVIS, AS THEY ARE AWFULLY FOND OF HIM.
HE'S THE KING.
INDEED. AND JUST AS MY BOYS ARE EXCITED TO MEET ELVIS, I HAVE VERY MUCH LOOKED FORWARD TO EARNING YOUR FRIENDSHIP.
ONE HUNDRED THOUSAND DOLLARS.
PARDON?
THAT'S WHAT THE FILM STUDIOS PAY ME AS A CONSULTANT ON ELVIS PITCHAS.
FOR ADVICE, ON THE SIDE. AND TO SECURE THE KING. BUT I'LL TALK TO YOU FOR FREE. BECAUSE I LIKE YOU.
WELL...I'M EXTREMELY WORRIED ABOUT SECURITY ON THE BEATLES' UPCOMING WORLD TOUR. IN PLACES LIKE THE PHILIPPINES--
I'VE NEVER HAD PROBLEMS TOURING, AND THE BEATLES AREN'T AS BIG AS ELVIS--SO YOU'VE GOT NOTHING TO WORRY ABOUT. ESPECIALLY IN PLACES LIKE PHILADELPHIA.
THE PHILIPPINES. IN THE FAR EAST.
WELL. ELVIS IS SO POPULAR, WE DON'T NEED TO TOUR THE WORLD.
THAT'S QUITE A...PERPLEXING LUXURY.
BUT SPEAKING OF HOLLYWOOD PICTURES, THERE IS THIS FILM COMPANY I'VE JUST SET UP--
HOW MUCH ARE YOU GONNA GIVE ELVIS TO PLAY THE LEAD?

97

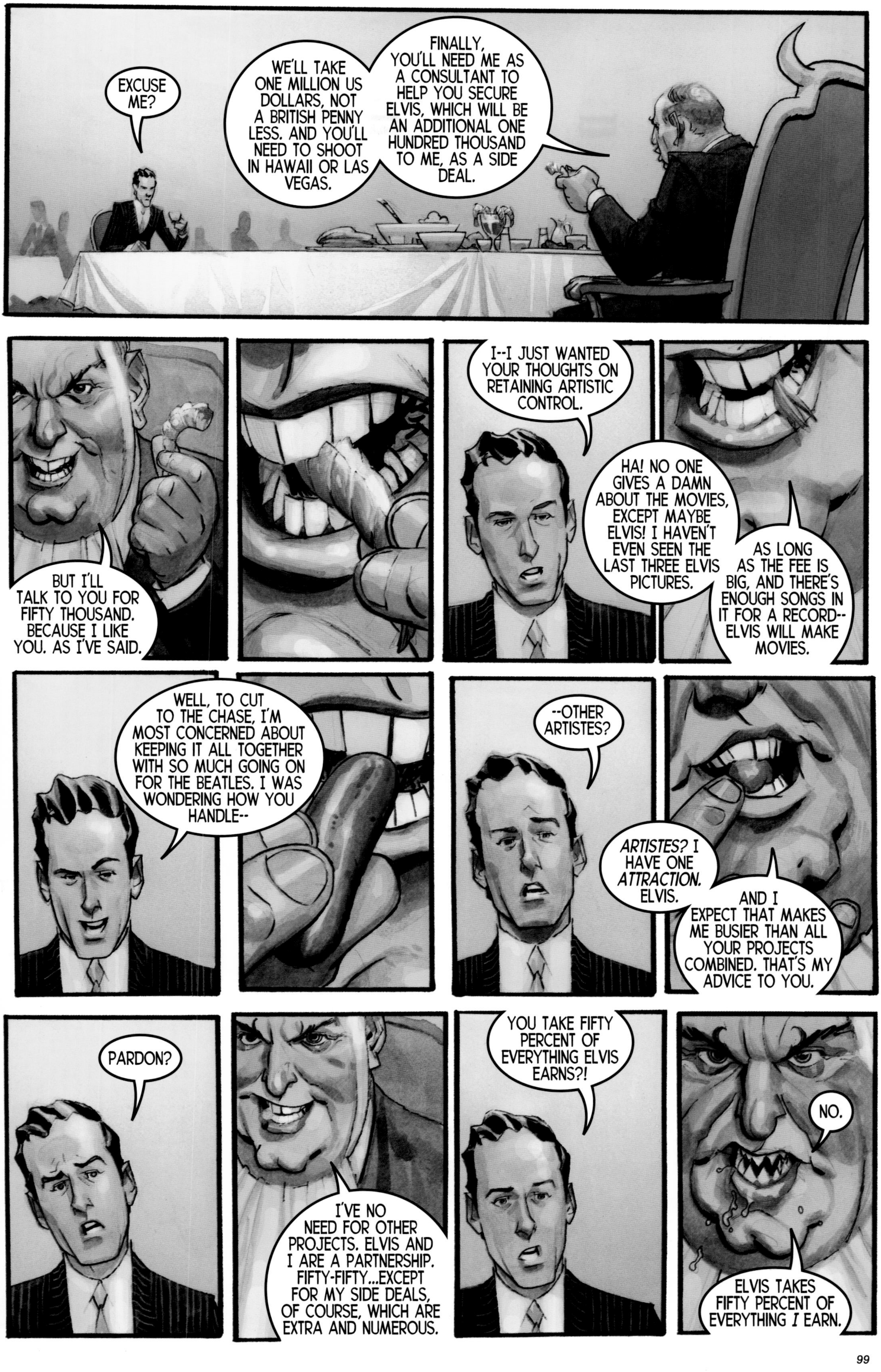
EXCUSE ME?
WE'LL TAKE ONE MILLION US DOLLARS, NOT A BRITISH PENNY LESS. AND YOU'LL NEED TO SHOOT IN HAWAII OR LAS VEGAS.
FINALLY, YOU'LL NEED ME AS A CONSULTANT TO HELP YOU SECURE ELVIS, WHICH WILL BE AN ADDITIONAL ONE HUNDRED THOUSAND TO ME, AS A SIDE DEAL.
BUT I'LL TALK TO YOU FOR FIFTY THOUSAND. BECAUSE I LIKE YOU. AS I'VE SAID.
I--I JUST WANTED YOUR THOUGHTS ON RETAINING ARTISTIC CONTROL.
HA! NO ONE GIVES A DAMN ABOUT THE MOVIES, EXCEPT MAYBE ELVIS! I HAVEN'T EVEN SEEN THE LAST THREE ELVIS PICTURES.
AS LONG AS THE FEE IS BIG, AND THERE'S ENOUGH SONGS IN IT FOR A RECORD-- ELVIS WILL MAKE MOVIES.
WELL, TO CUT TO THE CHASE, I'M MOST CONCERNED ABOUT KEEPING IT ALL TOGETHER WITH SO MUCH GOING ON FOR THE BEATLES. I WAS WONDERING HOW YOU HANDLE--
--OTHER ARTISTES?
ARTISTES? I HAVE ONE *ATTRACTION.* ELVIS.
AND I EXPECT THAT MAKES ME BUSIER THAN ALL YOUR PROJECTS COMBINED. THAT'S MY ADVICE TO YOU.
PARDON?
I'VE NO NEED FOR OTHER PROJECTS. ELVIS AND I ARE A PARTNERSHIP. FIFTY-FIFTY...EXCEPT FOR MY SIDE DEALS, OF COURSE, WHICH ARE EXTRA AND NUMEROUS.
YOU TAKE FIFTY PERCENT OF EVERYTHING ELVIS EARNS?!
NO.
ELVIS TAKES FIFTY PERCENT OF EVERYTHING *I* EARN.

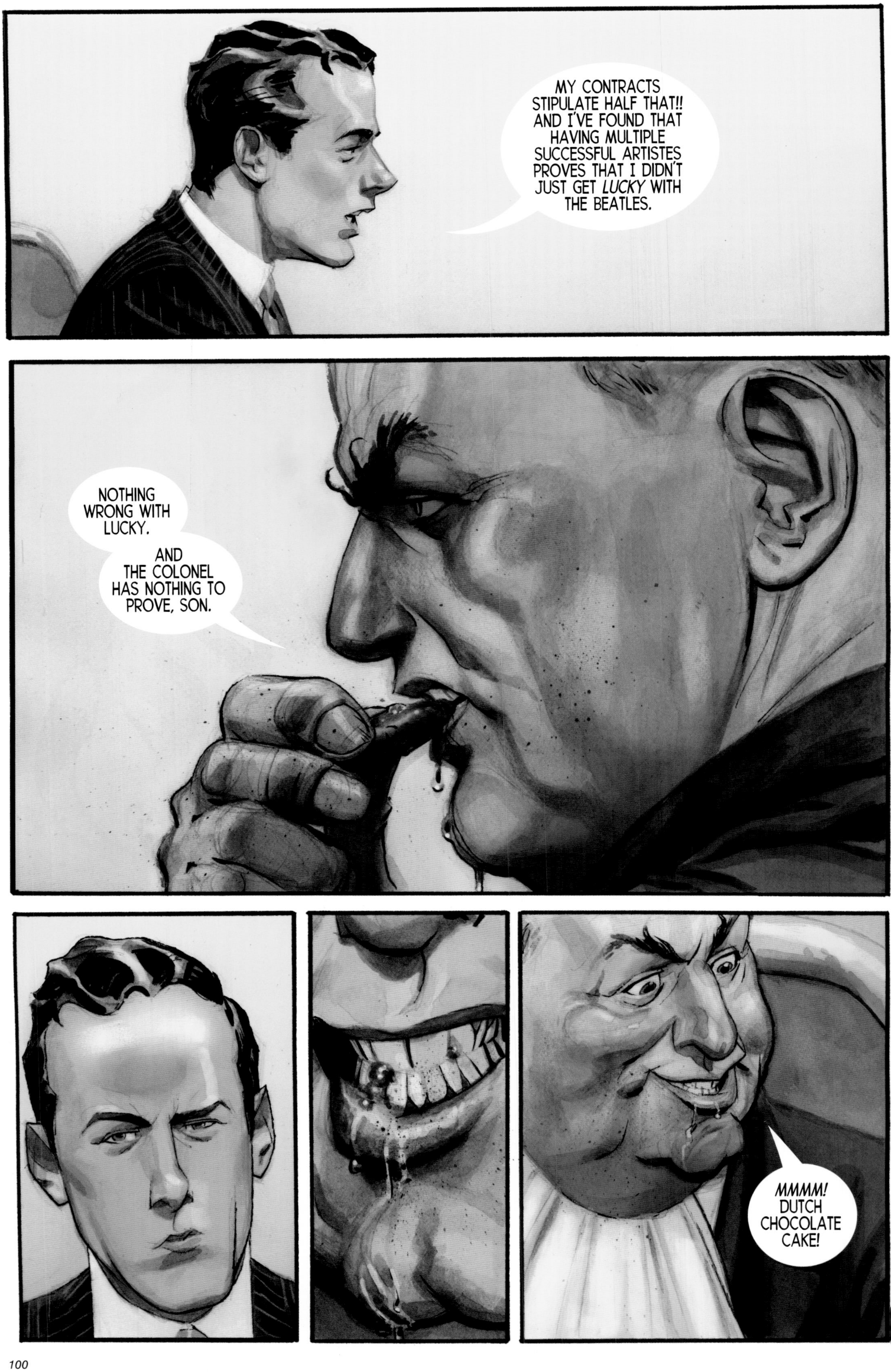
MY CONTRACTS STIPULATE HALF THAT!! AND I'VE FOUND THAT HAVING MULTIPLE SUCCESSFUL ARTISTES PROVES THAT I DIDN'T JUST GET *LUCKY* WITH THE BEATLES.
NOTHING WRONG WITH LUCKY.
AND THE COLONEL HAS NOTHING TO PROVE, SON.
MMMM! DUTCH CHOCOLATE CAKE!

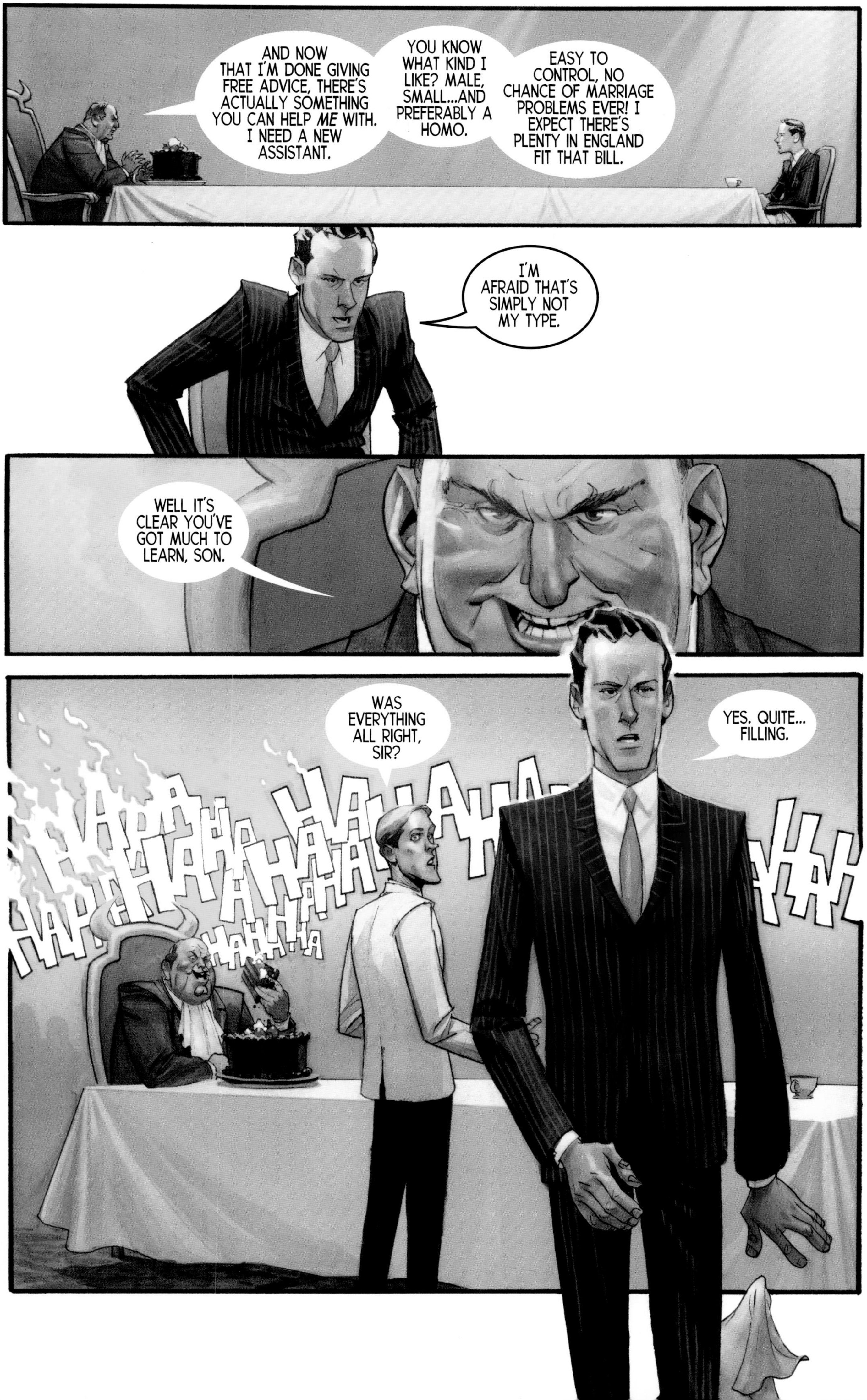
AND NOW THAT I'M DONE GIVING FREE ADVICE, THERE'S ACTUALLY SOMETHING YOU CAN HELP *ME* WITH. I NEED A NEW ASSISTANT.
YOU KNOW WHAT KIND I LIKE? MALE, SMALL...AND PREFERABLY A HOMO.
EASY TO CONTROL, NO CHANCE OF MARRIAGE PROBLEMS EVER! I EXPECT THERE'S PLENTY IN ENGLAND FIT THAT BILL.
I'M AFRAID THAT'S SIMPLY NOT MY TYPE.
WELL IT'S CLEAR YOU'VE GOT MUCH TO LEARN, SON.
WAS EVERYTHING ALL RIGHT, SIR?
YES. QUITE... FILLING.

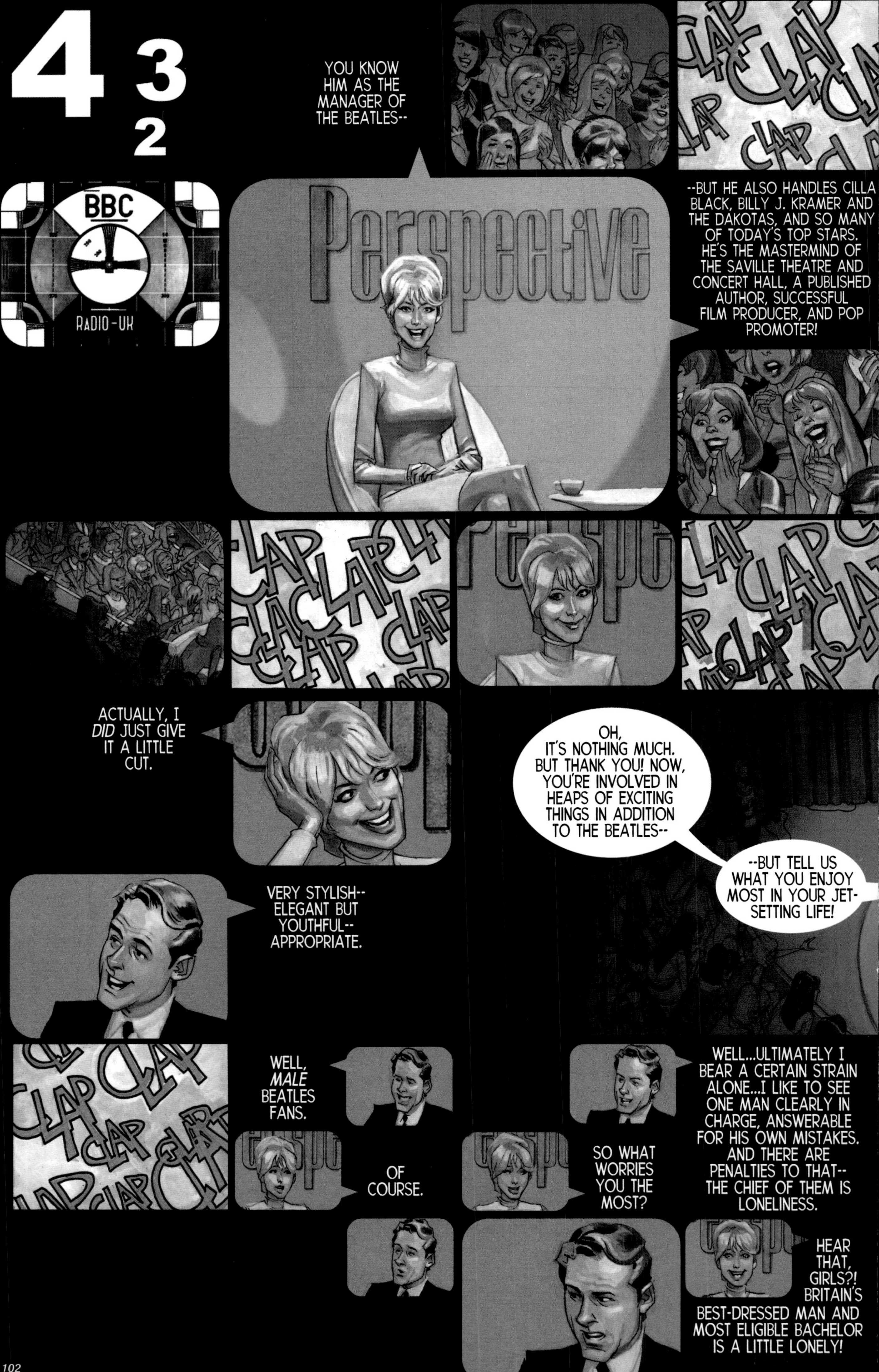
4
3
2
BBC
RADIO-UK
YOU KNOW HIM AS THE MANAGER OF THE BEATLES--
Perspective
--BUT HE ALSO HANDLES CILLA BLACK, BILLY J. KRAMER AND THE DAKOTAS, AND SO MANY OF TODAY'S TOP STARS. HE'S THE MASTERMIND OF THE SAVILLE THEATRE AND CONCERT HALL, A PUBLISHED AUTHOR, SUCCESSFUL FILM PRODUCER, AND POP PROMOTER!
CLAP CLAP CLAP
ACTUALLY, I *DID* JUST GIVE IT A LITTLE CUT.
VERY STYLISH-- ELEGANT BUT YOUTHFUL-- APPROPRIATE.
OH, IT'S NOTHING MUCH. BUT THANK YOU! NOW, YOU'RE INVOLVED IN HEAPS OF EXCITING THINGS IN ADDITION TO THE BEATLES--
--BUT TELL US WHAT YOU ENJOY MOST IN YOUR JET-SETTING LIFE!
WELL, *MALE* BEATLES FANS.
OF COURSE.
SO WHAT WORRIES YOU THE MOST?
WELL...ULTIMATELY I BEAR A CERTAIN STRAIN ALONE...I LIKE TO SEE ONE MAN CLEARLY IN CHARGE, ANSWERABLE FOR HIS OWN MISTAKES. AND THERE ARE PENALTIES TO THAT-- THE CHIEF OF THEM IS LONELINESS.
HEAR THAT, GIRLS?! BRITAIN'S BEST-DRESSED MAN AND MOST ELIGIBLE BACHELOR IS A LITTLE LONELY!

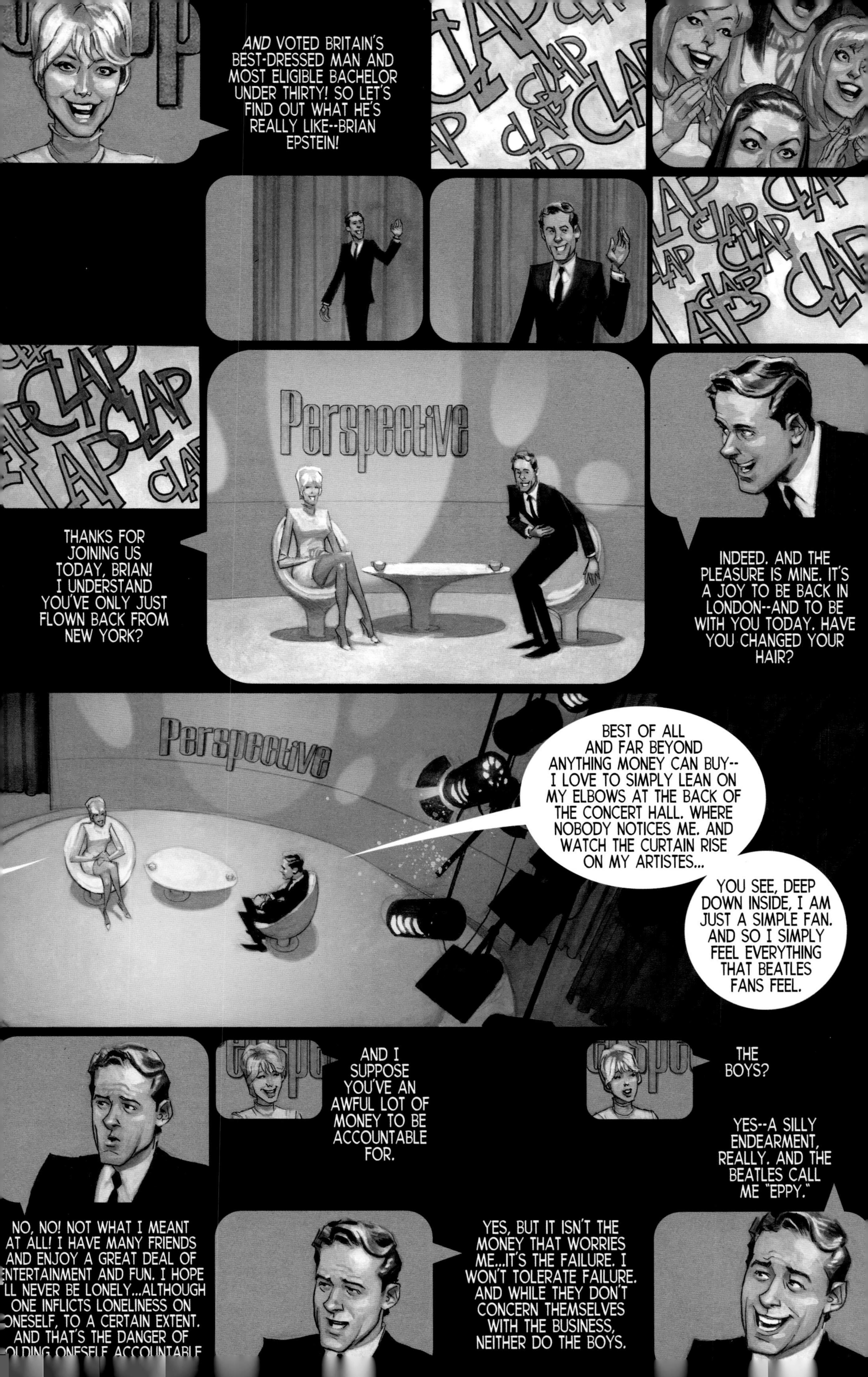
AND VOTED BRITAIN'S BEST-DRESSED MAN AND MOST ELIGIBLE BACHELOR UNDER THIRTY! SO LET'S FIND OUT WHAT HE'S REALLY LIKE--BRIAN EPSTEIN!
CLAP CLAP CLAP CLAP
CLAP CLAP CLAP CLAP
CLAP CLAP CLAP
Perspective
THANKS FOR JOINING US TODAY, BRIAN! I UNDERSTAND YOU'VE ONLY JUST FLOWN BACK FROM NEW YORK?
INDEED. AND THE PLEASURE IS MINE. IT'S A JOY TO BE BACK IN LONDON--AND TO BE WITH YOU TODAY. HAVE YOU CHANGED YOUR HAIR?
Perspective
BEST OF ALL AND FAR BEYOND ANYTHING MONEY CAN BUY-- I LOVE TO SIMPLY LEAN ON MY ELBOWS AT THE BACK OF THE CONCERT HALL. WHERE NOBODY NOTICES ME. AND WATCH THE CURTAIN RISE ON MY ARTISTES...
YOU SEE, DEEP DOWN INSIDE, I AM JUST A SIMPLE FAN. AND SO I SIMPLY FEEL EVERYTHING THAT BEATLES FANS FEEL.
AND I SUPPOSE YOU'VE AN AWFUL LOT OF MONEY TO BE ACCOUNTABLE FOR.
NO, NO! NOT WHAT I MEANT AT ALL! I HAVE MANY FRIENDS AND ENJOY A GREAT DEAL OF ENTERTAINMENT AND FUN. I HOPE I'LL NEVER BE LONELY...ALTHOUGH ONE INFLICTS LONELINESS ON ONESELF, TO A CERTAIN EXTENT. AND THAT'S THE DANGER OF HOLDING ONESELF ACCOUNTABLE
YES, BUT IT ISN'T THE MONEY THAT WORRIES ME...IT'S THE FAILURE. I WON'T TOLERATE FAILURE. AND WHILE THEY DON'T CONCERN THEMSELVES WITH THE BUSINESS, NEITHER DO THE BOYS.
THE BOYS?
YES--A SILLY ENDEARMENT, REALLY. AND THE BEATLES CALL ME "EPPY."

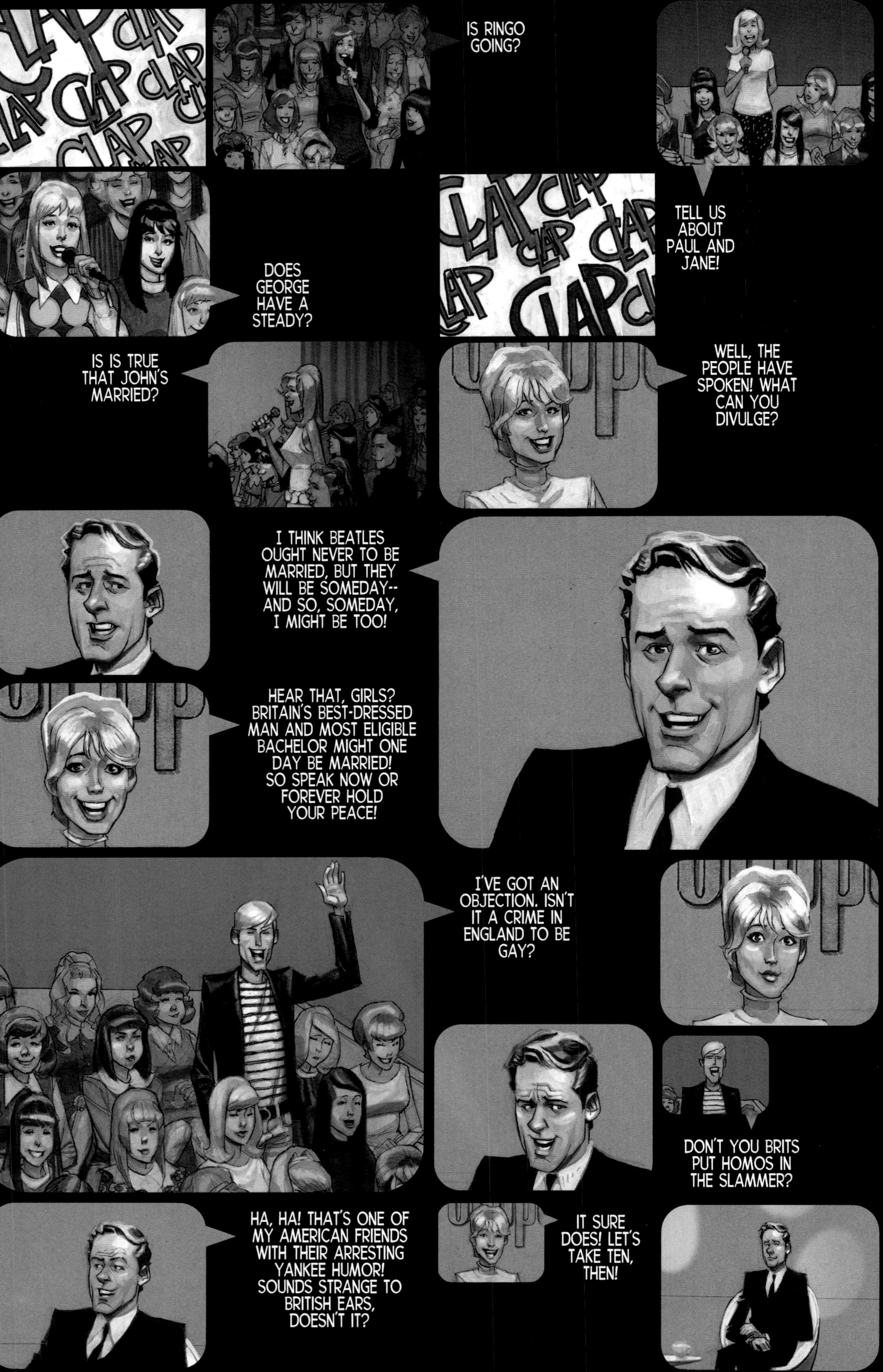

CLAP CLAP CLAP CLAP CLAP CLAP
IS RINGO GOING?
DOES GEORGE HAVE A STEADY?
CLAP CLAP CLAP CLAP CLAP CLAP
TELL US ABOUT PAUL AND JANE!
IS IS TRUE THAT JOHN'S MARRIED?
WELL, THE PEOPLE HAVE SPOKEN! WHAT CAN YOU DIVULGE?
I THINK BEATLES OUGHT NEVER TO BE MARRIED, BUT THEY WILL BE SOMEDAY-- AND SO, SOMEDAY, I MIGHT BE TOO!
HEAR THAT, GIRLS? BRITAIN'S BEST-DRESSED MAN AND MOST ELIGIBLE BACHELOR MIGHT ONE DAY BE MARRIED! SO SPEAK NOW OR FOREVER HOLD YOUR PEACE!
I'VE GOT AN OBJECTION. ISN'T IT A CRIME IN ENGLAND TO BE GAY?
DON'T YOU BRITS PUT HOMOS IN THE SLAMMER?
HA, HA! THAT'S ONE OF MY AMERICAN FRIENDS WITH THEIR ARRESTING YANKEE HUMOR! SOUNDS STRANGE TO BRITISH EARS, DOESN'T IT?
IT SURE DOES! LET'S TAKE TEN, THEN!

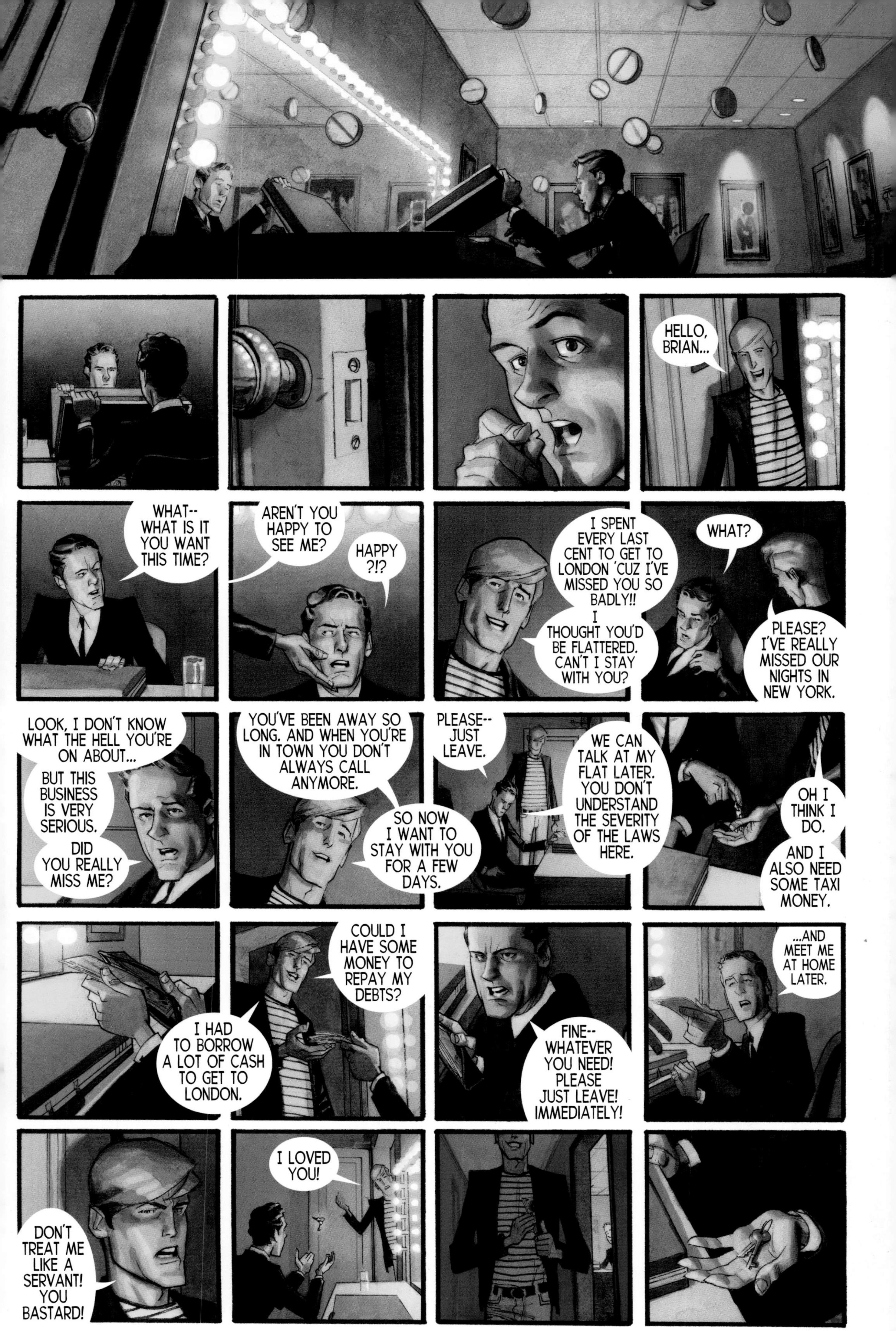
HELLO, BRIAN...
WHAT-- WHAT IS IT YOU WANT THIS TIME?
AREN'T YOU HAPPY TO SEE ME?
HAPPY ?!?
I SPENT EVERY LAST CENT TO GET TO LONDON 'CUZ I'VE MISSED YOU SO BADLY!!
I THOUGHT YOU'D BE FLATTERED. CAN'T I STAY WITH YOU?
WHAT?
PLEASE? I'VE REALLY MISSED OUR NIGHTS IN NEW YORK.
LOOK, I DON'T KNOW WHAT THE HELL YOU'RE ON ABOUT...
BUT THIS BUSINESS IS VERY SERIOUS.
DID YOU REALLY MISS ME?
YOU'VE BEEN AWAY SO LONG. AND WHEN YOU'RE IN TOWN YOU DON'T ALWAYS CALL ANYMORE.
SO NOW I WANT TO STAY WITH YOU FOR A FEW DAYS.
PLEASE-- JUST LEAVE.
WE CAN TALK AT MY FLAT LATER. YOU DON'T UNDERSTAND THE SEVERITY OF THE LAWS HERE.
OH I THINK I DO.
AND I ALSO NEED SOME TAXI MONEY.
COULD I HAVE SOME MONEY TO REPAY MY DEBTS?
I HAD TO BORROW A LOT OF CASH TO GET TO LONDON.
FINE-- WHATEVER YOU NEED! PLEASE JUST LEAVE! IMMEDIATELY!
...AND MEET ME AT HOME LATER.
DON'T TREAT ME LIKE A SERVANT! YOU BASTARD!
I LOVED YOU!

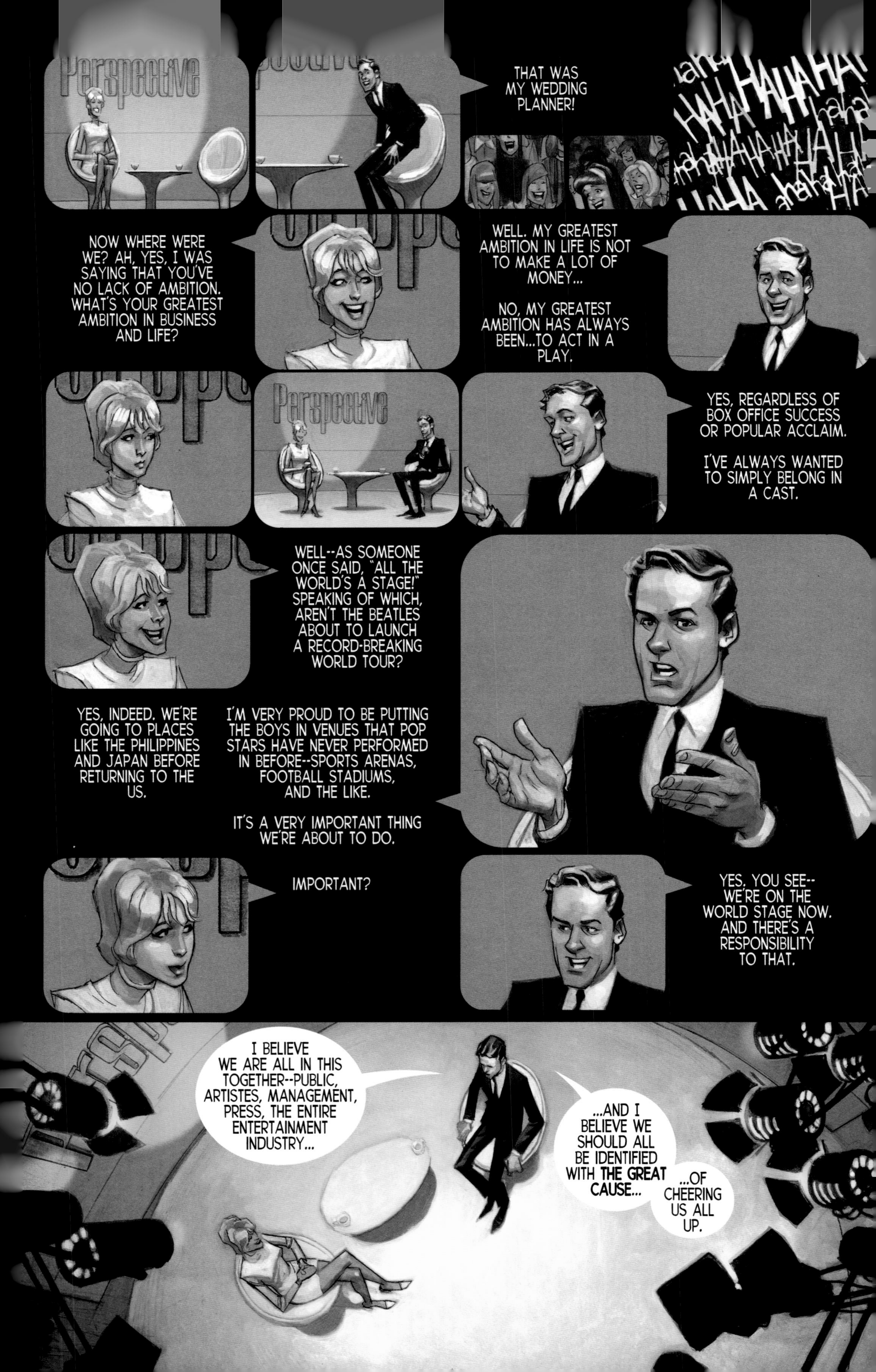

THAT WAS MY WEDDING PLANNER!
HAHAHA HAHAHA hahaha
NOW WHERE WERE WE? AH, YES, I WAS SAYING THAT YOU'VE NO LACK OF AMBITION. WHAT'S YOUR GREATEST AMBITION IN BUSINESS AND LIFE?
WELL. MY GREATEST AMBITION IN LIFE IS NOT TO MAKE A LOT OF MONEY...
NO, MY GREATEST AMBITION HAS ALWAYS BEEN...TO ACT IN A PLAY.
Perspective
YES, REGARDLESS OF BOX OFFICE SUCCESS OR POPULAR ACCLAIM.
I'VE ALWAYS WANTED TO SIMPLY BELONG IN A CAST.
WELL--AS SOMEONE ONCE SAID, "ALL THE WORLD'S A STAGE!" SPEAKING OF WHICH, AREN'T THE BEATLES ABOUT TO LAUNCH A RECORD-BREAKING WORLD TOUR?
YES, INDEED. WE'RE GOING TO PLACES LIKE THE PHILIPPINES AND JAPAN BEFORE RETURNING TO THE US.
I'M VERY PROUD TO BE PUTTING THE BOYS IN VENUES THAT POP STARS HAVE NEVER PERFORMED IN BEFORE--SPORTS ARENAS, FOOTBALL STADIUMS, AND THE LIKE.
IT'S A VERY IMPORTANT THING WE'RE ABOUT TO DO.
IMPORTANT?
YES, YOU SEE--WE'RE ON THE WORLD STAGE NOW. AND THERE'S A RESPONSIBILITY TO THAT.
I BELIEVE WE ARE ALL IN THIS TOGETHER--PUBLIC, ARTISTES, MANAGEMENT, PRESS, THE ENTIRE ENTERTAINMENT INDUSTRY...
...AND I BELIEVE WE SHOULD ALL BE IDENTIFIED WITH **THE GREAT CAUSE**...
...OF CHEERING US ALL UP.

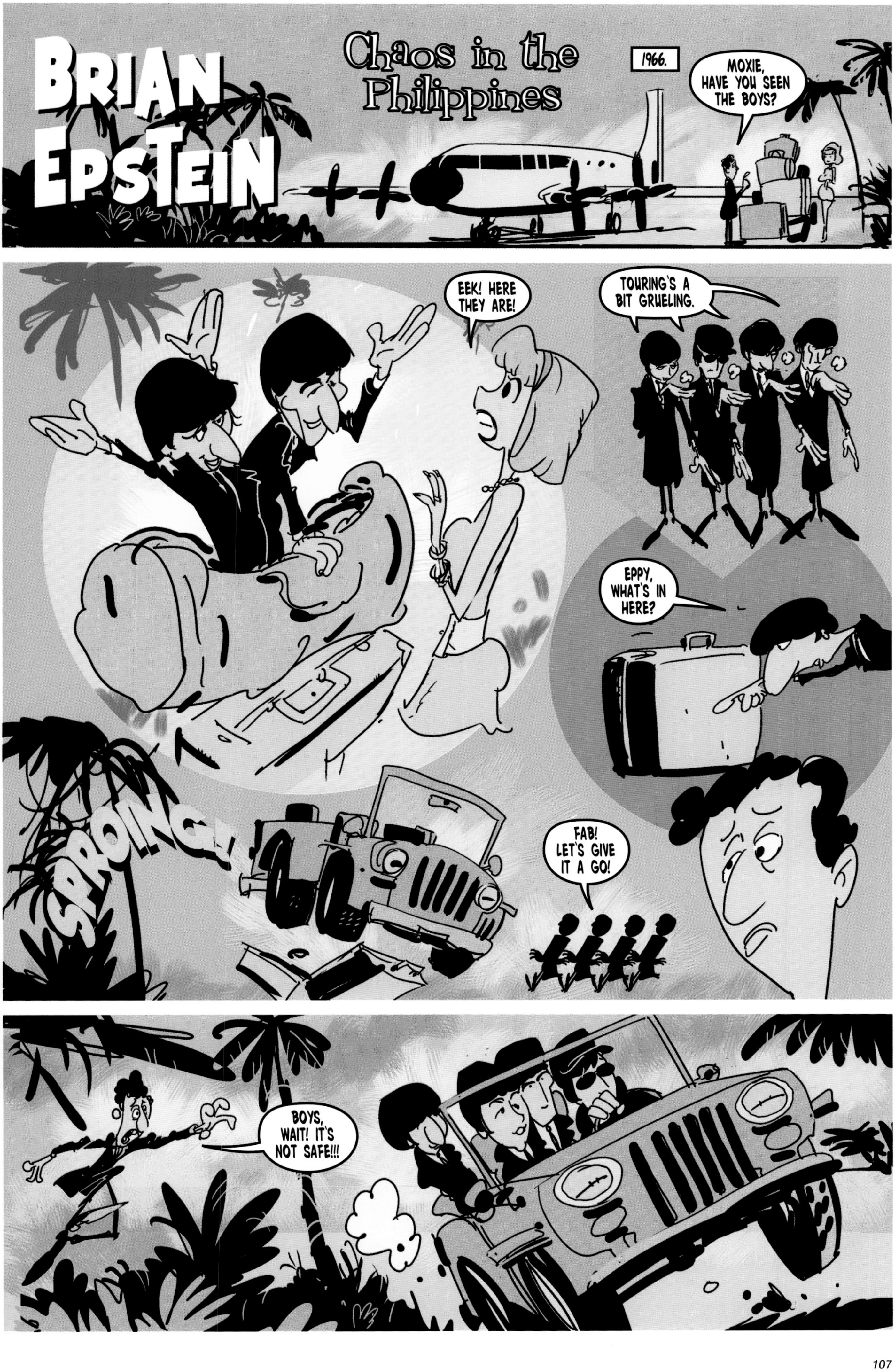
BRIAN EPSTEIN
Chaos in the Philippines
1966.
MOXIE, HAVE YOU SEEN THE BOYS?
EEK! HERE THEY ARE!
TOURING'S A BIT GRUELING.
EPPY, WHAT'S IN HERE?
SPROING!
FAB! LET'S GIVE IT A GO!
BOYS, WAIT! IT'S NOT SAFE!!!

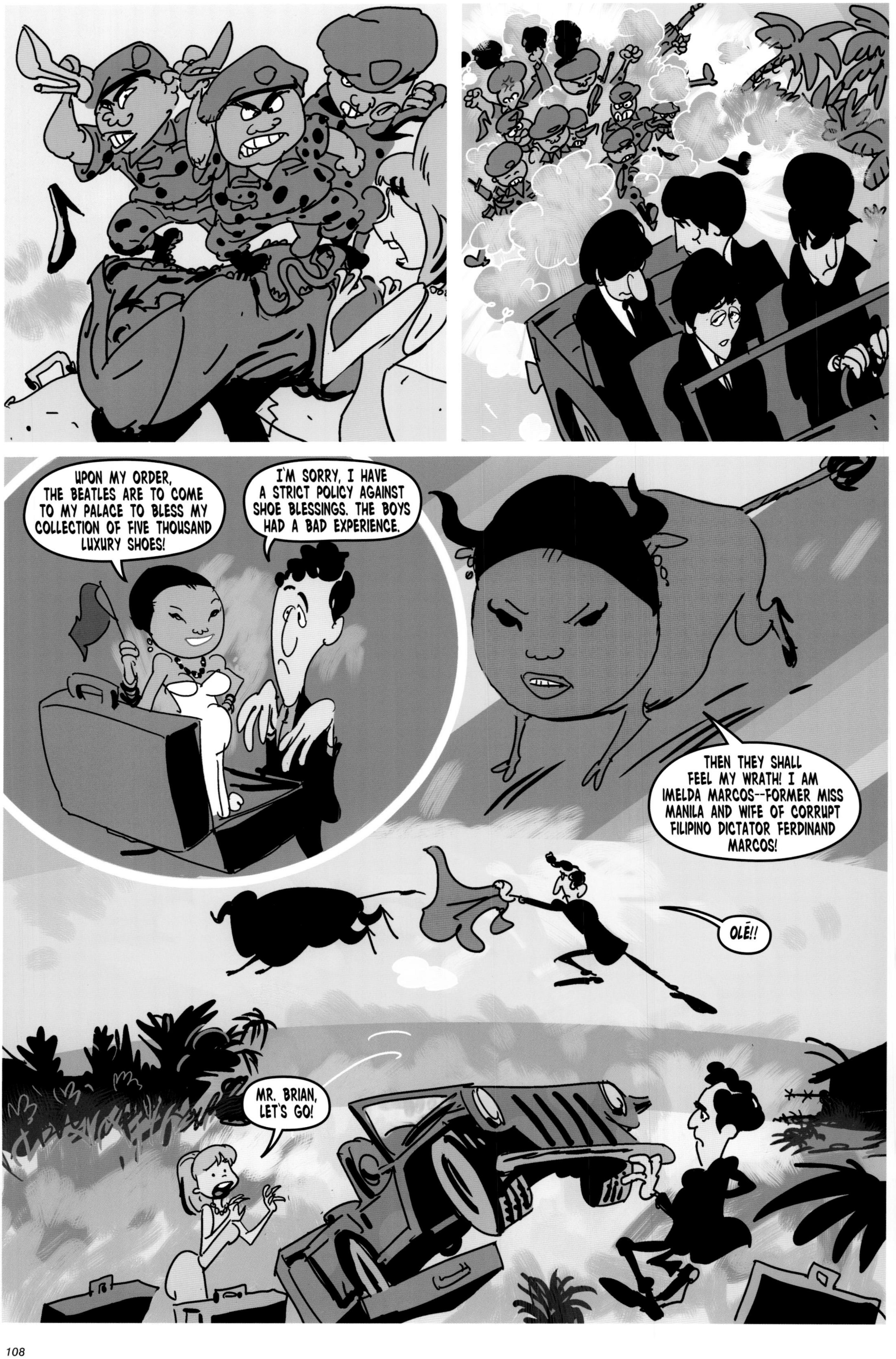
UPON MY ORDER, THE BEATLES ARE TO COME TO MY PALACE TO BLESS MY COLLECTION OF FIVE THOUSAND LUXURY SHOES!
I'M SORRY, I HAVE A STRICT POLICY AGAINST SHOE BLESSINGS. THE BOYS HAD A BAD EXPERIENCE.
THEN THEY SHALL FEEL MY WRATH! I AM IMELDA MARCOS--FORMER MISS MANILA AND WIFE OF CORRUPT FILIPINO DICTATOR FERDINAND MARCOS!
OLÉ!!
MR. BRIAN, LET'S GO!

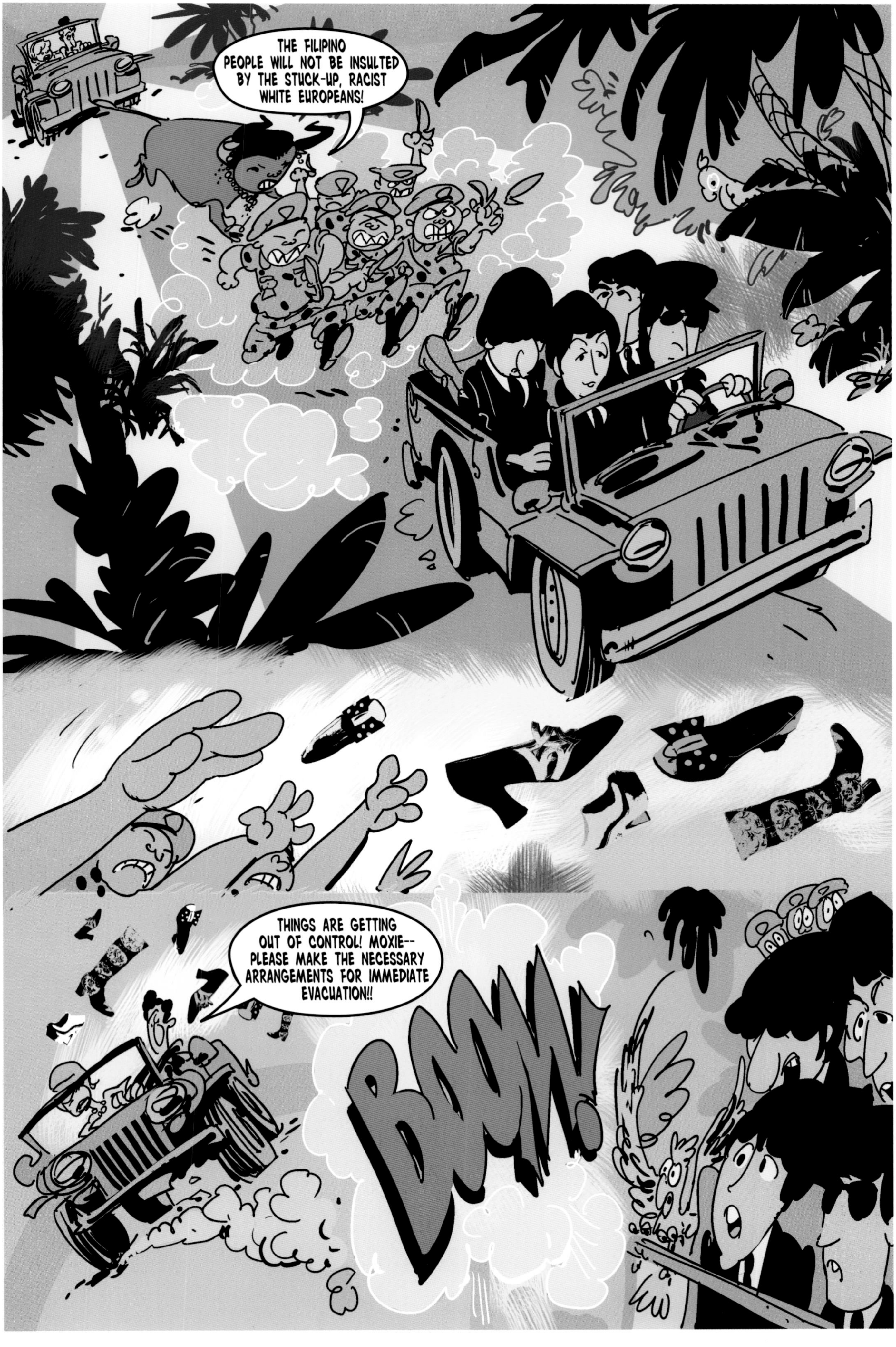
THE FILIPINO PEOPLE WILL NOT BE INSULTED BY THE STUCK-UP, RACIST WHITE EUROPEANS!
THINGS ARE GETTING OUT OF CONTROL! MOXIE-- PLEASE MAKE THE NECESSARY ARRANGEMENTS FOR IMMEDIATE EVACUATION!!
BOOM!

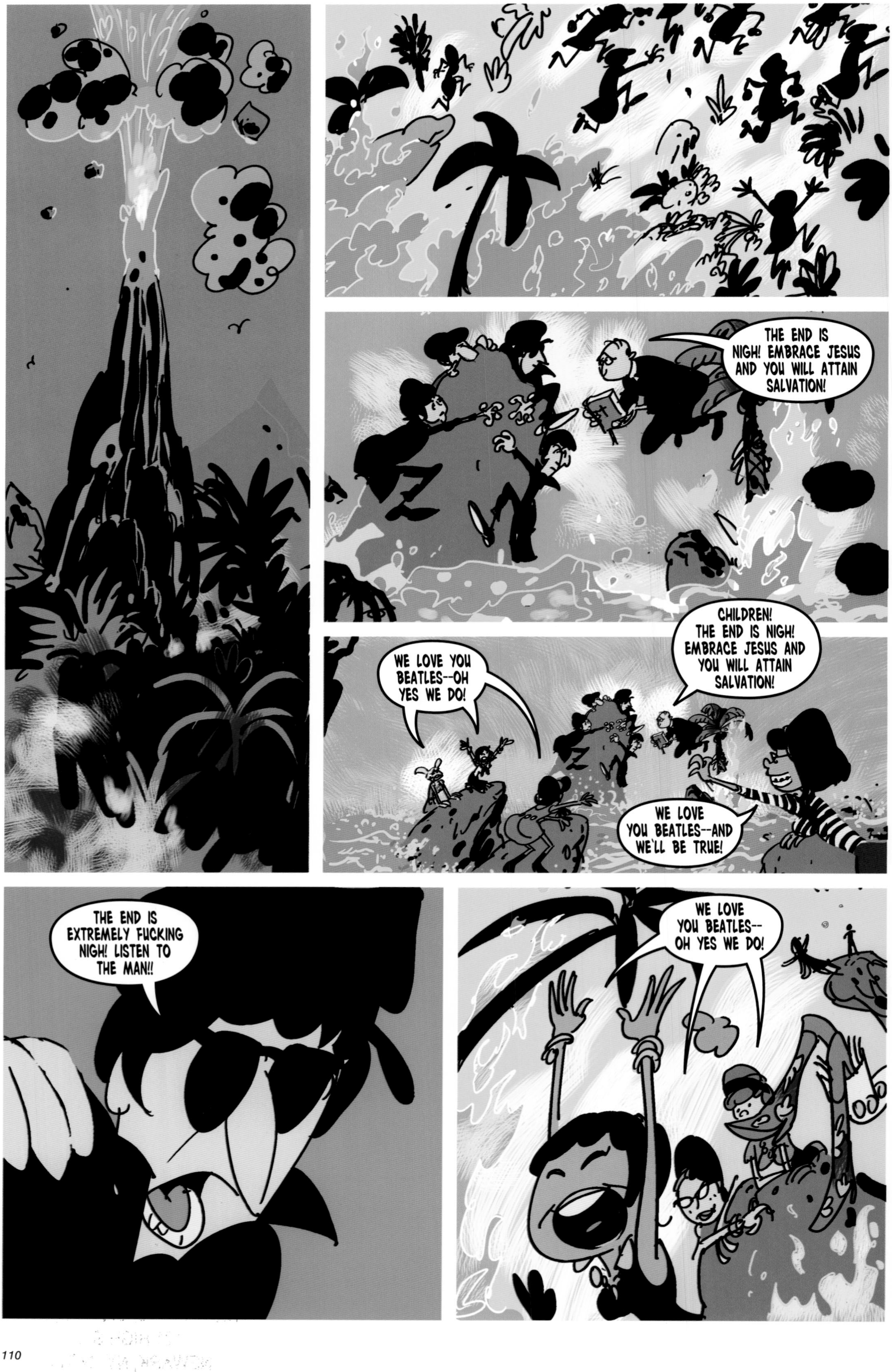
THE END IS NIGH! EMBRACE JESUS AND YOU WILL ATTAIN SALVATION!
CHILDREN! THE END IS NIGH! EMBRACE JESUS AND YOU WILL ATTAIN SALVATION!
WE LOVE YOU BEATLES--OH YES WE DO!
WE LOVE YOU BEATLES--AND WE'LL BE TRUE!
THE END IS EXTREMELY FUCKING NIGH! LISTEN TO THE MAN!!
WE LOVE YOU BEATLES--OH YES WE DO!

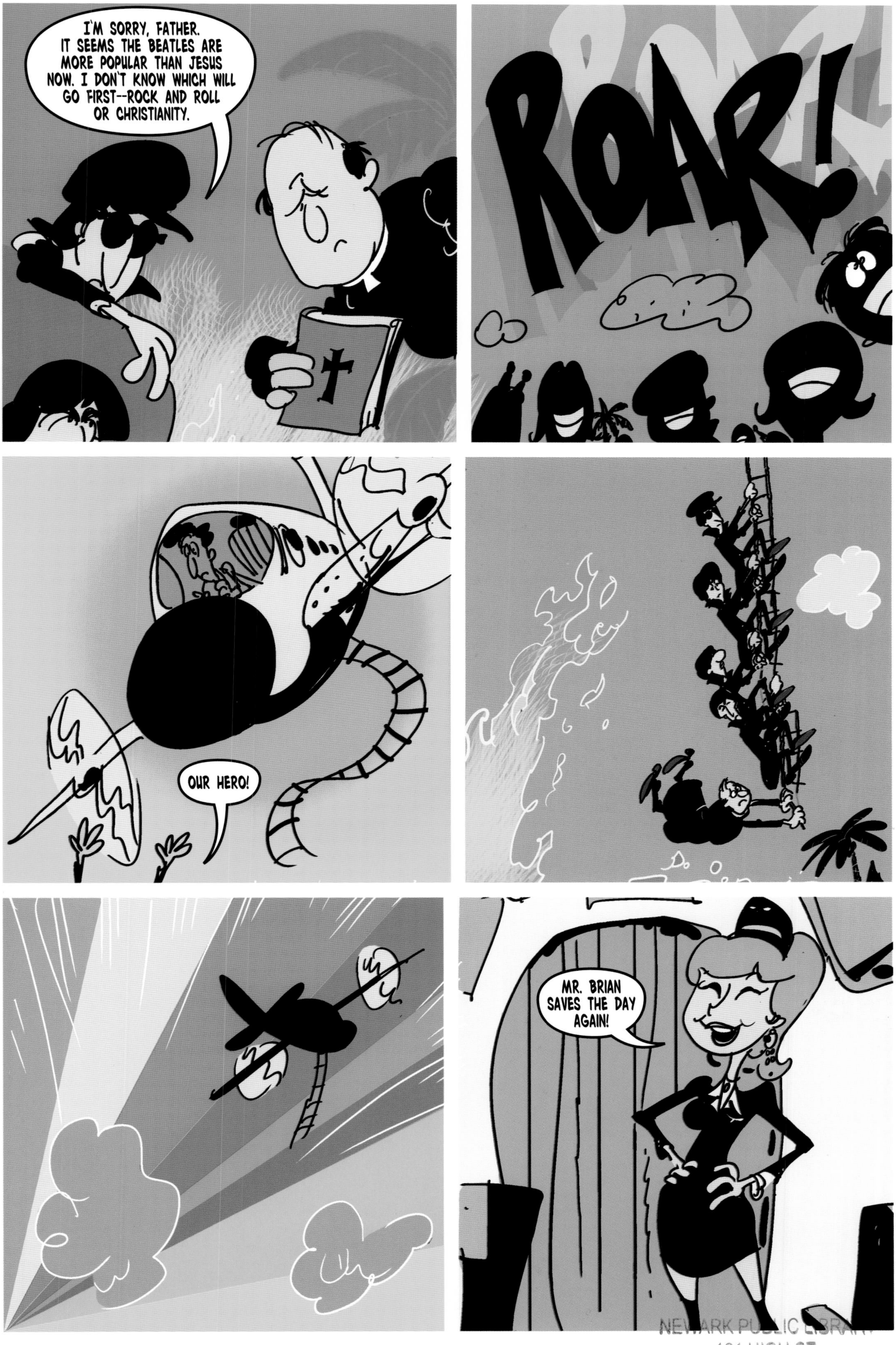
I'M SORRY, FATHER. IT SEEMS THE BEATLES ARE MORE POPULAR THAN JESUS NOW. I DON'T KNOW WHICH WILL GO FIRST--ROCK AND ROLL OR CHRISTIANITY.
ROAR!
OUR HERO!
MR. BRIAN SAVES THE DAY AGAIN!

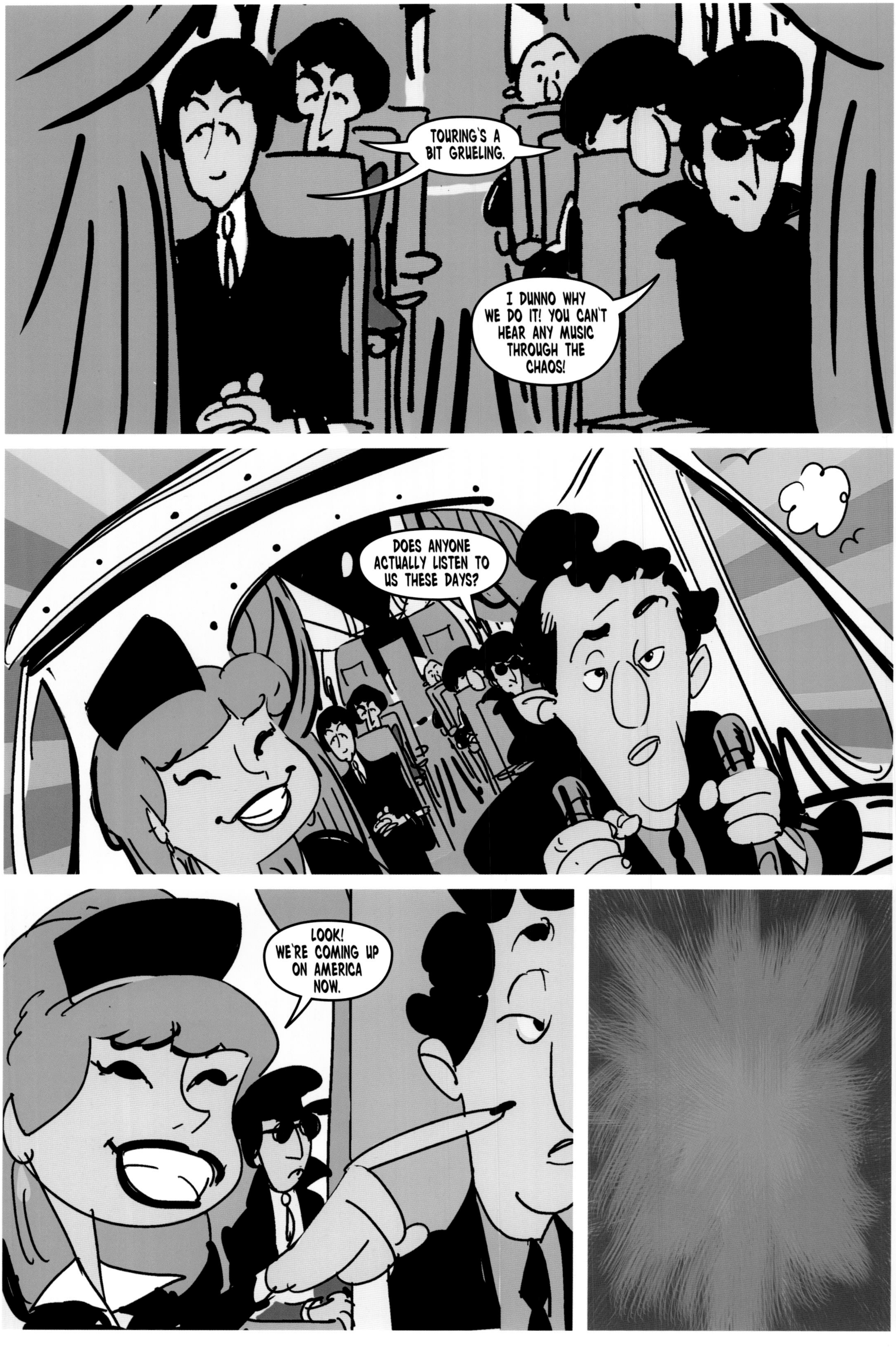
TOURING'S A BIT GRUELING.
I DUNNO WHY WE DO IT! YOU CAN'T HEAR ANY MUSIC THROUGH THE CHAOS!
DOES ANYONE ACTUALLY LISTEN TO US THESE DAYS?
LOOK! WE'RE COMING UP ON AMERICA NOW.

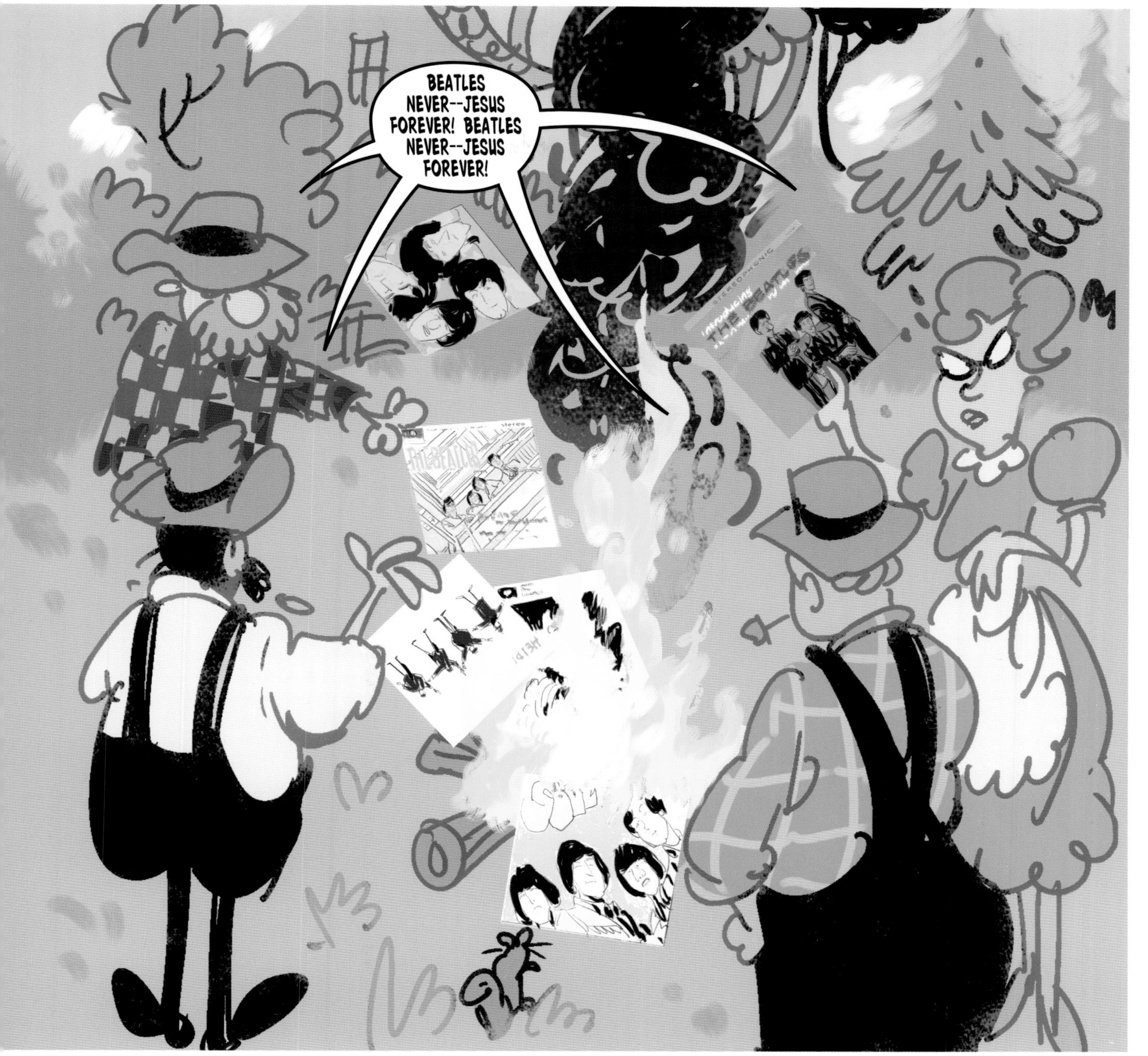
BEATLES NEVER--JESUS FOREVER! BEATLES NEVER--JESUS FOREVER!

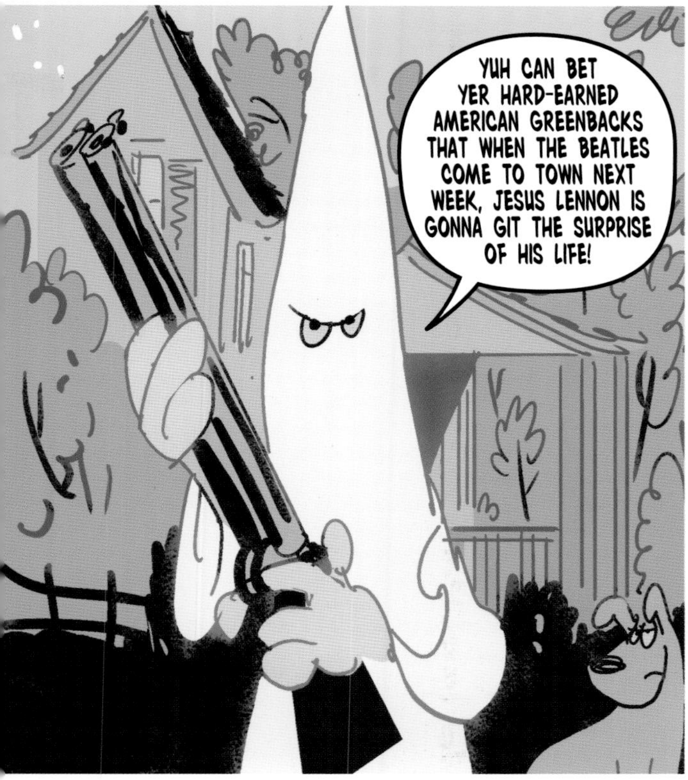
YUH CAN BET YER HARD-EARNED AMERICAN GREENBACKS THAT WHEN THE BEATLES COME TO TOWN NEXT WEEK, JESUS LENNON IS GONNA GIT THE SURPRISE OF HIS LIFE!

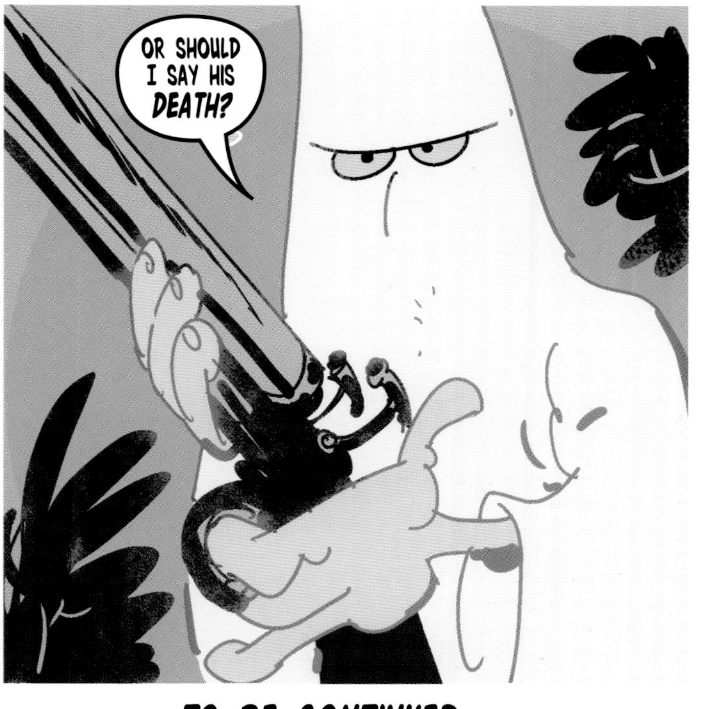
OR SHOULD I SAY HIS *DEATH?*

TO BE CONTINUED...

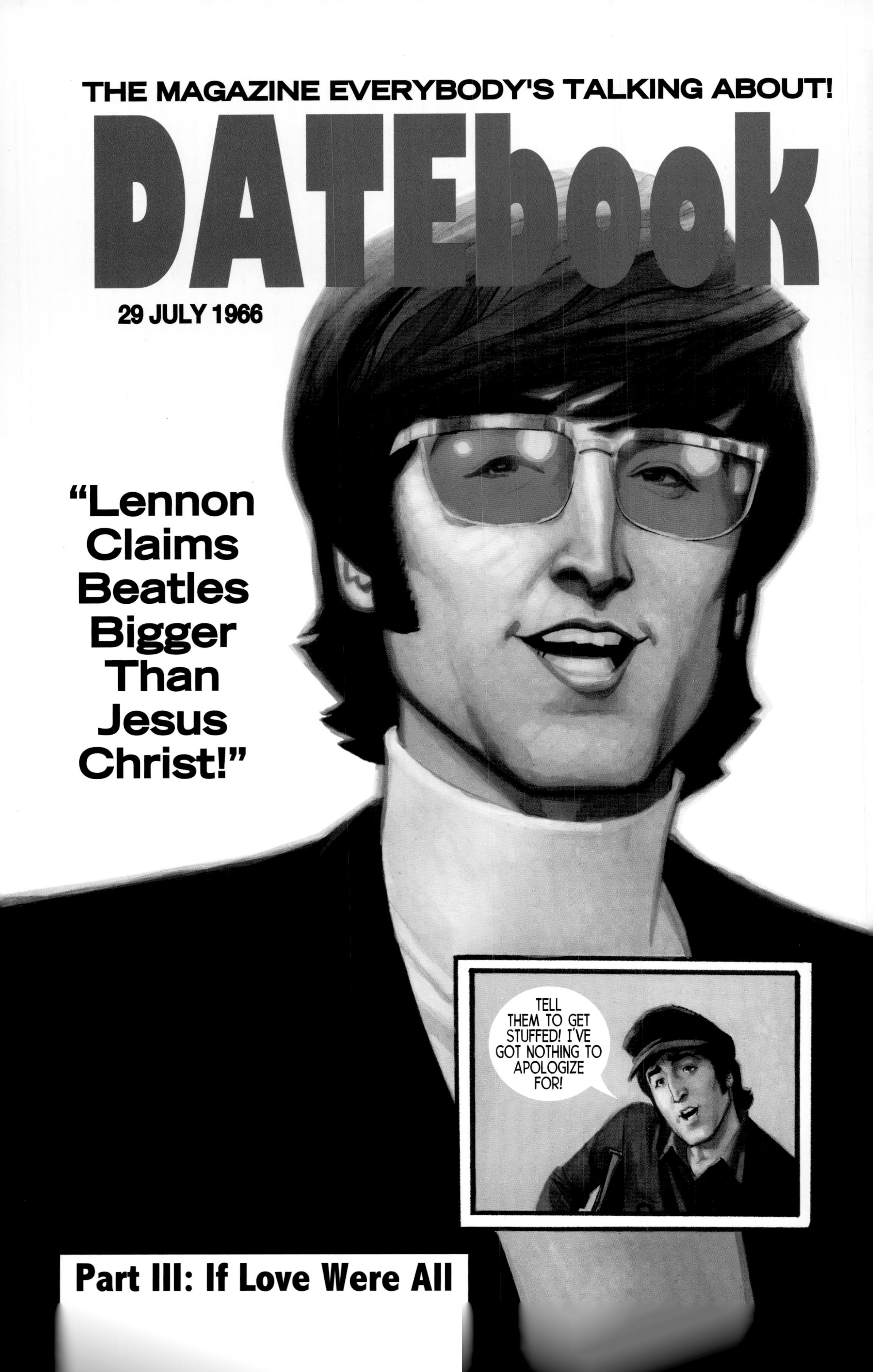
THE MAGAZINE EVERYBODY'S TALKING ABOUT!
DATEbook
29 JULY 1966
"Lennon Claims Beatles Bigger Than Jesus Christ!"
TELL THEM TO GET STUFFED! I'VE GOT NOTHING TO APOLOGIZE FOR!
Part III: If Love Were All

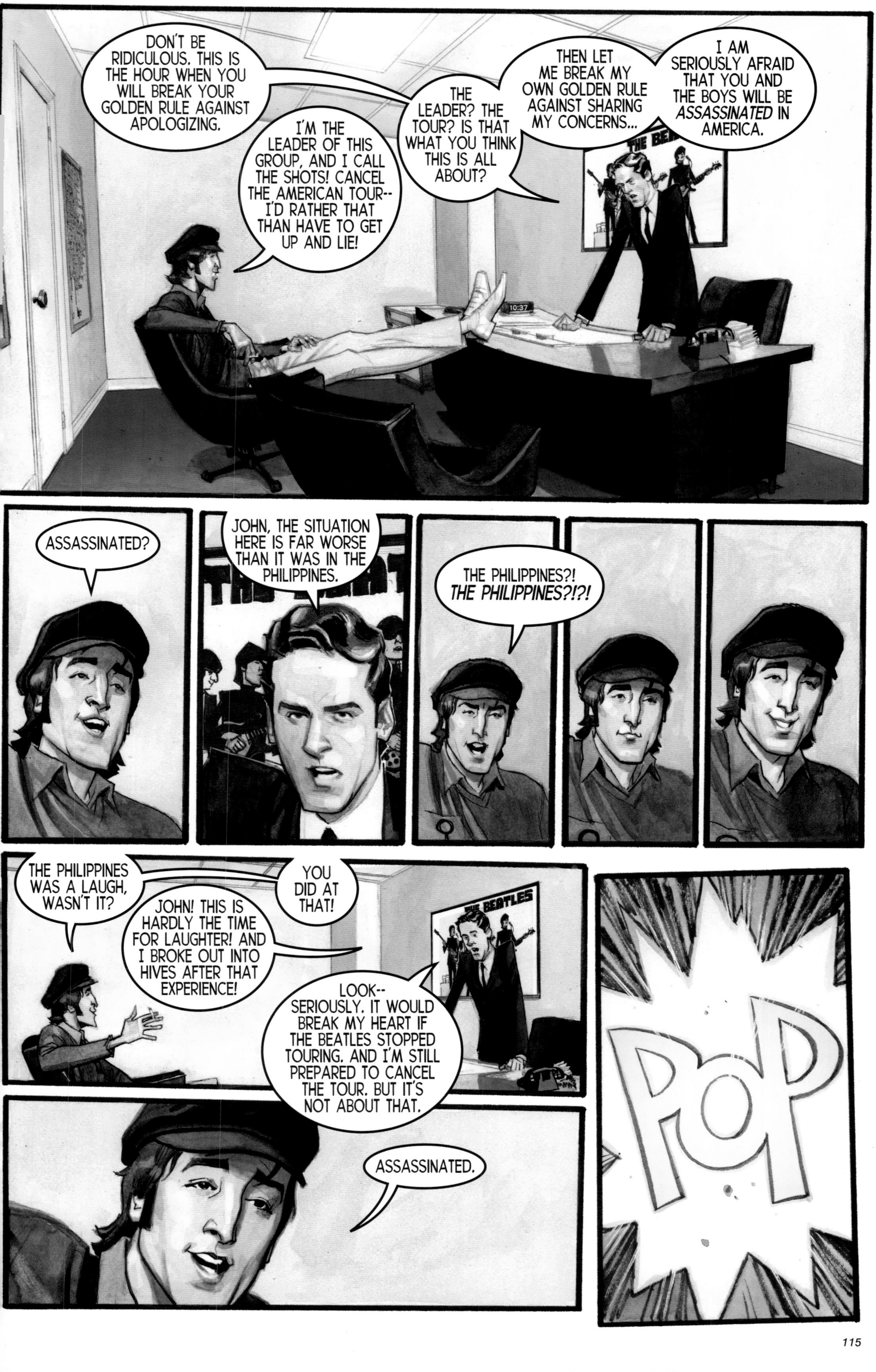
DON'T BE RIDICULOUS. THIS IS THE HOUR WHEN YOU WILL BREAK YOUR GOLDEN RULE AGAINST APOLOGIZING.
I'M THE LEADER OF THIS GROUP, AND I CALL THE SHOTS! CANCEL THE AMERICAN TOUR--I'D RATHER THAT THAN HAVE TO GET UP AND LIE!
THE LEADER? THE TOUR? IS THAT WHAT YOU THINK THIS IS ALL ABOUT?
THEN LET ME BREAK MY OWN GOLDEN RULE AGAINST SHARING MY CONCERNS...
I AM SERIOUSLY AFRAID THAT YOU AND THE BOYS WILL BE *ASSASSINATED* IN AMERICA.
10:37
ASSASSINATED?
JOHN, THE SITUATION HERE IS FAR WORSE THAN IT WAS IN THE PHILIPPINES.
THE PHILIPPINES?! *THE PHILIPPINES?!?!*
THE PHILIPPINES WAS A LAUGH, WASN'T IT?
YOU DID AT THAT!
JOHN! THIS IS HARDLY THE TIME FOR LAUGHTER! AND I BROKE OUT INTO HIVES AFTER THAT EXPERIENCE!
THE BEATLES
LOOK-- SERIOUSLY. IT WOULD BREAK MY HEART IF THE BEATLES STOPPED TOURING. AND I'M STILL PREPARED TO CANCEL THE TOUR. BUT IT'S NOT ABOUT THAT.
ASSASSINATED.
POP

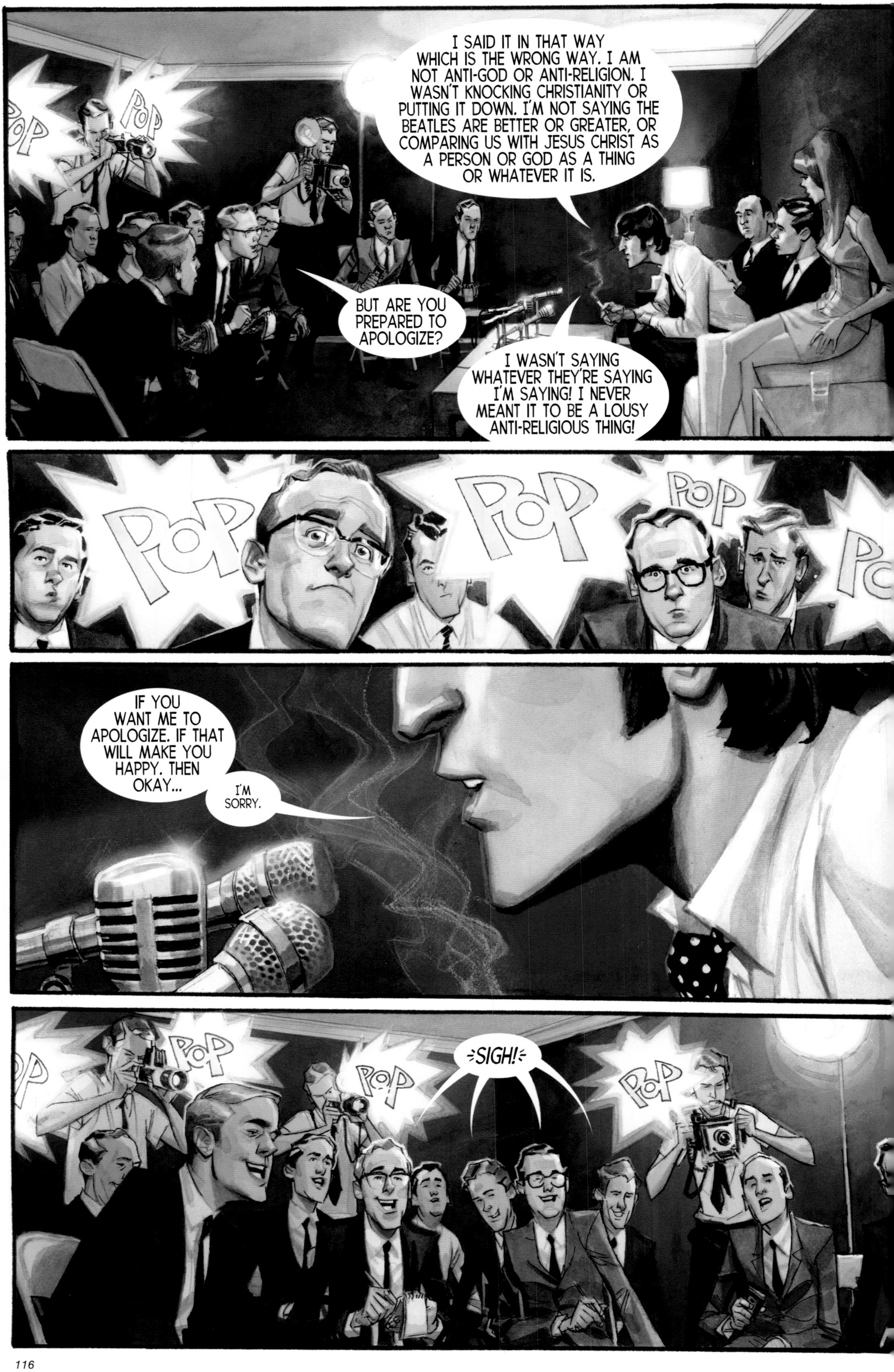
POP
POP
I SAID IT IN THAT WAY WHICH IS THE WRONG WAY. I AM NOT ANTI-GOD OR ANTI-RELIGION. I WASN'T KNOCKING CHRISTIANITY OR PUTTING IT DOWN. I'M NOT SAYING THE BEATLES ARE BETTER OR GREATER, OR COMPARING US WITH JESUS CHRIST AS A PERSON OR GOD AS A THING OR WHATEVER IT IS.
BUT ARE YOU PREPARED TO APOLOGIZE?
I WASN'T SAYING WHATEVER THEY'RE SAYING I'M SAYING! I NEVER MEANT IT TO BE A LOUSY ANTI-RELIGIOUS THING!
POP
POP
POP
IF YOU WANT ME TO APOLOGIZE. IF THAT WILL MAKE YOU HAPPY. THEN OKAY...
I'M SORRY.
POP
POP
SIGH!
POP

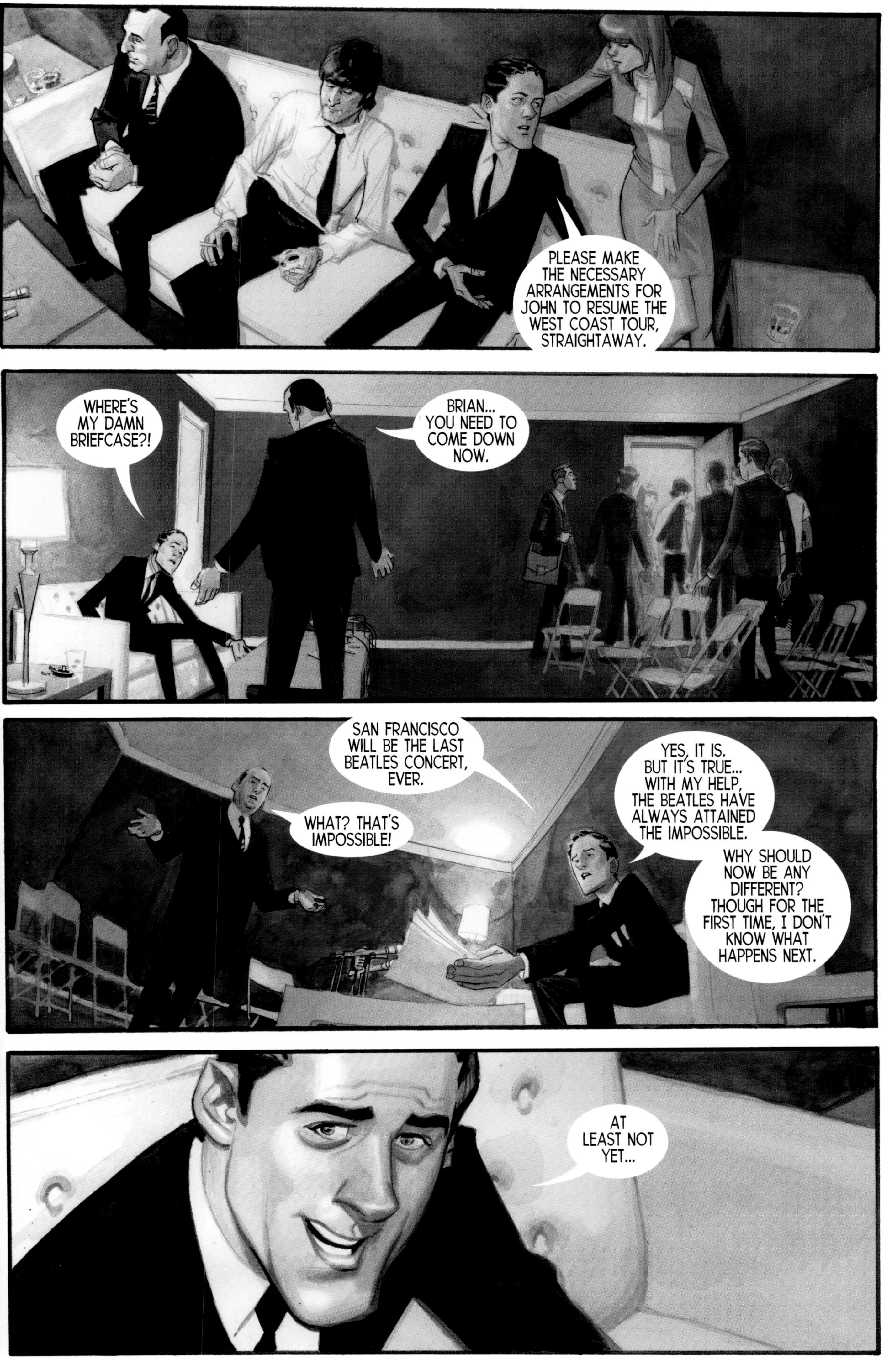
PLEASE MAKE THE NECESSARY ARRANGEMENTS FOR JOHN TO RESUME THE WEST COAST TOUR, STRAIGHTAWAY.
WHERE'S MY DAMN BRIEFCASE?!
BRIAN... YOU NEED TO COME DOWN NOW.
SAN FRANCISCO WILL BE THE LAST BEATLES CONCERT, EVER.
WHAT? THAT'S IMPOSSIBLE!
YES, IT IS. BUT IT'S TRUE... WITH MY HELP, THE BEATLES HAVE ALWAYS ATTAINED THE IMPOSSIBLE.
WHY SHOULD NOW BE ANY DIFFERENT? THOUGH FOR THE FIRST TIME, I DON'T KNOW WHAT HAPPENS NEXT.
AT LEAST NOT YET...

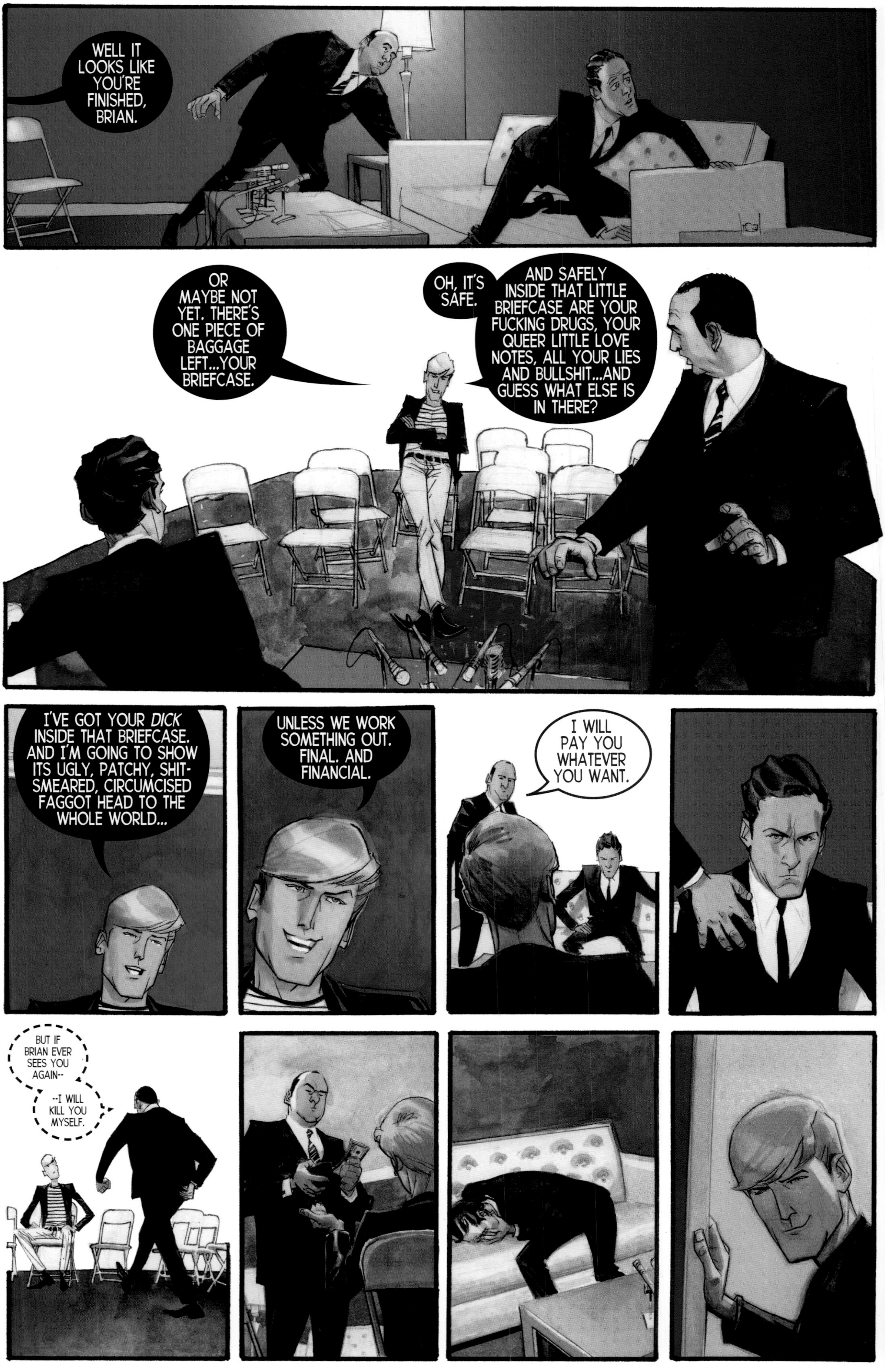
WELL IT LOOKS LIKE YOU'RE FINISHED, BRIAN.
OR MAYBE NOT YET. THERE'S ONE PIECE OF BAGGAGE LEFT...YOUR BRIEFCASE.
OH, IT'S SAFE.
AND SAFELY INSIDE THAT LITTLE BRIEFCASE ARE YOUR FUCKING DRUGS, YOUR QUEER LITTLE LOVE NOTES, ALL YOUR LIES AND BULLSHIT...AND GUESS WHAT ELSE IS IN THERE?
I'VE GOT YOUR *DICK* INSIDE THAT BRIEFCASE. AND I'M GOING TO SHOW ITS UGLY, PATCHY, SHIT-SMEARED, CIRCUMCISED FAGGOT HEAD TO THE WHOLE WORLD...
UNLESS WE WORK SOMETHING OUT. FINAL. AND FINANCIAL.
I WILL PAY YOU WHATEVER YOU WANT.
BUT IF BRIAN EVER SEES YOU AGAIN--
--I WILL KILL YOU MYSELF.

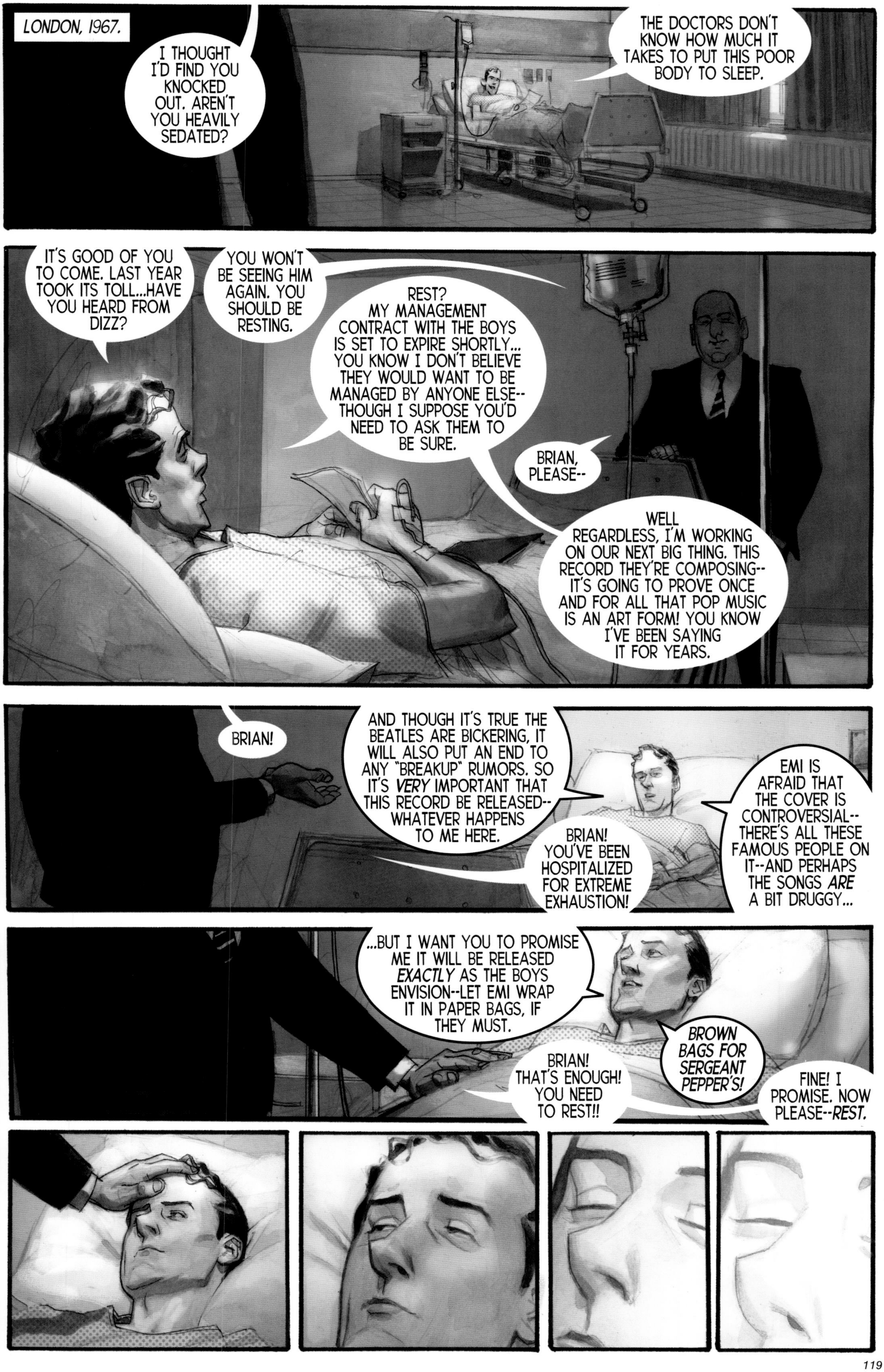
LONDON, 1967.
I THOUGHT I'D FIND YOU KNOCKED OUT. AREN'T YOU HEAVILY SEDATED?
THE DOCTORS DON'T KNOW HOW MUCH IT TAKES TO PUT THIS POOR BODY TO SLEEP.
IT'S GOOD OF YOU TO COME. LAST YEAR TOOK ITS TOLL...HAVE YOU HEARD FROM DIZZ?
YOU WON'T BE SEEING HIM AGAIN. YOU SHOULD BE RESTING.
REST? MY MANAGEMENT CONTRACT WITH THE BOYS IS SET TO EXPIRE SHORTLY... YOU KNOW I DON'T BELIEVE THEY WOULD WANT TO BE MANAGED BY ANYONE ELSE-- THOUGH I SUPPOSE YOU'D NEED TO ASK THEM TO BE SURE.
BRIAN, PLEASE--
WELL REGARDLESS, I'M WORKING ON OUR NEXT BIG THING. THIS RECORD THEY'RE COMPOSING-- IT'S GOING TO PROVE ONCE AND FOR ALL THAT POP MUSIC IS AN ART FORM! YOU KNOW I'VE BEEN SAYING IT FOR YEARS.
BRIAN!
AND THOUGH IT'S TRUE THE BEATLES ARE BICKERING, IT WILL ALSO PUT AN END TO ANY "BREAKUP" RUMORS. SO IT'S *VERY* IMPORTANT THAT THIS RECORD BE RELEASED-- WHATEVER HAPPENS TO ME HERE.
BRIAN! YOU'VE BEEN HOSPITALIZED FOR EXTREME EXHAUSTION!
EMI IS AFRAID THAT THE COVER IS CONTROVERSIAL-- THERE'S ALL THESE FAMOUS PEOPLE ON IT--AND PERHAPS THE SONGS *ARE* A BIT DRUGGY...
...BUT I WANT YOU TO PROMISE ME IT WILL BE RELEASED *EXACTLY* AS THE BOYS ENVISION--LET EMI WRAP IT IN PAPER BAGS, IF THEY MUST.
BROWN BAGS FOR SERGEANT PEPPER'S!
BRIAN! THAT'S ENOUGH! YOU NEED TO REST!!
FINE! I PROMISE. NOW PLEASE--*REST.*

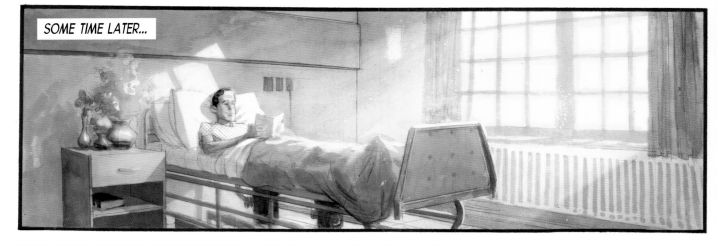

SOME TIME LATER...

"I'M SORRY WE HAVEN'T BEEN ROUND MORE THESE PAST FEW MONTHS, BUT YOU KNOW I LOVE YOU, EPPY, I REALLY DO. —JOHN"

EPPY! IT'S DONE! AND IT'S PERFECT.

IT'S NOT PERFECT AT ALL. BUT IT IS BRILLIANT.

NONSENSE. IT'S PERFECT.

WHATEVER YOU SAY, SIR PAUL.

ENOUGH! KNOWING YOU TWO, IT'S BOTH PERFECT *AND* BRILLIANT. AND IT CALLS FOR CELEBRATION. WE MUST THROW A PRESS EVENT AND A RELEASE PARTY IMMEDIATELY!

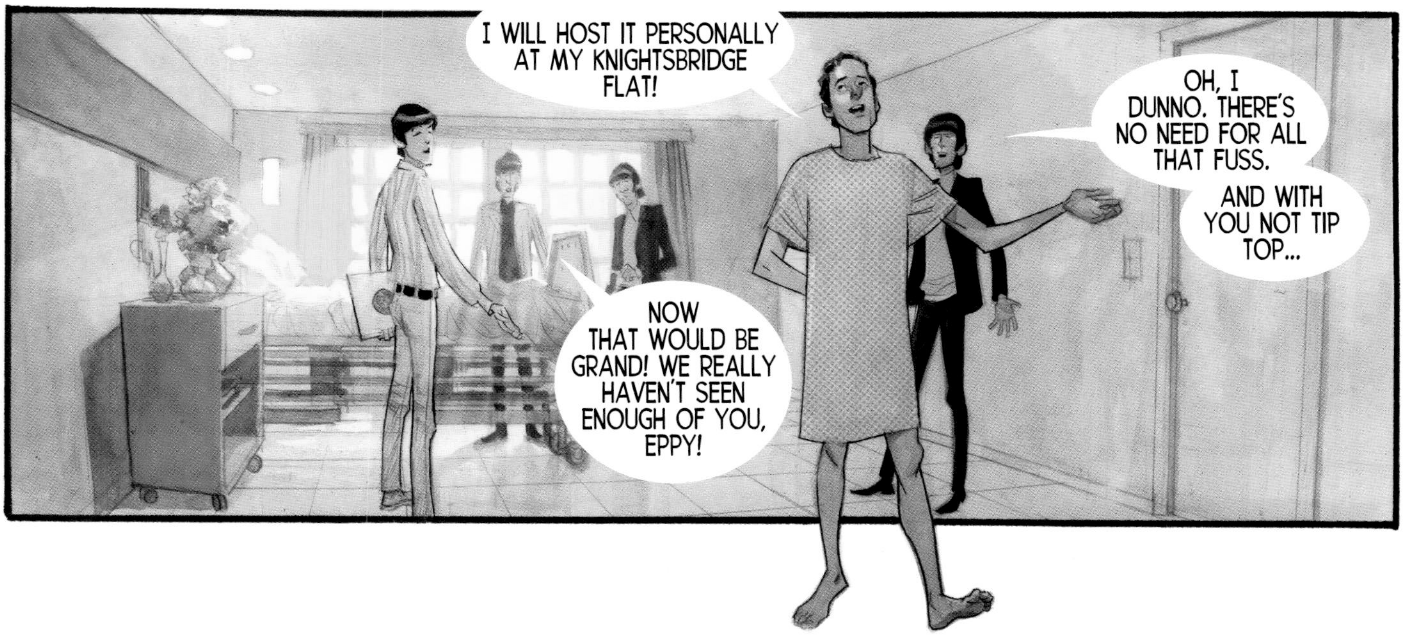
I WILL HOST IT PERSONALLY AT MY KNIGHTSBRIDGE FLAT!
OH, I DUNNO. THERE'S NO NEED FOR ALL THAT FUSS.
AND WITH YOU NOT TIP TOP...
NOW THAT WOULD BE GRAND! WE REALLY HAVEN'T SEEN ENOUGH OF YOU, EPPY!

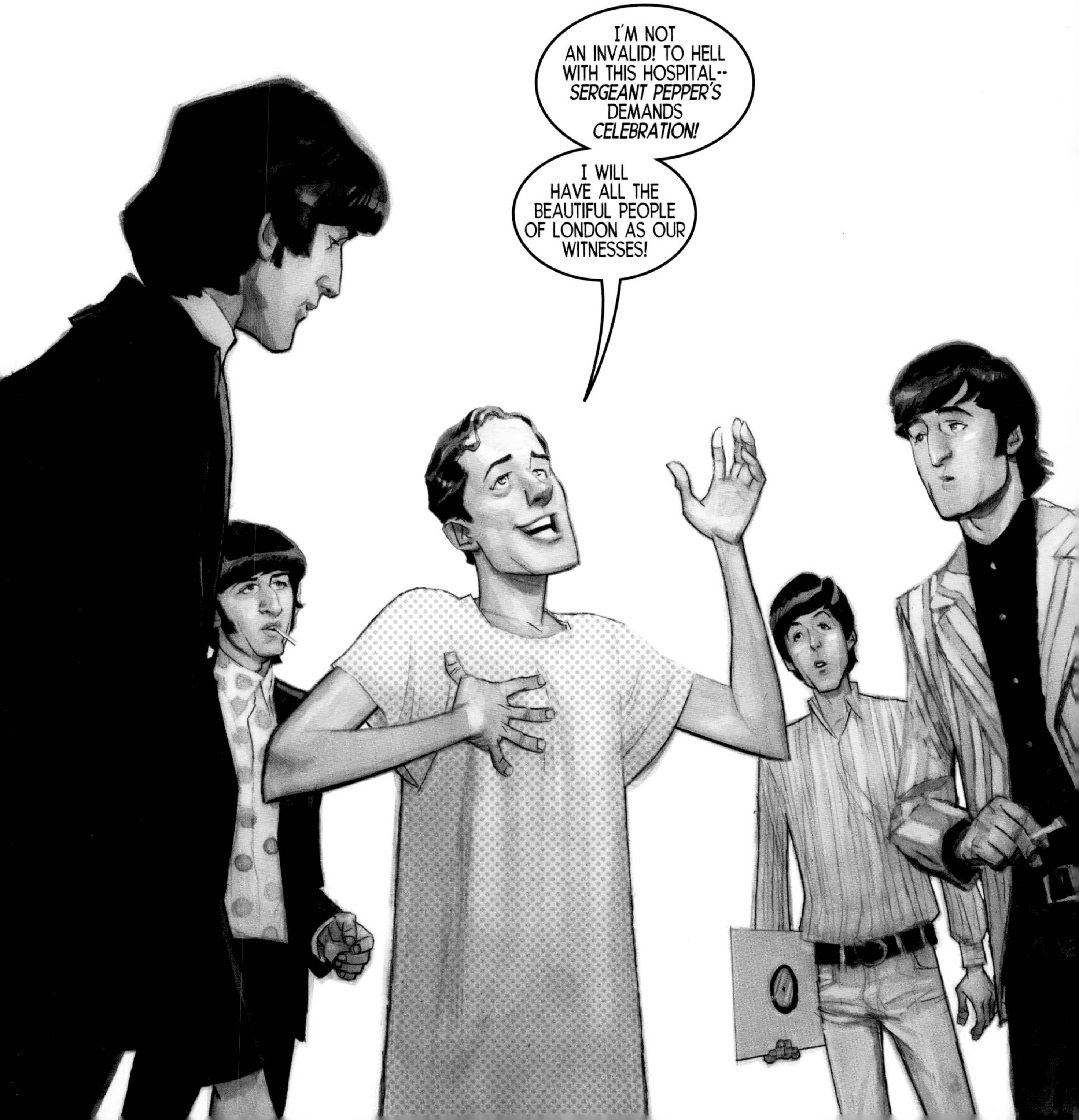
I'M NOT AN INVALID! TO HELL WITH THIS HOSPITAL-- *SERGEANT PEPPER'S* DEMANDS *CELEBRATION!*
I WILL HAVE ALL THE BEAUTIFUL PEOPLE OF LONDON AS OUR WITNESSES!

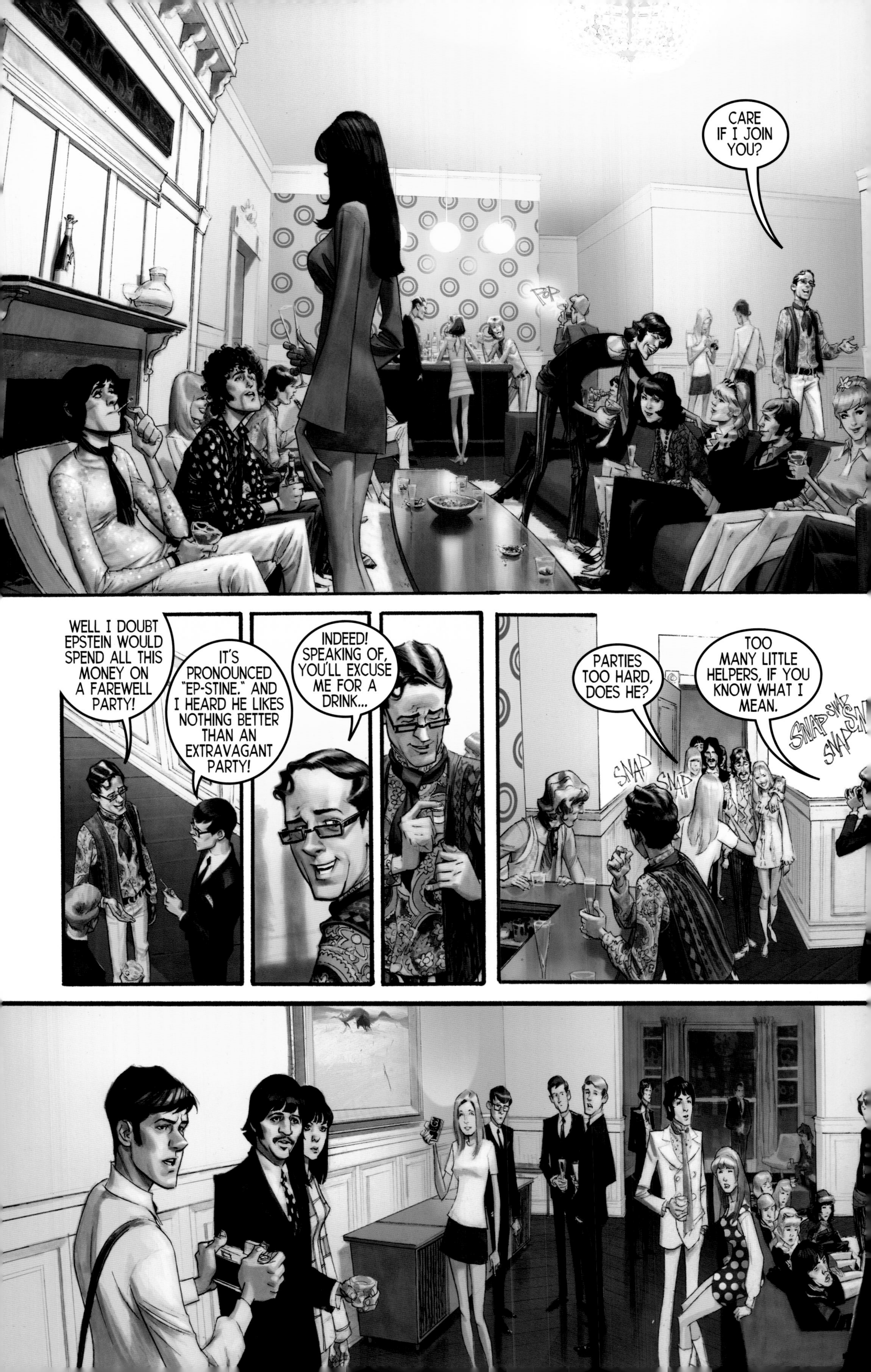
CARE IF I JOIN YOU?
POP
WELL I DOUBT EPSTEIN WOULD SPEND ALL THIS MONEY ON A FAREWELL PARTY!
IT'S PRONOUNCED "EP-STINE." AND I HEARD HE LIKES NOTHING BETTER THAN AN EXTRAVAGANT PARTY!
INDEED! SPEAKING OF, YOU'LL EXCUSE ME FOR A DRINK...
PARTIES TOO HARD, DOES HE?
TOO MANY LITTLE HELPERS, IF YOU KNOW WHAT I MEAN.
SNAP
SNAP

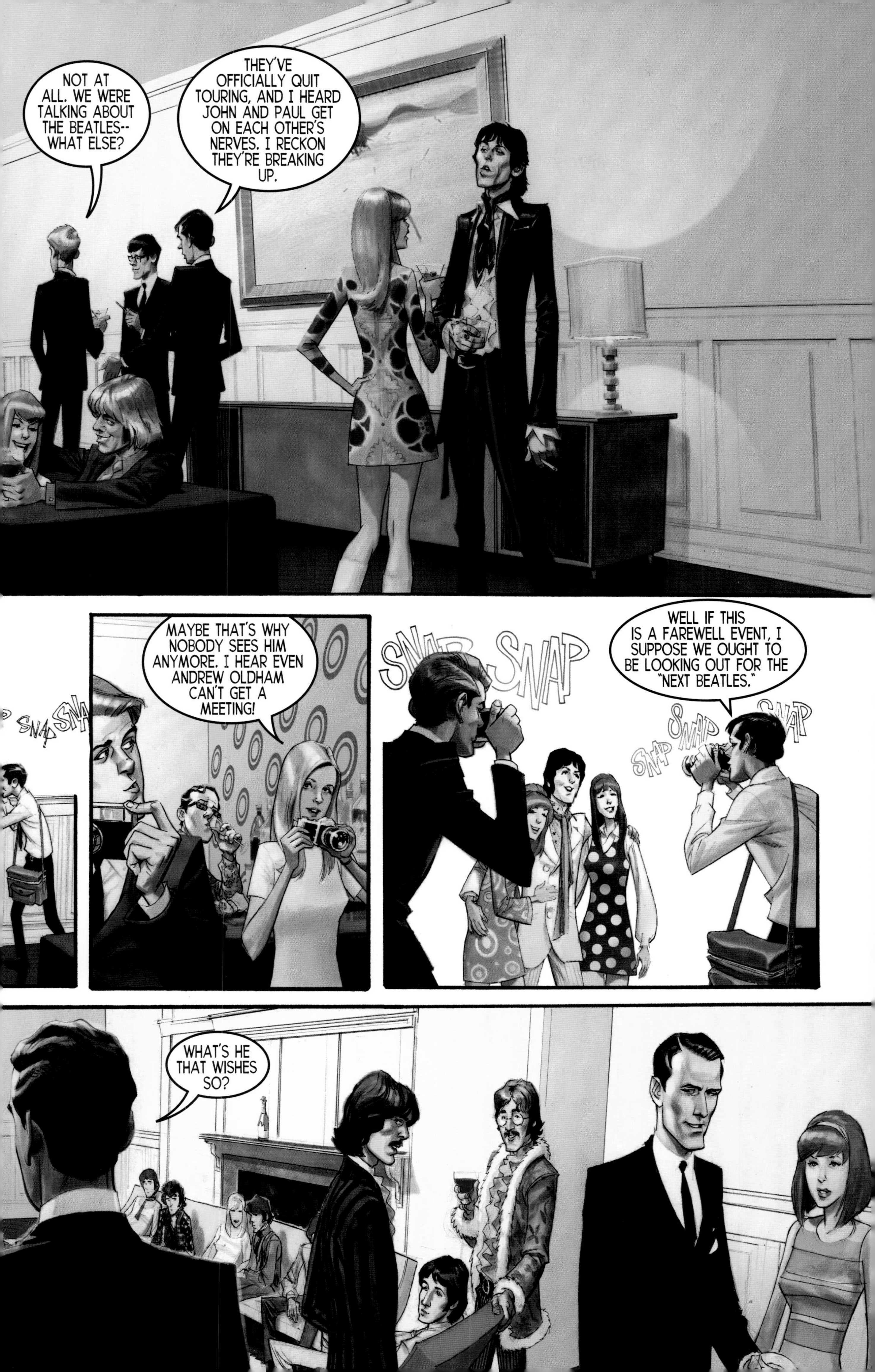

NOT AT ALL. WE WERE TALKING ABOUT THE BEATLES-- WHAT ELSE?
THEY'VE OFFICIALLY QUIT TOURING, AND I HEARD JOHN AND PAUL GET ON EACH OTHER'S NERVES. I RECKON THEY'RE BREAKING UP.
SNAP SNAP
MAYBE THAT'S WHY NOBODY SEES HIM ANYMORE. I HEAR EVEN ANDREW OLDHAM CAN'T GET A MEETING!
SNAP SNAP
WELL IF THIS IS A FAREWELL EVENT, I SUPPOSE WE OUGHT TO BE LOOKING OUT FOR THE "NEXT BEATLES."
SNAP SNAP SNAP
WHAT'S HE THAT WISHES SO?

For if I am mark'd to die, the Beatles have done enough to do our country loss; and if to live, the fewer Beatles, the greater share of honor! God's will, I pray thee not wish for one Beatles more. Though welcome Rolling Stones.
Being for the benefit of all uptight, there will be a new Beatles record released tonight!
And he that drops this day will stand a' trip-toes and rouse him at the title of **Sergeant Pepper's**!
He will yearly on the vigil feast his children and their children, and say, "'Twas twenty years ago today." And he'll remember with advantages what new sounds he heard that day.
This record shall the good man play his son; and this decade shall ne'er go by, from this day to the ending of the world, but we in it shall be remembered...
We few, we happy few, we Lonely Hearts Club Band of Brothers.
For he today that listens with me shall be our brother; be he ne'er so vile, a Summer of Love shall gentle his condition; and those too young and still unborn shall think themselves accursed they were not here; upon the day that **Sergeant Pepper's Lonely Hearts Club Band** be released!

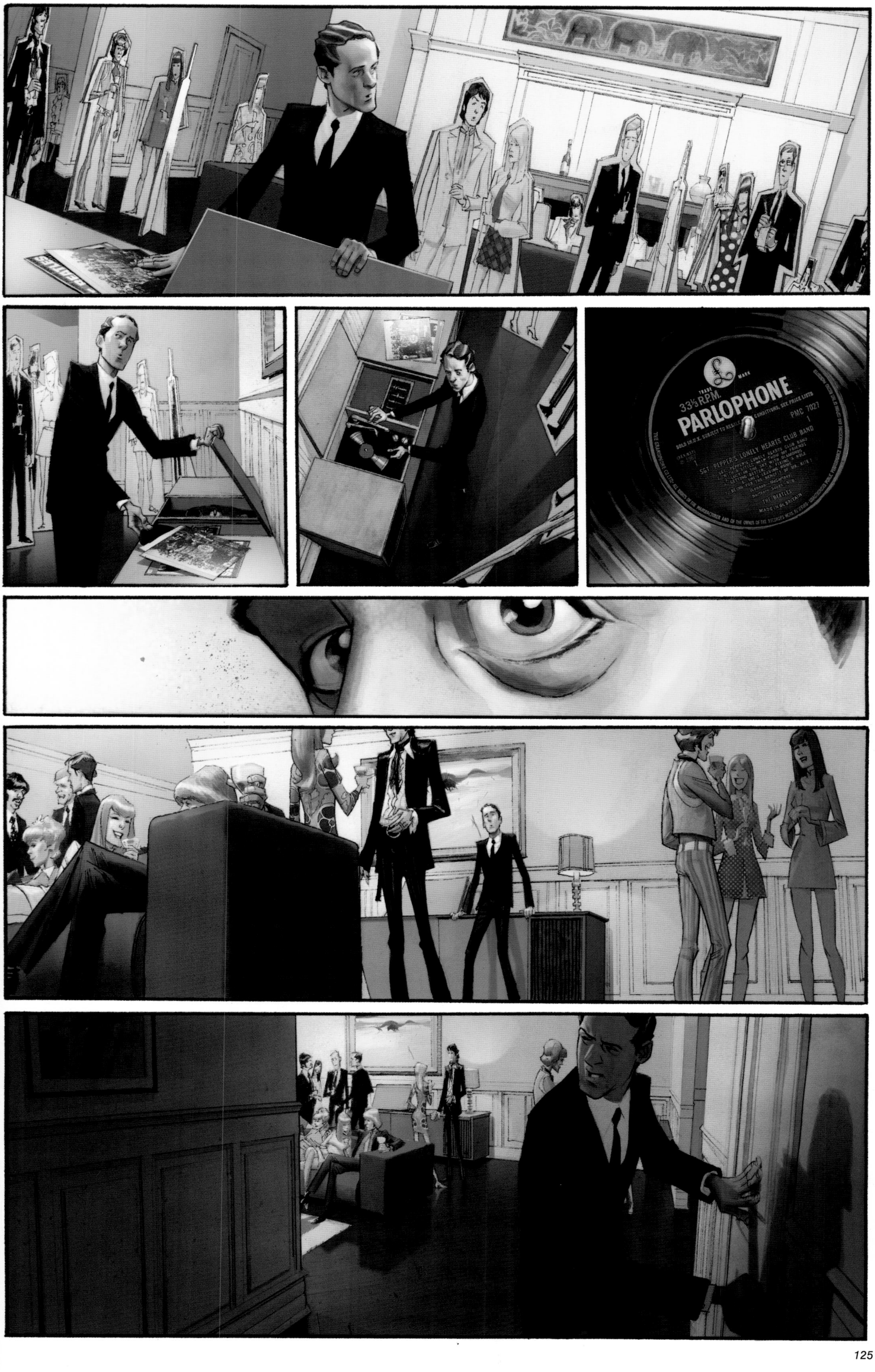
TRADE MARK
33⅓ R.P.M.
PARLOPHONE
CONDITIONS, SEE PRICE LISTS
PMC 7027
1
SGT. PEPPER'S LONELY HEARTS CLUB BAND
THE BEATLES
MADE IN GT. BRITAIN

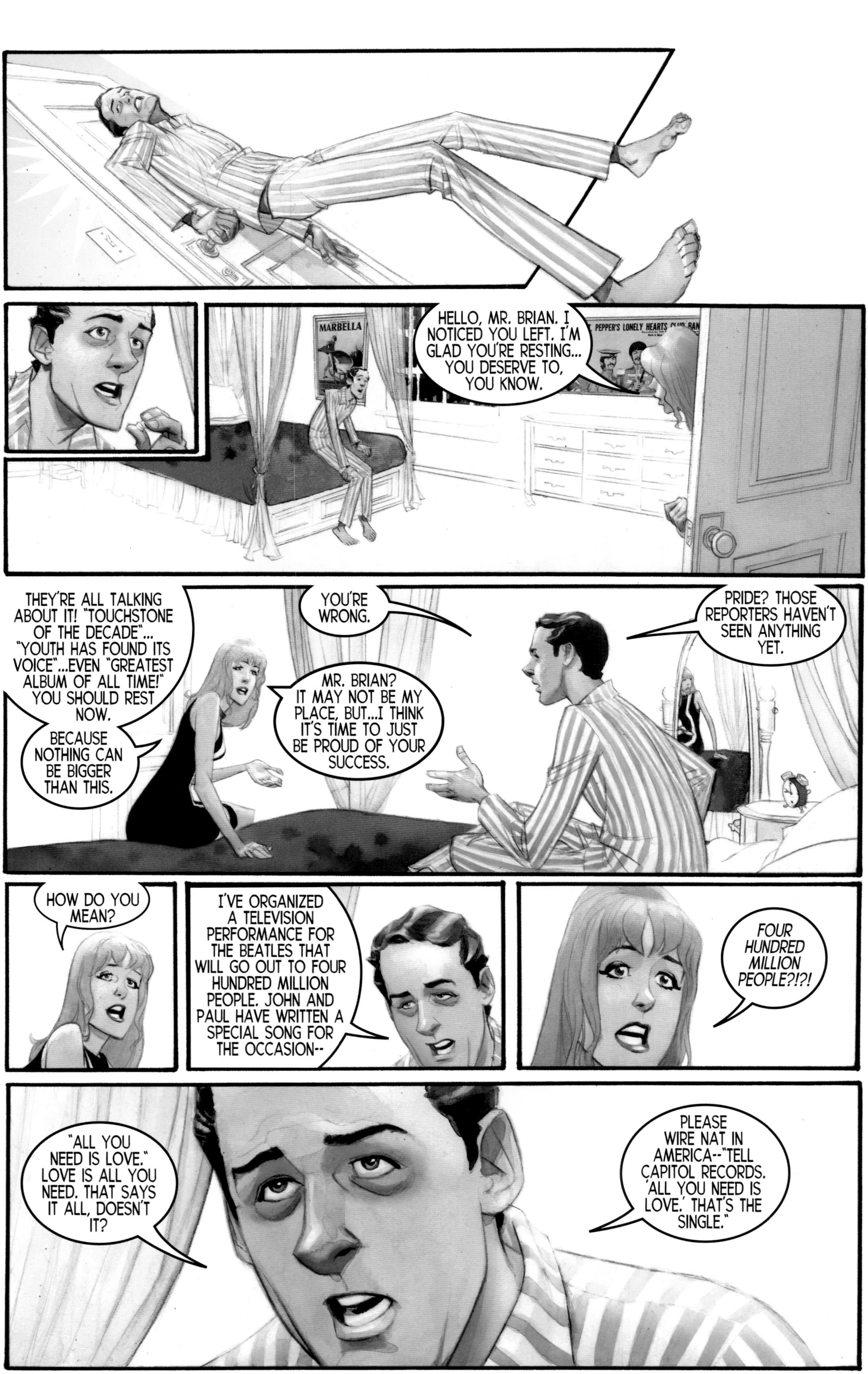
HELLO, MR. BRIAN. I NOTICED YOU LEFT. I'M GLAD YOU'RE RESTING... YOU DESERVE TO, YOU KNOW.
MARBELLA
SGT. PEPPER'S LONELY HEARTS CLUB BAND
THEY'RE ALL TALKING ABOUT IT! "TOUCHSTONE OF THE DECADE"... "YOUTH HAS FOUND ITS VOICE"...EVEN "GREATEST ALBUM OF ALL TIME!" YOU SHOULD REST NOW.
BECAUSE NOTHING CAN BE BIGGER THAN THIS.
YOU'RE WRONG.
MR. BRIAN? IT MAY NOT BE MY PLACE, BUT...I THINK IT'S TIME TO JUST BE PROUD OF YOUR SUCCESS.
PRIDE? THOSE REPORTERS HAVEN'T SEEN ANYTHING YET.
HOW DO YOU MEAN?
I'VE ORGANIZED A TELEVISION PERFORMANCE FOR THE BEATLES THAT WILL GO OUT TO FOUR HUNDRED MILLION PEOPLE. JOHN AND PAUL HAVE WRITTEN A SPECIAL SONG FOR THE OCCASION--
FOUR HUNDRED MILLION PEOPLE?!?!
"ALL YOU NEED IS LOVE." LOVE IS ALL YOU NEED. THAT SAYS IT ALL, DOESN'T IT?
PLEASE WIRE NAT IN AMERICA--"TELL CAPITOL RECORDS. 'ALL YOU NEED IS LOVE.' THAT'S THE SINGLE."

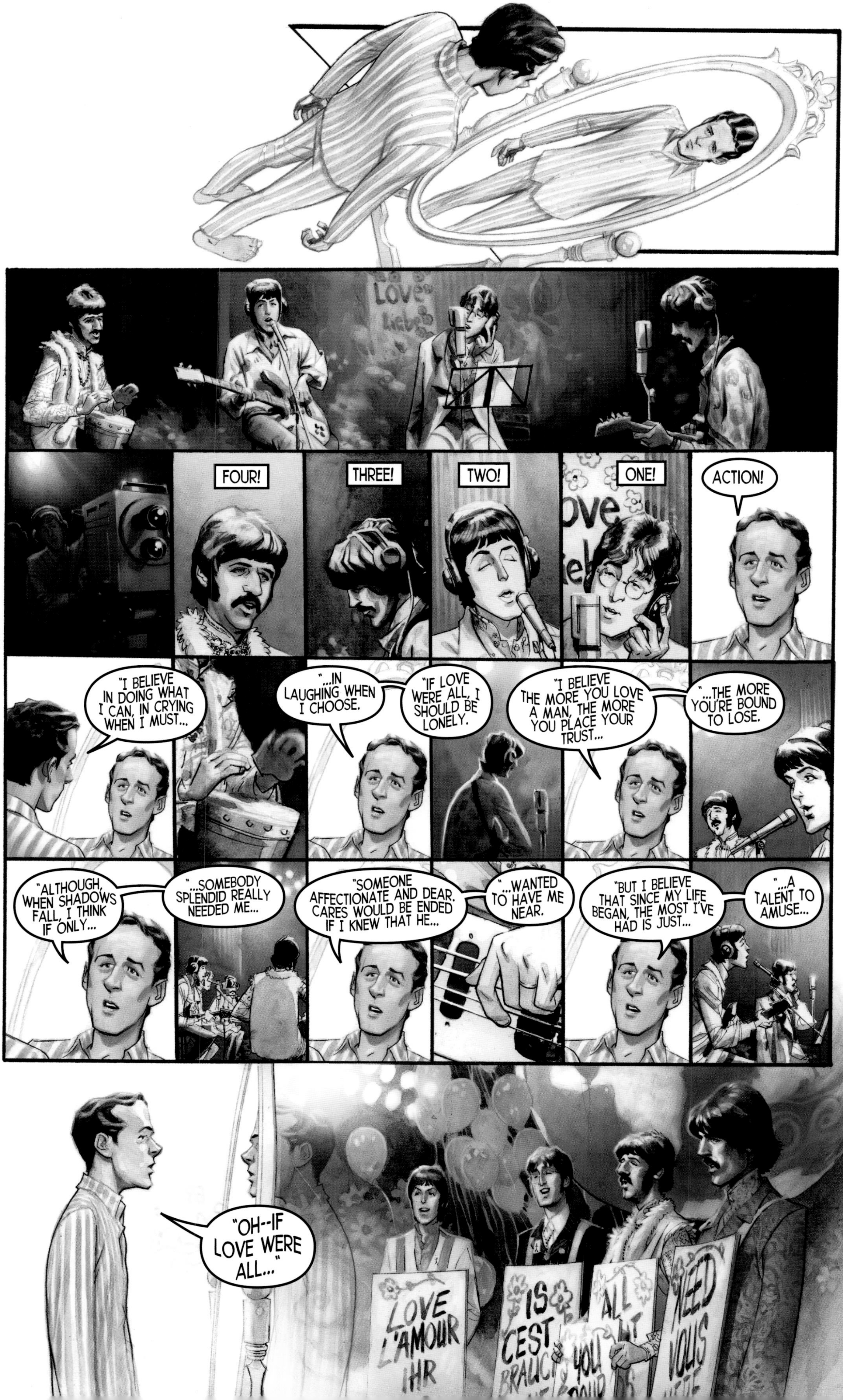
Love
Liebe
FOUR!
THREE!
TWO!
ONE!
ACTION!
"I BELIEVE IN DOING WHAT I CAN, IN CRYING WHEN I MUST...
"...IN LAUGHING WHEN I CHOOSE.
"IF LOVE WERE ALL, I SHOULD BE LONELY.
"I BELIEVE THE MORE YOU LOVE A MAN, THE MORE YOU PLACE YOUR TRUST...
"...THE MORE YOU'RE BOUND TO LOSE.
"ALTHOUGH, WHEN SHADOWS FALL, I THINK IF ONLY...
"...SOMEBODY SPLENDID REALLY NEEDED ME...
"SOMEONE AFFECTIONATE AND DEAR. CARES WOULD BE ENDED IF I KNEW THAT HE...
"...WANTED TO HAVE ME NEAR.
"BUT I BELIEVE THAT SINCE MY LIFE BEGAN, THE MOST I'VE HAD IS JUST...
"...A TALENT TO AMUSE...
"OH--IF LOVE WERE ALL..."
LOVE
L'AMOUR
IHR
IS
CEST
ALL
YOU
NEED
VOUS

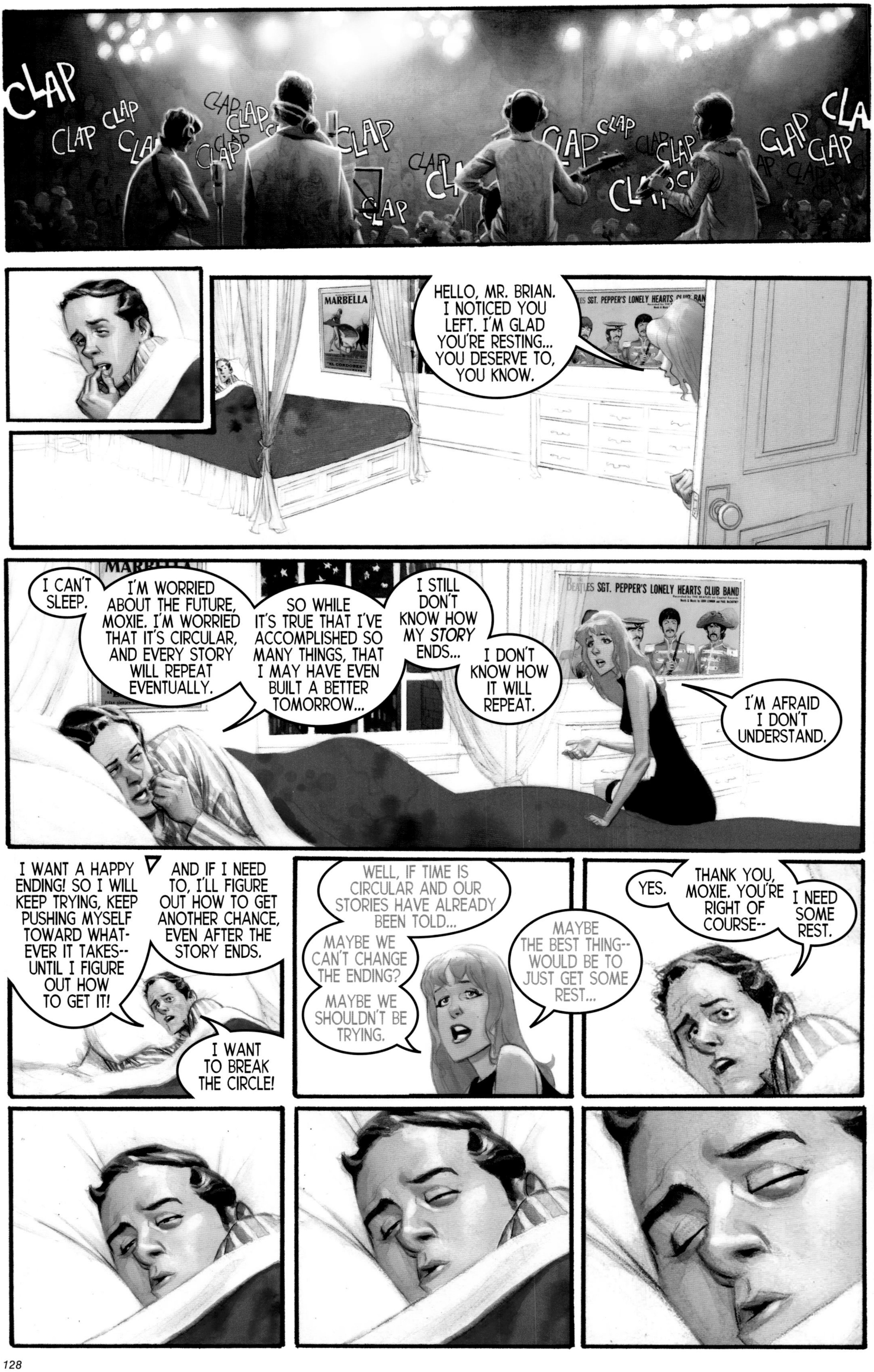
CLAP CLAP CLAP CLAP CLAP CLAP CLAP CLAP CLAP CLAP CLAP CLAP CLAP CLAP
MARBELLA
SGT. PEPPER'S LONELY HEARTS CLUB BAND
HELLO, MR. BRIAN. I NOTICED YOU LEFT. I'M GLAD YOU'RE RESTING... YOU DESERVE TO, YOU KNOW.
I CAN'T SLEEP.
I'M WORRIED ABOUT THE FUTURE, MOXIE. I'M WORRIED THAT IT'S CIRCULAR, AND EVERY STORY WILL REPEAT EVENTUALLY.
SO WHILE IT'S TRUE THAT I'VE ACCOMPLISHED SO MANY THINGS, THAT I MAY HAVE EVEN BUILT A BETTER TOMORROW...
I STILL DON'T KNOW HOW MY *STORY* ENDS...
I DON'T KNOW HOW IT WILL REPEAT.
I'M AFRAID I DON'T UNDERSTAND.
I WANT A HAPPY ENDING! SO I WILL KEEP TRYING, KEEP PUSHING MYSELF TOWARD WHATEVER IT TAKES-- UNTIL I FIGURE OUT HOW TO GET IT!
AND IF I NEED TO, I'LL FIGURE OUT HOW TO GET ANOTHER CHANCE, EVEN AFTER THE STORY ENDS.
I WANT TO BREAK THE CIRCLE!
WELL, IF TIME IS CIRCULAR AND OUR STORIES HAVE ALREADY BEEN TOLD...
MAYBE WE CAN'T CHANGE THE ENDING?
MAYBE WE SHOULDN'T BE TRYING.
MAYBE THE BEST THING-- WOULD BE TO JUST GET SOME REST...
YES.
THANK YOU, MOXIE. YOU'RE RIGHT OF COURSE--
I NEED SOME REST.

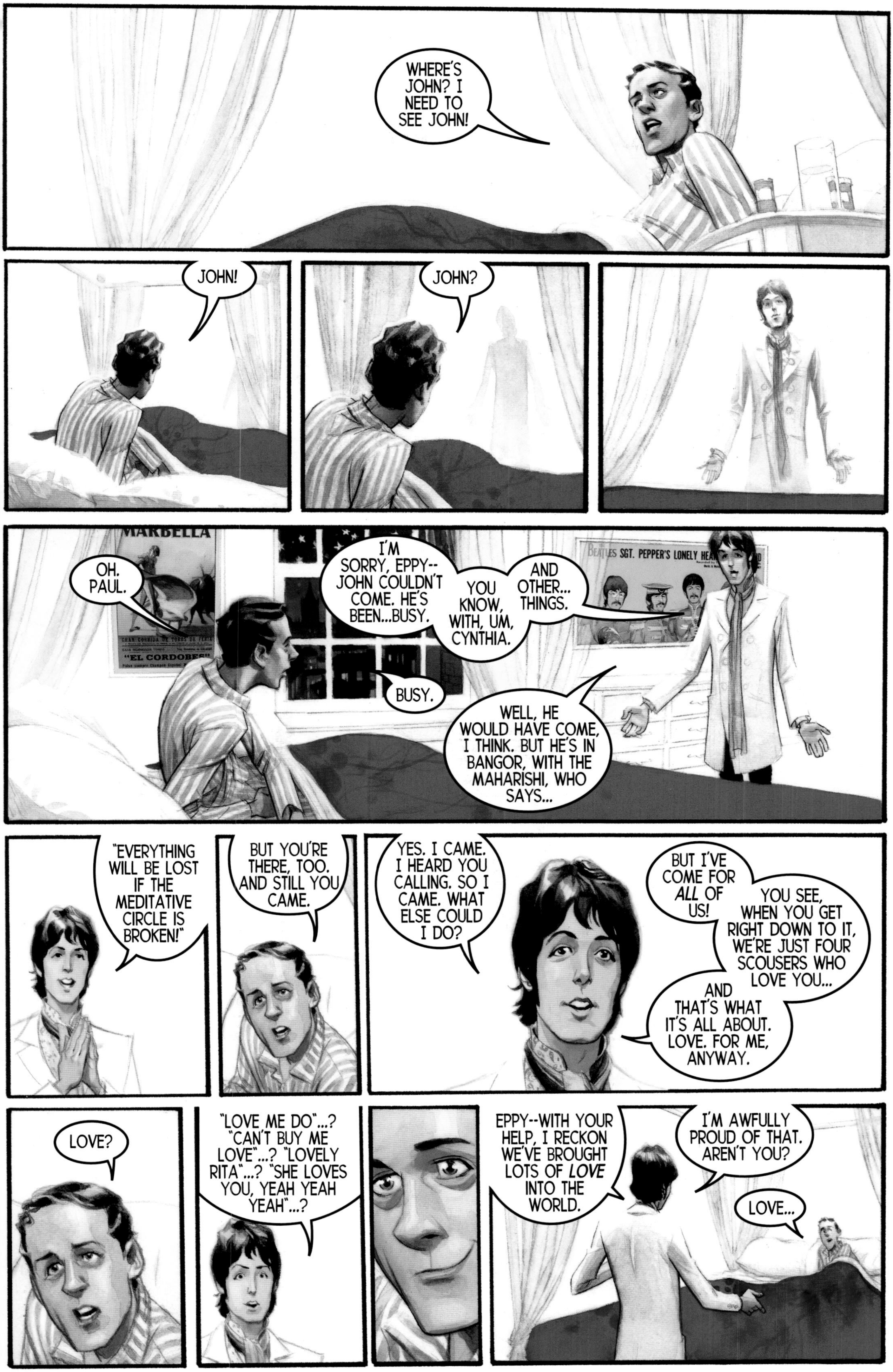
WHERE'S JOHN? I NEED TO SEE JOHN!
JOHN!
JOHN?
MARBELLA
"EL CORDOBES"
OH. PAUL.
I'M SORRY, EPPY--JOHN COULDN'T COME. HE'S BEEN...BUSY.
YOU KNOW, WITH, UM, CYNTHIA.
AND OTHER... THINGS.
BUSY.
WELL, HE WOULD HAVE COME, I THINK. BUT HE'S IN BANGOR, WITH THE MAHARISHI, WHO SAYS...
"EVERYTHING WILL BE LOST IF THE MEDITATIVE CIRCLE IS BROKEN!"
BUT YOU'RE THERE, TOO. AND STILL YOU CAME.
YES. I CAME. I HEARD YOU CALLING. SO I CAME. WHAT ELSE COULD I DO?
BUT I'VE COME FOR *ALL* OF US!
YOU SEE, WHEN YOU GET RIGHT DOWN TO IT, WE'RE JUST FOUR SCOUSERS WHO LOVE YOU...
AND THAT'S WHAT IT'S ALL ABOUT. LOVE. FOR ME, ANYWAY.
LOVE?
"LOVE ME DO"...? "CAN'T BUY ME LOVE"...? "LOVELY RITA"...? "SHE LOVES YOU, YEAH YEAH YEAH"...?
EPPY--WITH YOUR HELP, I RECKON WE'VE BROUGHT LOTS OF *LOVE* INTO THE WORLD.
I'M AWFULLY PROUD OF THAT. AREN'T YOU?
LOVE...

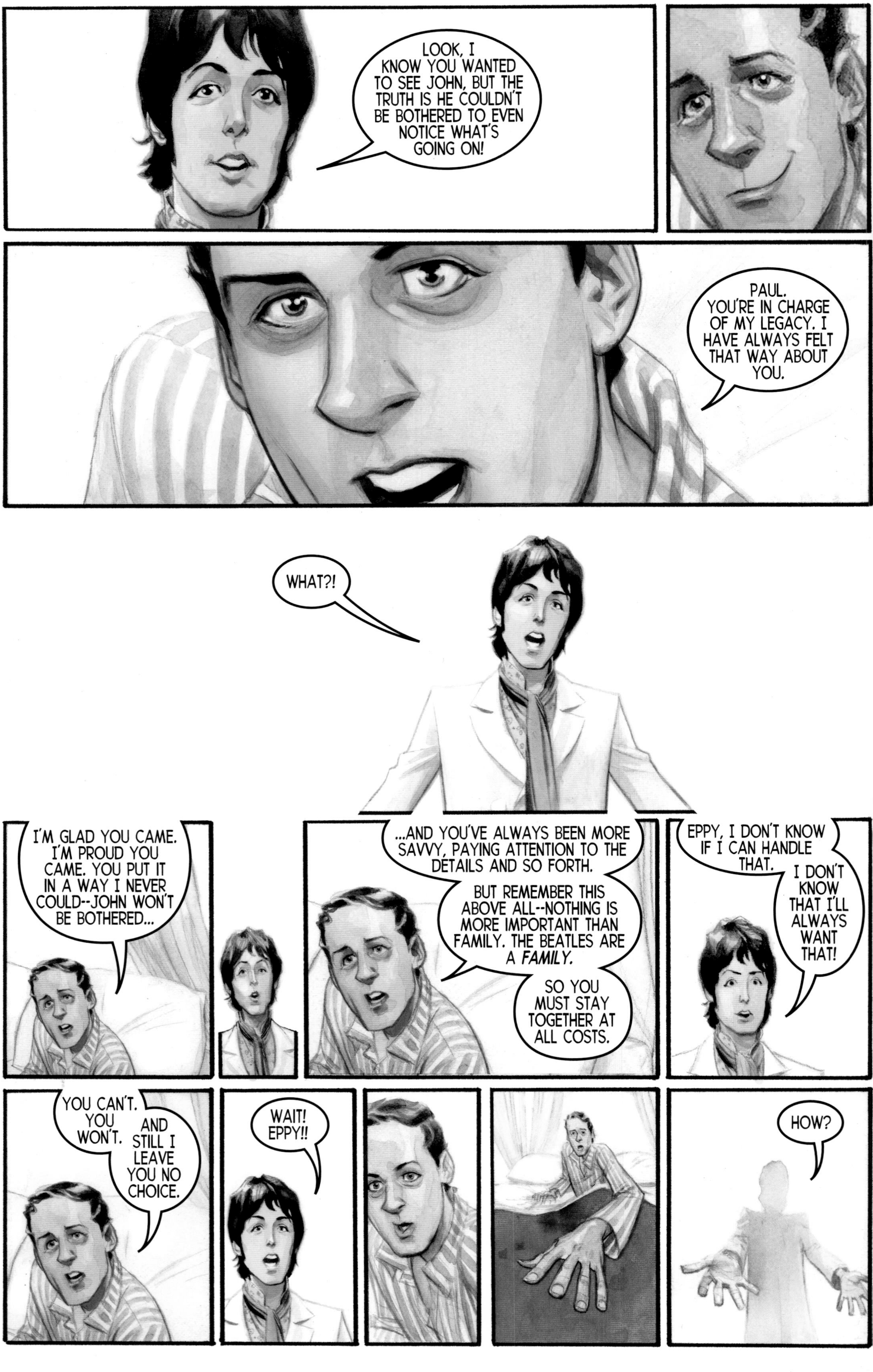
LOOK, I KNOW YOU WANTED TO SEE JOHN, BUT THE TRUTH IS HE COULDN'T BE BOTHERED TO EVEN NOTICE WHAT'S GOING ON!
PAUL. YOU'RE IN CHARGE OF MY LEGACY. I HAVE ALWAYS FELT THAT WAY ABOUT YOU.
WHAT?!
I'M GLAD YOU CAME. I'M PROUD YOU CAME. YOU PUT IT IN A WAY I NEVER COULD--JOHN WON'T BE BOTHERED...
...AND YOU'VE ALWAYS BEEN MORE SAVVY, PAYING ATTENTION TO THE DETAILS AND SO FORTH.
BUT REMEMBER THIS ABOVE ALL--NOTHING IS MORE IMPORTANT THAN FAMILY. THE BEATLES ARE A *FAMILY.*
SO YOU MUST STAY TOGETHER AT ALL COSTS.
EPPY, I DON'T KNOW IF I CAN HANDLE THAT.
I DON'T KNOW THAT I'LL ALWAYS WANT THAT!
YOU CAN'T. YOU WON'T.
AND STILL I LEAVE YOU NO CHOICE.
WAIT! EPPY!!
HOW?

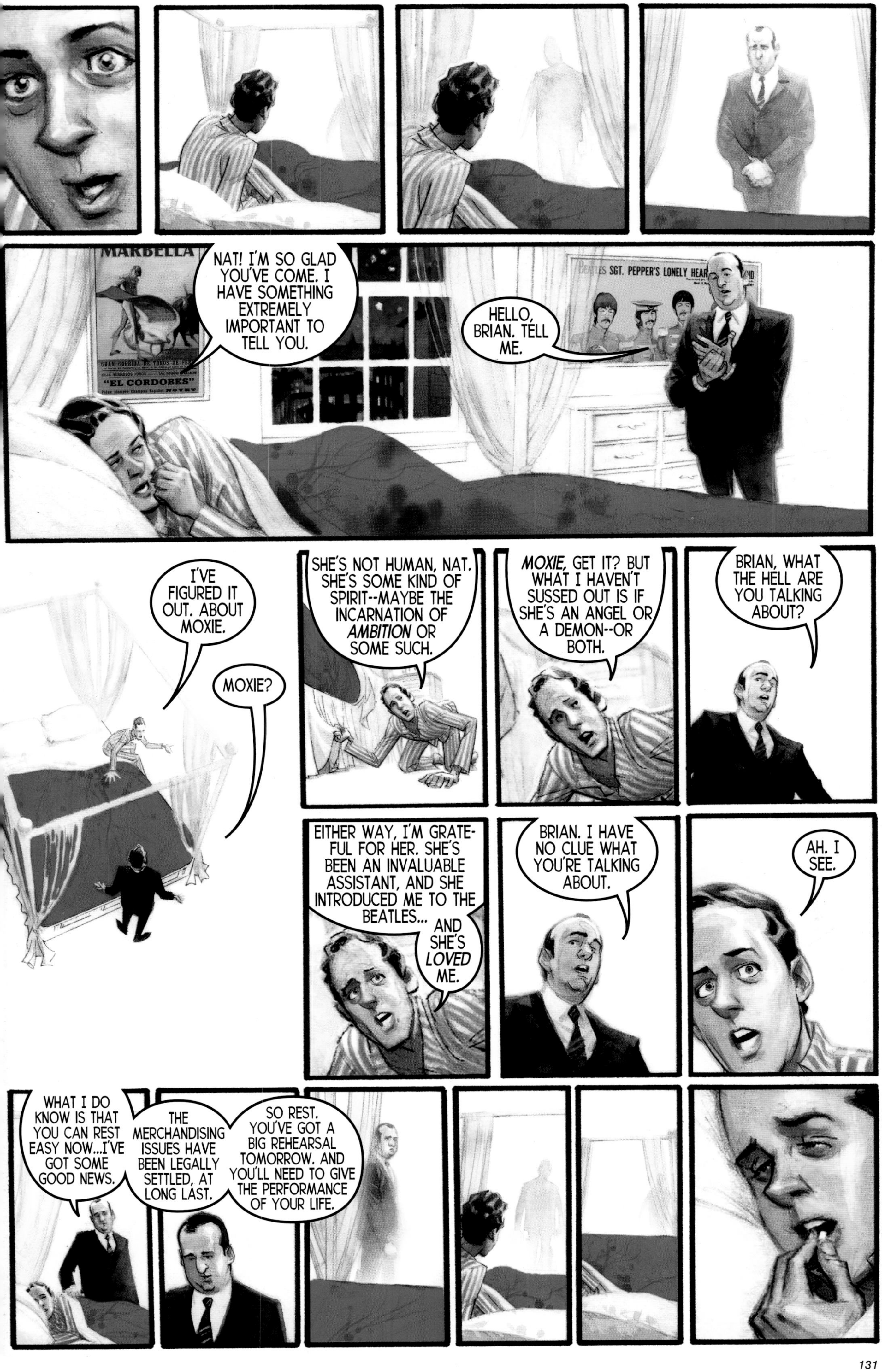
MARBELLA
GRAN CORRIDA DE TOROS DE FERIA
"EL CORDOBES"
NAT! I'M SO GLAD YOU'VE COME. I HAVE SOMETHING EXTREMELY IMPORTANT TO TELL YOU.
BEATLES SGT. PEPPER'S LONELY HEAR ND
HELLO, BRIAN. TELL ME.
I'VE FIGURED IT OUT. ABOUT MOXIE.
MOXIE?
SHE'S NOT HUMAN, NAT. SHE'S SOME KIND OF SPIRIT--MAYBE THE INCARNATION OF *AMBITION* OR SOME SUCH.
MOXIE, GET IT? BUT WHAT I HAVEN'T SUSSED OUT IS IF SHE'S AN ANGEL OR A DEMON--OR BOTH.
BRIAN, WHAT THE HELL ARE YOU TALKING ABOUT?
EITHER WAY, I'M GRATEFUL FOR HER. SHE'S BEEN AN INVALUABLE ASSISTANT, AND SHE INTRODUCED ME TO THE BEATLES...
AND SHE'S *LOVED* ME.
BRIAN. I HAVE NO CLUE WHAT YOU'RE TALKING ABOUT.
AH. I SEE.
WHAT I DO KNOW IS THAT YOU CAN REST EASY NOW...I'VE GOT SOME GOOD NEWS.
THE MERCHANDISING ISSUES HAVE BEEN LEGALLY SETTLED, AT LONG LAST.
SO REST. YOU'VE GOT A BIG REHEARSAL TOMORROW. AND YOU'LL NEED TO GIVE THE PERFORMANCE OF YOUR LIFE.

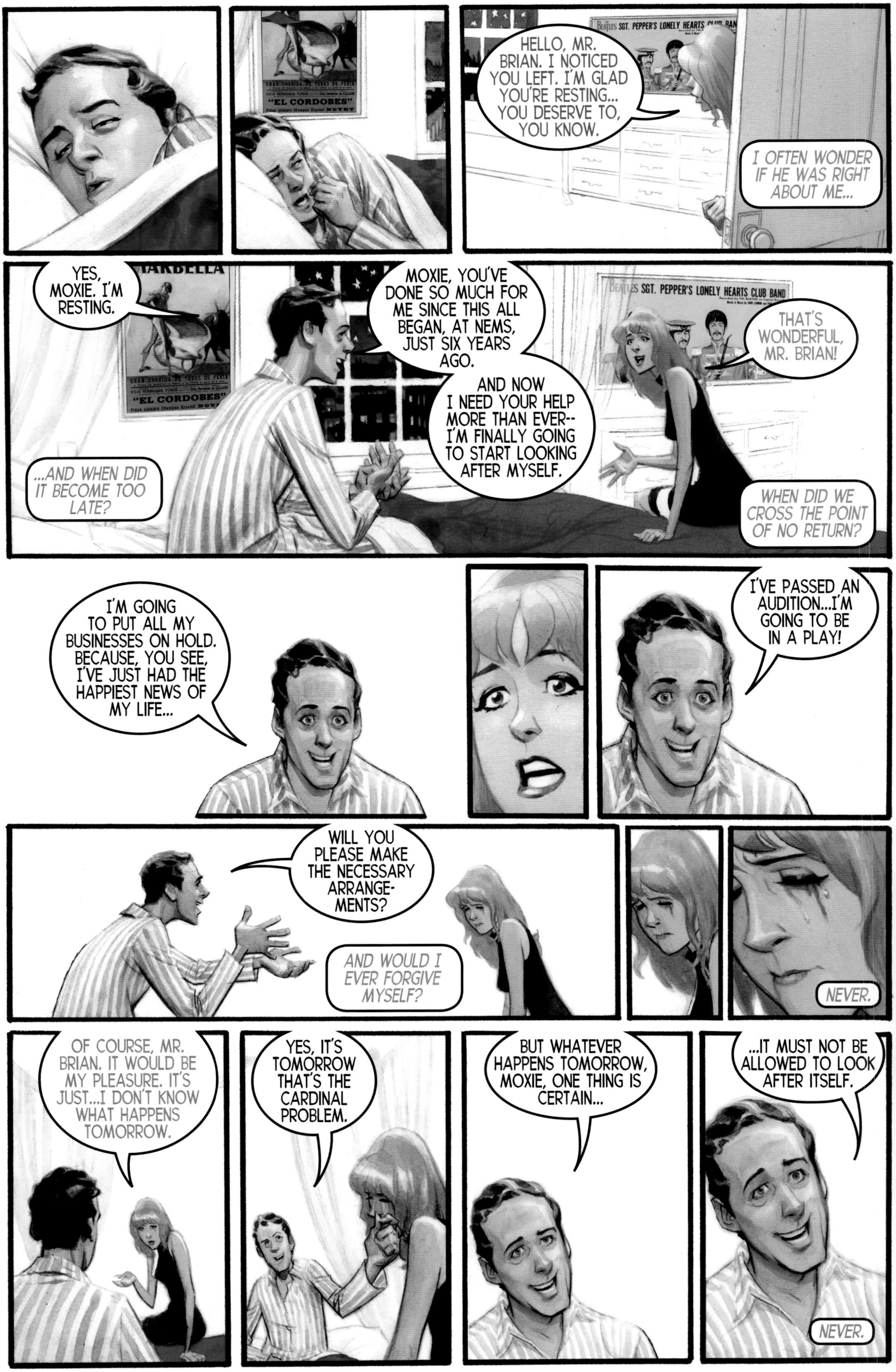

HELLO, MR. BRIAN. I NOTICED YOU LEFT. I'M GLAD YOU'RE RESTING... YOU DESERVE TO, YOU KNOW.
I OFTEN WONDER IF HE WAS RIGHT ABOUT ME...
SGT. PEPPER'S LONELY HEARTS CLUB BAND
YES, MOXIE. I'M RESTING.
MOXIE, YOU'VE DONE SO MUCH FOR ME SINCE THIS ALL BEGAN, AT NEMS, JUST SIX YEARS AGO.
AND NOW I NEED YOUR HELP MORE THAN EVER-- I'M FINALLY GOING TO START LOOKING AFTER MYSELF.
THAT'S WONDERFUL, MR. BRIAN!
...AND WHEN DID IT BECOME TOO LATE?
WHEN DID WE CROSS THE POINT OF NO RETURN?
I'M GOING TO PUT ALL MY BUSINESSES ON HOLD. BECAUSE, YOU SEE, I'VE JUST HAD THE HAPPIEST NEWS OF MY LIFE...
I'VE PASSED AN AUDITION...I'M GOING TO BE IN A PLAY!
WILL YOU PLEASE MAKE THE NECESSARY ARRANGE- MENTS?
AND WOULD I EVER FORGIVE MYSELF?
NEVER.
OF COURSE, MR. BRIAN. IT WOULD BE MY PLEASURE. IT'S JUST...I DON'T KNOW WHAT HAPPENS TOMORROW.
YES, IT'S TOMORROW THAT'S THE CARDINAL PROBLEM.
BUT WHATEVER HAPPENS TOMORROW, MOXIE, ONE THING IS CERTAIN...
...IT MUST NOT BE ALLOWED TO LOOK AFTER ITSELF.
NEVER.

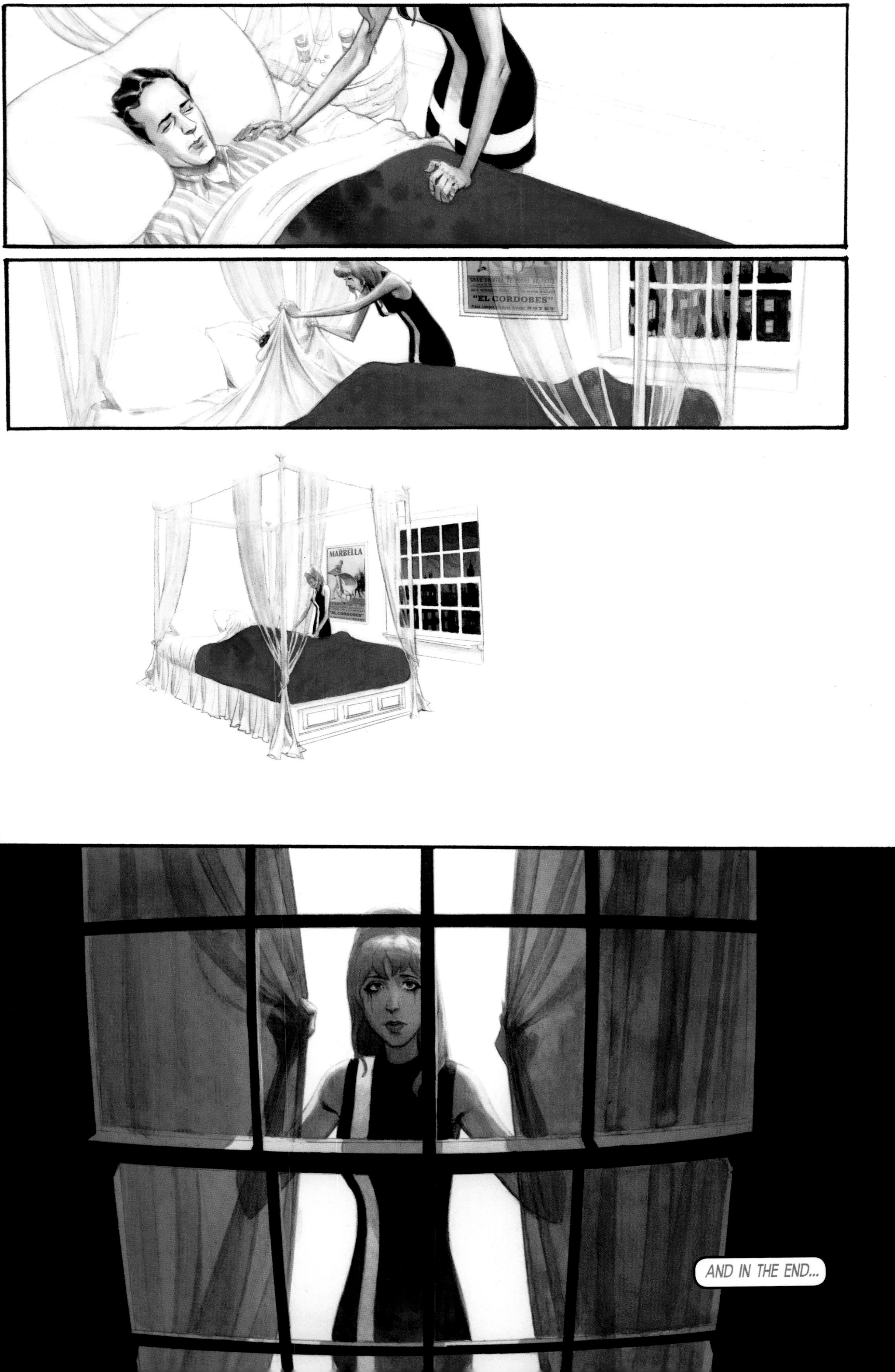
"EL CORDOBES"
MARBELLA
"EL CORDOBES"
AND IN THE END...

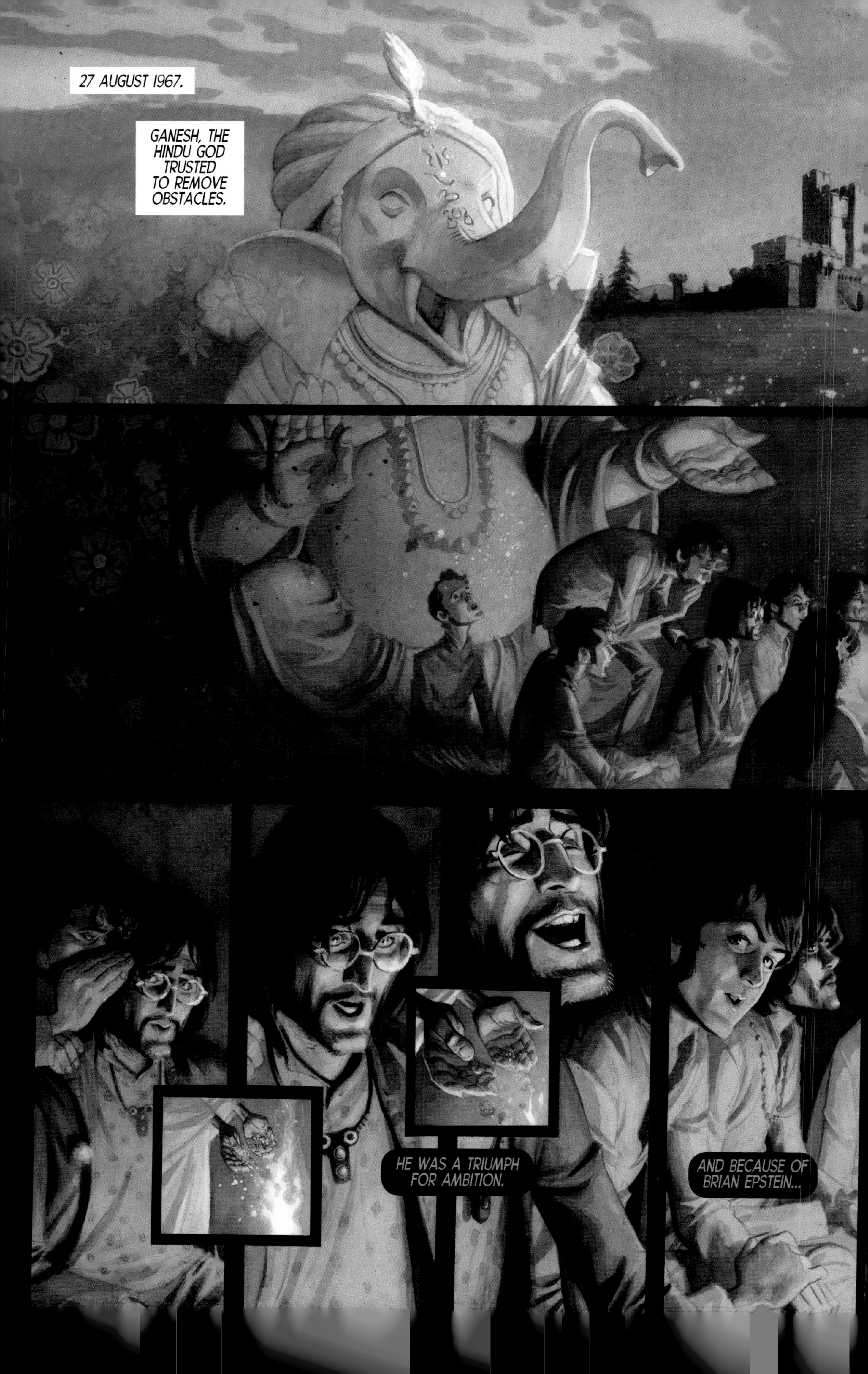
27 AUGUST 1967.
GANESH, THE HINDU GOD TRUSTED TO REMOVE OBSTACLES.
HE WAS A TRIUMPH FOR AMBITION.
AND BECAUSE OF BRIAN EPSTEIN...

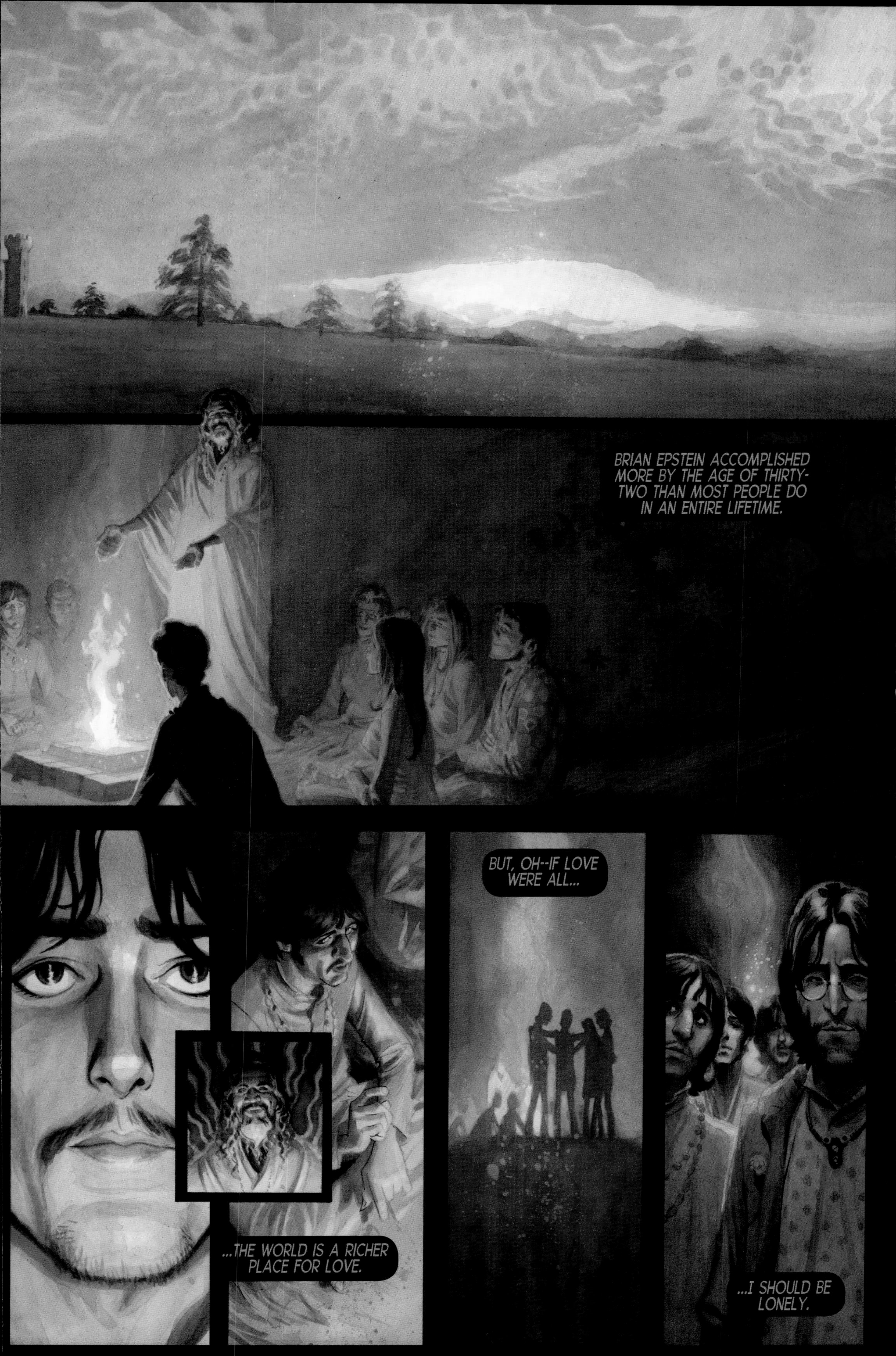
BRIAN EPSTEIN ACCOMPLISHED MORE BY THE AGE OF THIRTY-TWO THAN MOST PEOPLE DO IN AN ENTIRE LIFETIME.
...THE WORLD IS A RICHER PLACE FOR LOVE.
BUT, OH--IF LOVE WERE ALL...
...I SHOULD BE LONELY.

Within two years, the Beatles would disband in a very public sea of personal acrimony and professional lawsuits. Nevertheless, the legacy that Brian orchestrated and protected would insure that the Beatles remained among the best-loved and most inspirational artists—in any artistic discipline—for all time. Their message of Love would continue to burn brightly, even as the fire died.

"If anyone was the Fifth Beatle, it was Brian."

—Paul McCartney, 1999

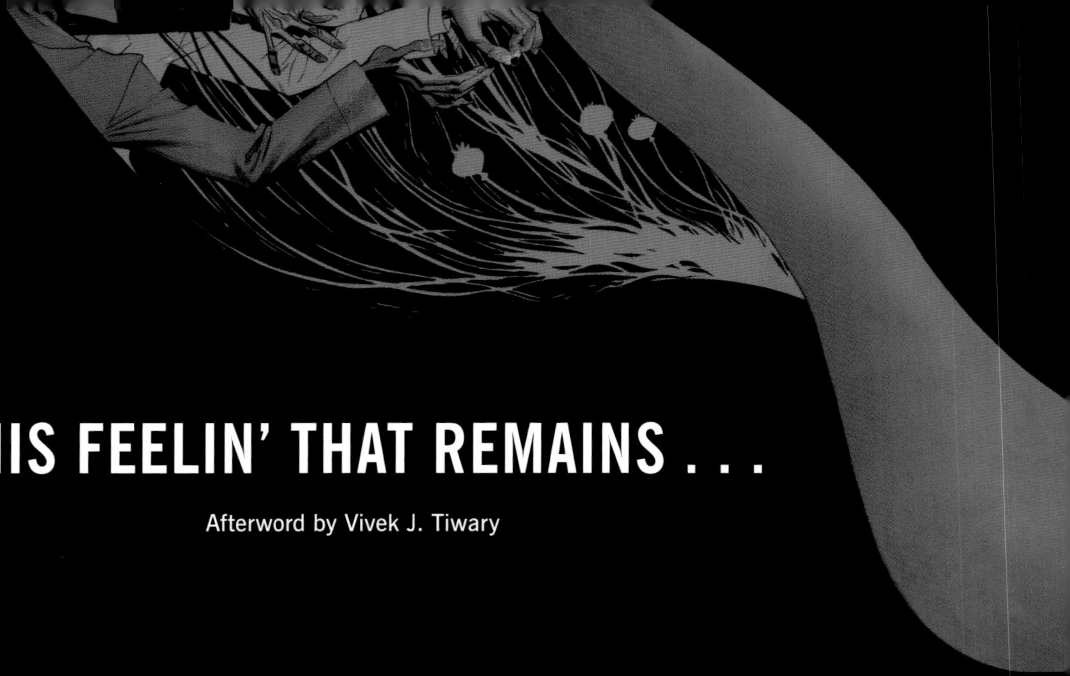

THIS FEELIN' THAT REMAINS . . .

Afterword by Vivek J. Tiwary

> *"Mythology is better and more fondly remembered than history! So we create legends rather than recount truths."*

The Fifth Beatle is a true labor of love. Telling the Brian Epstein story has been my "life's work"—as strange as it is to use that phrase, since I hope to have many more years ahead of me. But I've had an ongoing and unrequited love affair with the Brian Epstein story for more than half my life.

As romantic as that may sound, my fascination with Brian Epstein started with my head rather than my heart. I found my way to his story when I was a student at the Wharton School of Business, dreaming of working in entertainment and managing bands, hungry for professional inspiration. My mother, Nandini Beharry Tiwary, always taught me not only to work hard in the present—but to study the past, find inspiration wherever you can, and carve your own future. She also filled my childhood home with the sounds of classical music . . . and the Beatles.

I was stunned to discover how little information there is available about Brian Epstein and the management of the Beatles, and so I dove deeply into intense research that has literally gone on for over two decades. Over those years I've had the good fortune of breaking bread with a number of people who were important to Brian—from artists he managed, to coworkers, to members of the Epstein family, to those few people who he considered close friends. In truth, some were reluctant to speak with me at first. But I did my best to convey my genuine interest and passion for Brian's legacy, and in the end each and every one of these fascinating folks proved warm and welcoming, freely sharing their memories (and in some cases, their memorabilia) about Brian.

The business student in me was of course richly rewarded with the "case study" I uncovered in Brian Epstein . . . But it was the human, emotional side of Brian's story that deeply resonated with me. Brian was an outsider in his chosen field—and I have often felt that way myself, as a first-generation American of Indian origin, wading my way through the changing tides of the film, television, and theater industries. Brian Epstein became my "historical mentor." He's a person whose history I've sought to learn from—both what to do and what *not* to do. Brian was a flawed and imperfect hero, but he was a hero all the same . . . *So like all worthy heroes, why shouldn't Brian Epstein have a life in comics?*

Now if I'm such an Epstein expert, Beatles historians might rightly question some points of history in *The Fifth Beatle*. Were the Beatles playing a gig in Taunton when John Lennon found out Cynthia was pregnant? Where is Pete Best in all of this? Did Ed Sullivan really negotiate with Brian using a ventriloquist's dummy? (Believe it or not, *that* actually happened.*) And who—or what—the hell is Moxie?

If *The Fifth Beatle* were a film, we might include an end credit like "This story is based on actual events. In certain cases incidents, characters, and timelines have been changed for dramatic purposes." But that disclaimer reads more like a legal attempt to cover one's ass than a heartfelt attempt to capture the essence of a man.

As it turns out, almost everything in the pages you've just read actually *did* happen. But conveying the truth—while important—has never been my primary goal. My goal with *The Fifth Beatle* is to use 130 pages of my words and Andrew C. Robinson's gorgeous art to reveal not just the facts but the *poetry* behind the Brian Epstein story. His is a painfully human story about the struggle to overcome seemingly insurmountable odds. A story about staggering ambition yielding staggering success. A story about wanting too much, too soon, while not focusing on the things that really matter. A story about being an outsider, and trying desperately to belong. A story of triumph and tragedy. A story full of dreams, hope, and music . . .

A story that changed my life.

I hope it will inspire yours, in some small but meaningful way. In which case, *The Fifth Beatle* will have been a life's work done well.

—VIVEK J. TIWARY
New York, 2013

*Or did it?

THE FREEDOM TO MARRY

"I think Beatles ought never to be married, but they will be someday—and someday, I might be too . . ."

—Brian Epstein, 1964

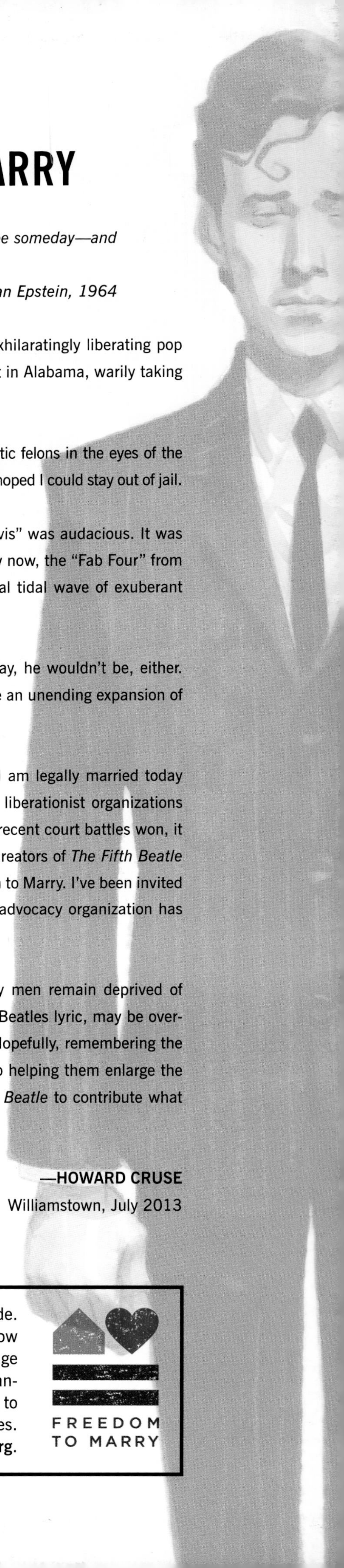

In 1964, while Brian Epstein was engaged in bringing the most exhilaratingly liberating pop phenomenon in history to America's shores, I was a college student in Alabama, warily taking stock of how my gayness might affect my prospects in life.

Both Brian and I, in our separate worlds, knew that we were automatic felons in the eyes of the law. Forget about being allowed to marry another man someday! I just hoped I could stay out of jail.

Epstein's dream of enabling the Beatles to become "bigger than Elvis" was audacious. It was modest, though, compared to what actually transpired. As we know now, the "Fab Four" from Liverpool were destined to both ride and help fuel the international tidal wave of exuberant social change that we call The Sixties.

I am no longer an automatic criminal, and if Brian were alive today, he wouldn't be, either. Beatles songs didn't make that happen, but their spirit helped make an unending expansion of human possibilities feel joyous instead of scary.

Indeed, far from trying to market my cartoons from behind bars, I am legally married today to a man whom I've loved for thirty-four years. Many heroes and liberationist organizations have played a part in making this possible, but in light of the most recent court battles won, it seems appropriate to single out one in particular. That's what the creators of *The Fifth Beatle* have done by forging a spiritual and economic alliance with Freedom to Marry. I've been invited to add these words to their endorsement because of the role that advocacy organization has played in enriching my own life.

There's more to be done. In thirty-seven states, lesbians and gay men remain deprived of their full rights of citizenship. "All You Need Is Love," that thrilling Beatles lyric, may be over-simplified as a rule of life, but all of us do need love an awful lot! Hopefully, remembering the Beatles' music and contemplating the energy one gay man put into helping them enlarge the world's view of love's potential will encourage readers of *The Fifth Beatle* to contribute what they can to Freedom to Marry so the good work can go on.

—HOWARD CRUSE
Williamstown, July 2013

Freedom to Marry is the campaign to win marriage nationwide. By working to win the freedom to marry in more states, grow the national majority for marriage, and end federal marriage discrimination, Freedom to Marry is creating the climate for another Supreme Court victory, one that will secure the freedom to marry throughout the country, in a matter of years, not decades. Learn more by visiting them at **www.freedomtomarry.org**.

FREEDOM TO MARRY

VIVEK J. TIWARY

Vivek's earliest childhood memories include browsing the comic-book racks at Forbidden Planet with his parents and listening to their Beatles records at home. He would grow up to be an award-winning producer of theater, film, and television with productions including Green Day's *American Idiot*, *The Addams Family*, and *A Raisin in the Sun*, among others. *The Fifth Beatle: The Brian Epstein Story* is his first book, and he is currently writing the screenplay for its film adaptation. He lives in New York City with his inspiring wife, Tracy, their two delightful children, Kavi and Nandini, and a feisty papillon named Sukhi. Visit him at TiwaryEnt.com.

ANDREW C. ROBINSON

Growing up on the family farm in Florida, Andrew C. Robinson was quite the daydreamer, with a huge fascination for artists like Frank Frazetta, Walt Simonson, and his influential older brother Roby. Before graduating from the Savannah College of Art and Design, Andrew landed his first professional comic-book job. His career began illustrating short stories for *Dark Horse Presents*. Since then, he has seen his paintings published by all major comic-book publishers in the industry, contributing beautifully illustrated covers for such titles as *King Conan*, *Detective Comics* (Batman), *Hawkman*, *Starman*, *Action Comics* (Superman), *Iron Man*, *X-Man*, and *Justice Society of America*. Andrew is also a writer and a creator, currently working on his own creation—*Dusty Star*. Andrew lives in Altadena, California, with his lovely Leah and their daughter Ella. To learn more about his art and projects, visit NextExitComics.com.

KYLE BAKER

Kyle Baker grew up a fan of the old Beatles cartoons, and the Beatles were his first favorite band. As a toddler, he could often be found singing "Ob-La-Di, Ob-La-Da" and "The Continuing Story of Bungalow Bill." Today, Kyle is an award-winning cartoonist, comic book writer/artist, and animator known for his graphic novels (including *Why I Hate Saturn* and *Nat Turner*) and for a 2000s revival of the classic series *Plastic Man*. He has won numerous Eisner Awards and Harvey Awards for his work in the comics field, and has worked for such companies as Disney, Warner Bros. Feature Animation, HBO, DreamWorks, Cartoon Network, Marvel Comics, DC Entertainment, Saatchi & Saatchi, Watson-Guptill, RCA/BMG, Random House, *Nickelodeon Magazine*, *Rugrats*, Scholastic, *Goosebumps*, and others.

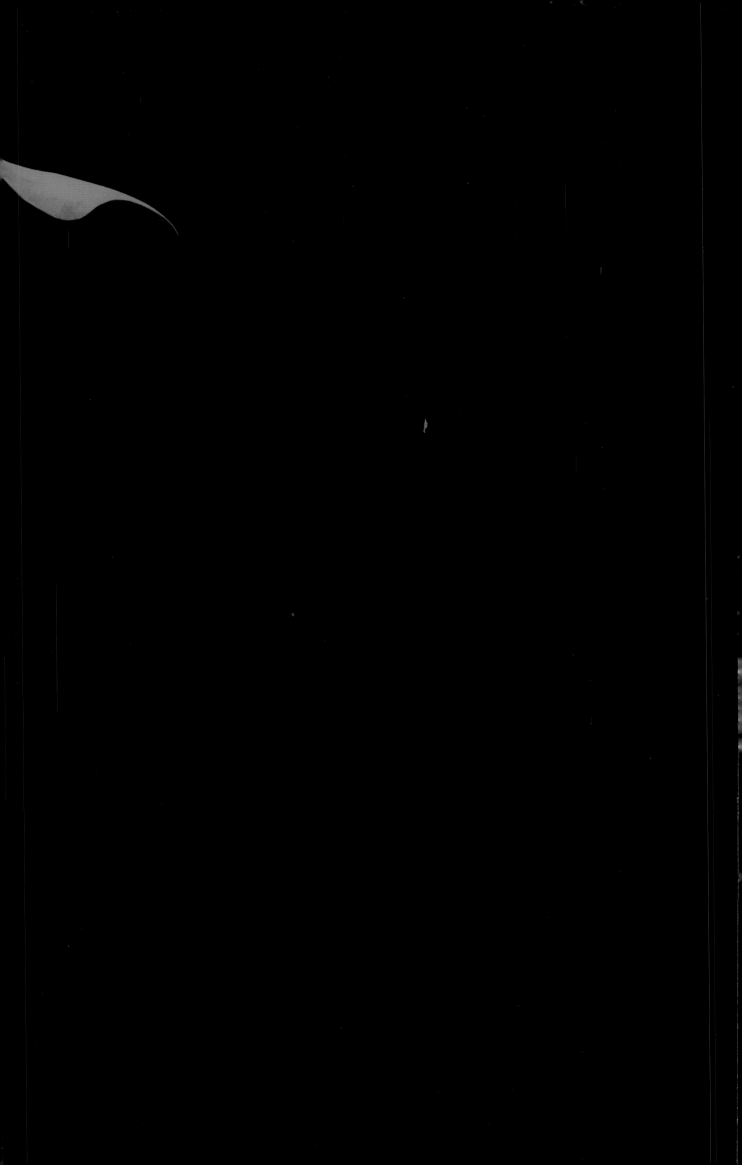